Agriculture and Rural Development in the People's Republic of the Congo

About the Book and Author

This comprehensive study outlines the current transformation in agriculture and its effect on the demography, development, and economy of the People's Republic of the Congo. G. Nguyen Tien Hung analyzes fundamental structural changes within the economy and the impact of the application of the Marxist model of development upon the performance and growth of the agricultural sector. The course of rural development over the past fifteen years is charted with an emphasis on migration, welfare, and the influence of aid on small farming communities. Dr. Hung assesses the constraints on agricultural production and marketing and the effectiveness of farmer cooperatives in overcoming these limitations. This study explores the prospects for future development in the Congo and provides an analysis applicable to other African states.

G. Nguyen Tien Hung is professor of economics at Howard University in Washington, D.C. He is the author of *Economic Development of Socialist Vietnam, 1955-1980*. His other publications include works on development planning and financing and on African development.

Agriculture and Rural Development in the People's Republic of the Congo

G. Nguyen Tien Hung
with José Alfaro, Richard E. Downs,
Winfred Biddier, and Russell Barbour

Routledge
Taylor & Francis Group
LONDON AND NEW YORK

First published 1987 by Westview Press

Published 2018 by Routledge
52 Vanderbilt Avenue, New York, NY 10017
2 Park Square, Milton Park, Abingdon, Oxon OX14 4RN

Routledge is an imprint of the Taylor & Francis Group, an informa business

Copyright © 1987 by Taylor & Francis

All rights reserved. No part of this book may be reprinted or reproduced or utilised in any form or by any electronic, mechanical, or other means, now known or hereafter invented, including photocopying and recording, or in any information storage or retrieval system, without permission in writing from the publishers.

Notice:
Product or corporate names may be trademarks or registered trademarks, and are used only for identification and explanation without intent to infringe.

Library of Congress Cataloging-in-Publication Data
Hung, Gregory Nguyen Tien, 1935-
  Agriculture and rural development in the People's
Republic of the Congo.
  (Westview special studies on Africa)
  Bibliography: p.
  1. Agriculture--Economic aspects--Congo
(Brazzaville) 2. Rural development--Congo
(Brazzaville) 3. congo (Brazzaville)--Economic
policy. I. Title. II. Series.
HD2138.N48 1987   338.1'0967'24   85-32333
ISBN 0-8133-7067-1

ISBN 13: 978-0-367-00879-6 (hbk)
ISBN 13: 978-0-367-15866-8 (pbk)

To

Christine, Daniel, and Michael

Contents

LIST OF TABLES, FIGURES, AND MAPS	xiii
PREFACE	xix
ACKNOWLEDGMENTS	xxi

PART I
AN OVERVIEW

1	HISTORICAL SETTING	1
	GEOGRAPHICAL ENVIRONMENT	8
	Major Geographical Regions	8
	Climate	10
	GENERAL CHARACTERISTICS OF THE POPULATION	10
	Size and Distribution	10
	Ethnic Groups	13
2	ECONOMIC AND FINANCIAL CONDITIONS BEARING ON AGRICULTURE, 1960-1985	16
	BACKGROUND	16
	The Sixties	16
	The Seventies	17
	First Half of the Eighties	18
	The 1982-1986 Five-Year Plan	18
	STRUCTURAL DISEQUILIBRIUM	20
	BEHIND THE $1,000 PER CAPITA INCOME	21
	QUANTITATIVE TRENDS	23
	Gross Domestic Product (GDP)	23
	Sectorial Growth	25
	Fiscal Performance	33

International Trade and Finance	37
The Other Side of Oil	40
Planning for Development: Toward Agriculture	46

PART II
THE AGRICULTURAL SECTOR

3 AGRICULTURE IN THE CONGOLESE ECONOMY 49

    A Shrinking Sector 49
    The Socialist Option 51
    Agriculture Research 57

4 AGRONOMIC AND ENGINEERING ASPECTS 61

    Climatic Resources 61
    Management of Climatic Resources 76
    Water and Land Resources 81
    Geology and Ground Water Resources 84
    Natural Vegetation 89
    Rural Roads 91

5 AGRICULTURAL PERFORMANCE 97

    The Three Sectors 97
    Agricultural Production 100
    Livestock 109

6 AGRICULTURAL MARKETING 117

    The Markets 117
    The Marketing System 119

7 THE RURAL MILIEU 123

    The Small Farmers 123
    Cultural and Social Characteristics 126
    Farmers' Income and Welfare 133
    Behind the Rural Exodus 139

8 THE FARMING SYSTEMS 142

    Food Crops System 145
    Soil Fertility Maintenance 150

9 FARMERS' ORGANIZATIONS:
   THE COOPERATIVES   152

   Types of Cooperatives   152
   Membership of the Cooperatives   153
   Organization and Level of
      Development   153
   Potential Roles for Marketing
      Cooperatives   156
   The Non-Viability of Production
      Cooperatives   160
   Constraints on the Cooperatives
      Movement   161
   Policy Implications for Cooperatives
      Program   164

10 SMALL FARMERS' PARTICIPATION IN THE
   ECONOMY   170

   Domestic Resources   170
   External Assistance   179
   Expansion of Cash Crops Cultivation   181
   Animal Husbandry Development   182
   Other Assistance   182

PART III

PROBLEMS AND PROSPECTS

11 CONSTRAINTS TO AGRICULTURE AND RURAL
   DEVELOPMENT   184

   At the Farms   184
   Beyond the Farms   187
   Policy Constraints   190
   Natural Constraints   191

12 SUPPORTING AGRICULTURE AND RURAL
   DEVELOPMENT   193

   Feasibility   194
   Cost-Benefit   194
   Speed of Implementation   195
   Past Experiences   195

APPENDIXES   197

Tables, Figures, and Maps

TABLES

1.1	Population Trend	6
1.2	The Congolese Population by Age and Sex (1983)	11
2.1	The Five-Year Development Plan (1982-1986)	19
2.2	Behind the High Per-Capita Income (1983)	22
2.3	Gross Domestic Product (GDP), Gross National Product (GNP) (1970-1983)	24
2.4	Labor and Employment in Selected Years (1964-1983)	31
2.5	Employment in the Government Sector (1971-1982)	32
2.6	Fiscal Performance (1970-1983)	34
2.7	Commodity Exports (1970-1982)	36
2.8	Commodity Imports (1976-1982)	39
2.9	Balance of Payments (1970-1982)	41
2.10	External Public Debt (1970-1983)	42
2.11	The Other Side of Oil: Some Rough Indicators (1973-1980)	44
2.12	Planning for Development (1978-1986)	48
3.1	Agriculture: Indicators of a Shrinking Sector (1960-1980)	50
3.2	Major State Farms: Locations and Products	52
3.3	Land Utilization by Regions	56

4.1	Annual Surface Water Hydrological Balance for the Nine Sub-Zones of Congo	83
4.2	Roads Needed and Estimated Cost: The 1978 Program	94
4.3	Equipment Needed and Cost: The 1979 Program	95
5.1	Share of Agricultural Production by Sectors	98
5.2	Food Crops: Estimated Area Under Cultivation Production and Yields	103
5.3	Marketed Production of Food Crops (1973-1982)	105
5.4	Marketed Production of Cash Crops	108
5.5	Livestock Population	111
5.6	The Volume of Fish Landed at Pointe-Noire by Commercial Fishermen (1970-1980)	114
6.1	Composition of Coffee Prices and Marketing Costs (1973-1979)	118
6.2	Composition of Cocoa Prices and Marketing Costs (1973-1979)	122
7.1	Distribution of Rural Population, Number of Holdings and Area Under Cultivation by Regions	124
7.2	Distribution of Active Farm Family Members By Age, Sex and Region	125
7.3	Estimation of Per Capita Agricultural Income (1970-1982)	136
7.4	Number of Students at Different Levels of Education	137
7.5	The Congolese Diet	140

8.1	Distribution of Farms by Regions and According to Crops	143
8.2	Land Cultivated According to Number of Family Members and by Regions	144
9.1	The Pre-Cooperatives	154
9.2	Participation of Women in the Cooperatives of Pool and Plateaux Regions (1971-1980)	155
10.1	Financial Inflow to Agriculture (1960-1986)	171
10.2	Average Number of Small Tools Per Farm Family in Niari and Pool Regions	172
10.3	Loans for Tool and Seed Purchases in the Pool Area	173
10.4	OCV Seed Distribution	175
10.5	Administrative Employees Funded By the Government in the Pool and Plateau Rural Development Program	176
10.6	Support Personnel for the Pool and Koukouya Plateau Rural Development Program	178

FIGURES

1.1	Population Pyramid	12
2.1	Gross National Product (1970-1983)	26
2.2	Growth of Agriculture & Forestry; Mining; Manufacturing & Construction; Transport, Communications & Services (1970-1983)	28
4.1	Position of Air Masses During Southern Winter and Summer	62
4.2	Duration of Long Dry Season in Days	64

4.3	Duration in Days and Ending Dates of Short Dry Season	65
4.4	Annual Rainfall Variability at Pointe-Noire (1950-1975)	67
4.5	Annual Rainfall At Loubomo (1950-1980)	68
4.6	Annual Rainfall At Impfondo (1950-1980)	70
4.7	Mean Annual Precipitation in MM (1951-1975)	71
4.8	Mean Monthly Values of Precipitation and Potential Evapotranspiration: Loubomo, Mouyondzi, Brazzaville	72
4.9	Mean Monthly Values of Precipitation and Potential Evapotranspiration: Mpouya, Owando-Makoua, Ouesso	73
4.10	Distribution of Stations Within the Congo	74
4.11	Mean Annual Actual Evapotranspiration in Millimeters (1951-1975)	77
4.12	Mean Monthly Sunshine and Temperatures (1951-1975): Loubomo, Mouyondzi, Brazzaville	78
4.13	Mean Monthly Sunshine and Temperatures (1951-1975): Mpouya, Makoua, Ouesso	79
4.14	Hydrologically Homogeneous Sub-Zones and Drainage Areas	82

MAPS

	The People's Republic of the Congo	xxii
1.1	Administrative Divisions	9
1.2	Ethnic Groups	14
7.1	Rural Density	127
7.2	Small Farmer Cash Crop Producing Areas	135

Preface

In the hot, steamy capital city of Brazzaville on the Congo River, an experiment in socialist planning and economic development is taking place in what was once a center of the African slave trade.

The Congo is 342,000 square kilometers (132,000 square miles), slightly larger than the state of New Mexico. An estimated two-thirds of the Congo's population of 1.8 (1986) million people live in the two major cities of Brazzaville and Pointe Noire and along the Congo Ocean Railway line linking the two. The Congo has a coastline of only 160 kilometers and it is only 480 kilometers wide at its maximum width. About two-thirds of the country is covered with forest, the rest is savanna. In rural areas the Congolese live in small communities and have little outside contact. Just 50 miles outside of the capital there is little evidence of modern day development except for transistor radios that bring the outside world to the thatched clay and earthen homes without electricity or running water. Some 9,000 Europeans, mostly French, remain as residents.

The Congo was one of the four territories of the French Equatorial Africa; it became independent in 1960. Since 1968 the country turned to socialism in its economic orientation with the government increasing control of the economy and pushing agriculture toward a socialist transformation. The government began to establish state farms and ranches as well as grouping the farmers into cooperatives and pre-cooperatives.

As a result of these policies, agricultural production has declined steadily with farmers turning away from the rural areas to the cities, generating a continuing rise in unemployment. The unemployed work force must be absorbed by the public sector in order to avoid social and political unrest, thus straining the budget severely.

This book analyzes the fundamental structural changes within the Congolese economy and the impact of the application of a Marxist model of development upon the performance and growth of agriculture. The course of rural development over the past fifteen years is charted with an emphasis on migration, welfare, and the influence of external aid on small farming communities. An assessment is also made of the constraints on agricultural production and marketing and the effectiveness of farmer cooperatives in overcoming these limitations. The study explores the prospects for future development in the Congo as well as offering an analysis applicable to other African states.

In writing this book, I had in mind not only scholars and students of African development, but also the people of the Congo and their needs as well as the potential aid donors who will assist the Congo in its quest for progress. As a result, throughout the book I did not hesitate to discuss policy issues and recommend measures to improve existing conditions. At the end of the book there is a list of feasible projects to enhance the agriculture and rural development.

The Congo is facing problems that elude its ideology. They are the basic problems of a developing country: lack of capital and trained personnel, unemployment, economic underdevelopment and a rural, disguised urban population shift that intensifies the strains. The government's intervention in all phases of the economy has certainly exacerbated the problems. At the end of its second five-year plan (1982-1986) the Congolese development dreams, based on oil resources, were dashed by falling prices. The Congo remains an agricultural society, true to the symbols of its red flag with two green palm branches framing a crossed hoe and hammer, topped by a gold star.

In recent years, the economic problems of the country have been aggravated to the point of crisis, forcing the government to reorient its thinking on the merits of socialism. Though still pursuing the "socialist option," the government has now moved toward liberalization of the economy, granting more private ownership and incentives to farmers. It has accorded a high priority to "dynamizing the small farmers sector" with the aim of revitalizing agriculture. It is this new trend toward upgrading the private sector that promises to enhance future economic development of the Congo in the future.

G. Nguyen Tien Hung
Howard University

Acknowledgments

This book grew out of a report that I prepared for Development Associates, Inc. in the summer of 1980. I am grateful to Development Associates, Inc. for granting permission to use the materials in my original report and encouraging me to publish a more extensive book on the Congo to contribute to the area of African development, especially French- speaking Africa. Peter Davis, President, and John H. Sullivan, Vice President of Development Associates, were helpful in offering their encouragement and cooperation. For the past five years I have done additional research to revise and expand the study.

I would like to thank my colleagues who contributed substantially to several chapters in the book: José Alfaro, on the agronomic and engineering aspects of agriculture; Richard E. Downs, on the social, cultural, and historical development; Winfred Biddier, on the development of cooperatives, and Russell Barbour, on extension services. I, of course, am responsible for the interpretation and presentation of the material.

I am particularly indebted to the Earhart Foundation and its President, David B. Kennedy, for providing summer financial assistance for the research to complete the book, and for their continued interest in my work.

I am grateful to my friends Professor and Mrs. Lien Fu Huang, and to my graduate students, Ms. Sadie Gregory and Bijan Raffati, for assisting me in research, and Jerrold Schecter for reading the manuscript. My thanks to Martha Albershardt for reviewing the text and to Karen White and Laurie Hall for their skillful typing.

My wife, Therese Duong, has been a constant source of support and strength in helping me to complete the book.

G.N.T.H.

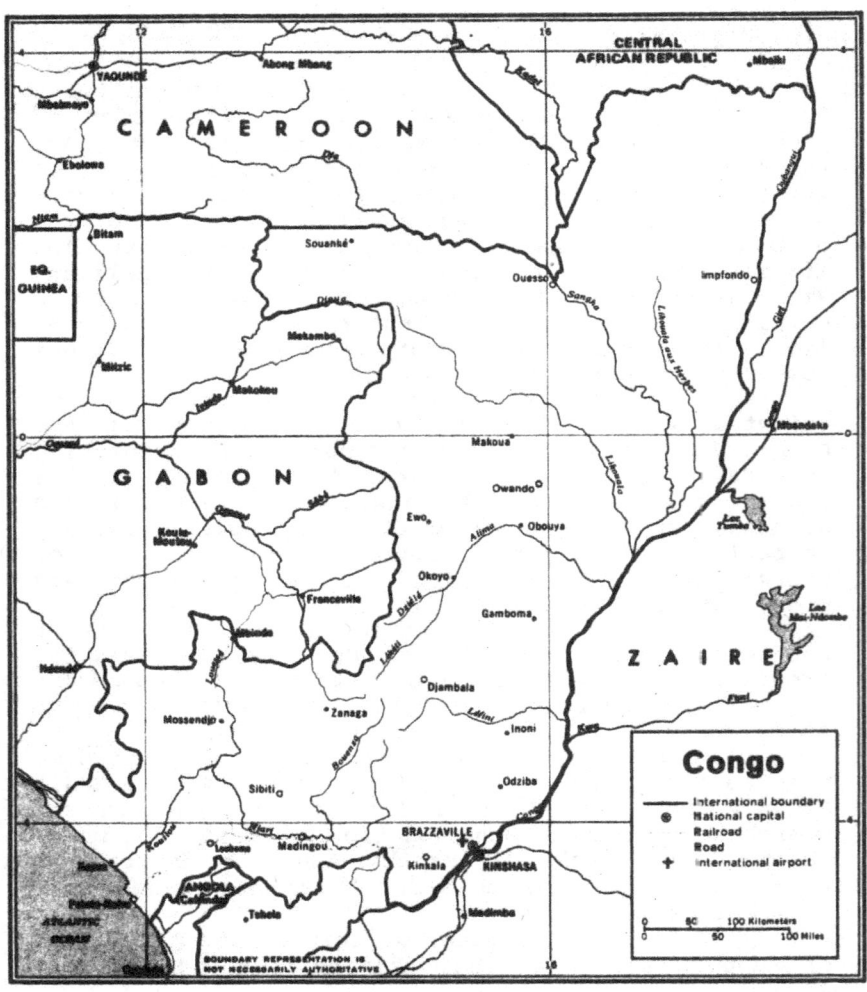

Source: U.S. Department of State, "Background Notes: Congo," December 1985.

PART I
AN OVERVIEW

1

Historical Setting

The Congo's character has been shaped by its relationship to France. The first European explorers, the Portuguese, established relations with the Congo tribal kingdom which dates back to the Fourth Century A.D. With the growth of the slave trade the Portuguese also dealt with the Loango and Teke kingdoms. French penetration of the Congo began when Savorgnan de Brazza set out in 1875 from Libreville in Gabon on the first of three expeditions. In 1880 he reached the Congo River and made a treaty with Makoko, the paramount chief of the Teke people, placing them under French protection and granting the French the site of present-day Brazzaville. In 1882 France created the French Congo, which comprised both Gabon and the modern Congo. Brazza was named the first French commissioner. The borders of the Congo Cabinda, the Belgian Congo, and Cameroon were established by international treaties in 1885 and 1887.

In the beginning, the rapid expansion of their conquests had obliged the French to rule indirectly through the native political institutions. After 1900, however, the French started to eliminate them wherever possible, substituting direct control by French officials. The consequences for the native political institutions are clearly expressed in a passage from a government circular dated August 15, 1917:

> ...but the village chiefs, poor devils designated as responsible by the family chiefs, carefully selected by the administration, maintained both because of lack of personnel and to keep contact with the population, became poorly paid petty officials who were transformed into miserable despots, endowed with European means of constraint in order to satisfy formerly

inconceivable demands (taxes, porterage, forced labor); dispossessed of their former prestige in fact they had no power of their own of any sort, for there are not two authorities in the circle, French authority and native authority; there is only one. Only the commandant of the circle commands; he is the only one responsible. The native chief is only an instrument, an auxiliary.[1]

This policy of direct rule resulted in a structure which a strictly hierarchical pyramidal system defined French authority "the African was involved only at the level of the village."[2]

As France gradually extended its control over the interior, it encountered numerous administrative difficulties, leading to a reorganization of all its territories in Central Africa from 1905-1910 into the Federation of French Equatorial Africa, comprising Moyen-Congo, Gabon, Oubangui-Chari, and Chad. Brazzaville was made the capital both of Moyen-Congo and the Federation. Because the capital of the Federation was located there, Moyen Congo benefited considerably at the expense of the other members with respect to construction of a railroad and government buildings and the provision of public services. This proved to be, however, a very mixed blessing.

The aim of the French government, driven by European industrialization and international competition, was from the start to exploit the supposed wealth of the Congo at the least possible cost. In 1899, 60,000,000 francs were thought to be sufficient to guarantee the success of 41 private companies (societes) to which the government accorded full rights of exploitation (except in mines) for thirty years over 70% of the 700,000 square kilometers making up the country (then including Gabon).

Unfortunately, this expectation was based on the wildest of demographic estimates. In 1901 it was thought that the presumed 10,000,000 inhabitants would produce 10,000 metric tons of rubber and 200,000 ivory tusks. The concessionaires were supposed to organize plantations on 9/10 of their land and make the peasants cultivate two-thirds of the 1/110 left to them in commercial crops. An

---

1. Samir Amin and Catherine Coquery-Vidrovitch, Histoire economique du Congo 1800-1968: Du Congo francais a l'union douaniere et economique d'afrique centrale. (Paris and Dakar: I.F.A.N., 1969), p. 25.
2. Ibid., p. 27.

attempt was made to plant rubber trees to replace the wild ones, but the project was abandoned in 1912 after almost 1,000,000 had been planted.[3]

The pacification of the country proceeded slowly and it was not complete till the end of the First World War. Neither the government nor the private companies had the knowledge or were willing to commit the resources that might have allowed them to succeed in producing the expected wealth.

After the war, the government decided to develop the infrastructure necessary for the evacuation not only of produce from the Congo, but from the whole Federation. At the time they pushed the commercial development of rubber and palm kernels and food crops (especially manioc) to feed the laborers involved in construction activities. The railroad from Pointe Noire to Brazzaville was started in 1921 (at first with forced labor) and finished by 1934. Plans to expand foreign-owned plantation agriculture throughout the country were frustrated during the thirties by the depression and its aftermath and finally the Second World War. The scope of the French development efforts were thus reduced and confined essentially to the south where an appropriate infrastructure was built up. The structure of rural society and traditional subsistence agriculture were left unchanged, except for the effects caused by an increasing exodus of young men toward the cities.

During the Second World War the Federation became a stronghold in sub-Saharan Africa for the Free French Forces under General de Gaulle, with Moyen-Congo serving as a base and transit area for the produce of the rest of the Federations. Under Felix Eboue from French Guyana as Governor-General, social and political reforms were made, many of which were incorporated into the constitution of the Fourth French Republic. Further reforms were made in 1945-46 and 1957, gradually increasing the autonomy of the country and enlarging the electorate to all adult Congolese.

During the post-war period, the French continued to push the development of the Congo along the lines already established. From 1946-1959 a hydroelectric dam on the Djoue river to supply Brazzaville, the ports of Pointe Noire and Brazzaville were built, along with the airport for Brazzaville. Dolisie (now Loubomo) and Gabon, and between Brazzaville and Kindala.

Postal service, telegraph, telephone, and radio were initiated or expanded, and cities were provided

---

3. Ibid., p. 43.

with electricity and water. In Brazzaville a hospital was built, lycees and colleges funded. In Pointe Noire a center for endemic diseases was established. Banks, insurance companies, and oil companies established themselves in the southern cities and various light industries were started to produce cloth, cigarettes, and basic consumer goods. The development included canning, sawmills, shipyards, and factories to fabricate aluminum housewares. At the same time the import-export business thrived. Exports of agricultural products were dominated by wood, sugar, and palm oil. Much of what was manufactured was also exported as well. Bertrand describes the "vocation" of the Congo for foreign capital, principally French, in 1975 in these terms:

> ...a country destined to ensure the majority of activities of a staging post for capital in the Customs Union. On the one hand services, both technical and financial, are much better developed there than elsewhere; numerous small metal working shops and various services begin to function, while almost half the credits destined for the Customs Union are delivered to the Congo. On the other hand transit activities rapidly expand, necessitating the enlargement of the port of Pointe Noire, the increase of the carrying capacity of the railroad and the river fleet on the Congo and the Ubangi; Comilog (Compagnie Miniere de l'Ogoue) begins construction of a railroad connecting southern Gabon (region of Franceville) to the Congo-Ocean line to evacuate manganese ore. Finally a certainly number of small and medium-sized industries produce for markets of the Customs Union (cigarettes, beer, etc.) or even the entire Community (sugar).[4]

A further large scale industrial project was planned in 1956-57 that would have made the Congo the most important industrial center in the French sphere of influence in Africa. Power for the project was to come from a major hydroelectric installation on the Kouilou river 70 km north of Pointe Noire. A major element of the project, however, was to be the production of aluminum from Guinean bauxite, and

---

4. Hughes Bertrand, <u>Le Congo, Formation Sociale et Mode de Developpement Economique</u>, (Paris, 1975), p. 86.

Guinea's refusal to join the Community seems to have stymied the construction of the dam.

The net effect of all this development activity in the post-war years was to further unbalance the economy of the Congo. As Table 1.1 shows, the urban population increased from an annual rate of 4.0% between 1950 and 1955, to 8.3% between 1955 and 1960. Rural population, on the other hand, which grew at an annual rate of 2.2% between 1950 and 1955, declined at a rate of .1% annually between 1955 and 1960. In 1930 Brazzaville had 17,000 inhabitants; in 1945, 43,000; and in 1959, 100,000. Pointe Noire grew from a few thousand in 1930 to 12,000 in 1945 and 57,000 in 1959. (In 1985,, population in the two cities rose to 450,000 and 225,000.)

By the end of the 1950's, the Congo was socially and psychologically ready for independence, but its economy lacked the infrastructure to sustain an independent nation.

As Samir Amin commented:

> The Congo of 1958 is certainly no longer that of Celine; it is 'modernized,' its population urbanised and proletarianized. But it is not 'developed.' The misshapen economy of this territory is not a national economy; it is neither structured, nor self-centered, nor self-dynamic. From a primitive country the Congo has become a true underdeveloped country; a peripheral region of the world capitalist system.

The People's Republic of the Congo became fully independent on August 15, 1960, after having voted in 1958 to become an autonomous member of the Franco-African Community. The Congo also signed agreements with regard to defense and cooperation with France and with respect to the coordination of various economic, financial, and cultural measures with the other states in the former French Equatorial Africa. In 1959 the Equatorial Customs Union (Union Douaniere Equatoriale -- U.D.E.), including Chad, the Central African Republic, Gabon, and the Congo was formed. In 1962 Cameroon joined the U.D.E. members in a common customs arrangement and in 1964 the same five countries created the Central African Customs and Economic Union (Union Douaniere et Economique de l'Afrique Centrale -- U.D.E.A.C.), which was to become effective on January 1, 1966. These countries share a common currency (Communaute Financiere Africaine Franc -- C.F.A.F.) linked to and freely convertible with the French franc at the rate of 50 to 1.

Table 1.1
Population Trend

	1950	1955	1960	1965	1970	1974	1980	1982	1985[1]	1986[1]
	(in thousands and percentages)									
TOTAL POPULATION (thousands)	815	885	969	1,069	1,191	1,320	1,550	1,635	1,764	1,811
URBAN POPULATION (thousands)	119	143	202	294	394	533	671	719	800	832
RURAL POPULATION (thousands)	696	771	767	775	797	787	880	916	965	979
PERCENT OF RURAL POPULATION	85	87	79	72	67	60	57	56	55	54

1. Estimated.
Sources: Population Census, 1974; Programme d'Action du Gouvernement 1978/79; Annuaire Statistiques, 1980 and 1982; and estimates by author.

After independence, foreign investments declined except in mining, forestry, and more recently oil, as they were redirected elsewhere in francophone Africa. On the other hand, the urbanization of the population continued at a high rate. Whereas in 1960 the rural population accounted for 79% of the total, for 1986 it is estimated at only 54%. The slowing pace of industrialization in the cities was not able to absorb the influx of labor from the rural areas which tended to be taken up to a large degree by employment in the public sector. The basic imbalance in the economy created during the colonial period has thus worsened. An ever increasing total population, which rose from 969,000 in 1960 to 1,811,000 in 1986, cannot be fed by a shrinking rural population while still employing its traditional methods of agriculture on soils of declining fertility. Most of the food must be imported for the urban population at a high cost, which has only proved possible thanks to revenues derived primarily from exports of wood, potash (for a few years), and oil.

The Congo has had notable success in maintaining the high level of literacy (more than 50% inherited from the colonial period. The government devotes 15% of its operating budget to education. The government encourages parents to send their children to school, and university enrollment has increased to the point where it strains existing budgets and facilities. The rising expectations created by education have not been fulfilled in terms of employment opportunities.

Most of the population engages in subsistence farming, producing corn, bananas, cassava, rice, peanuts, tropical fruits, goats and chickens; cash crops include palm kernels, sugar cane, bananas, peanuts, tobacco, coffee and cocoa beans. Most commercial agriculture is directed by a state marketing board and the government has established Party "ranches" in an attempt to develop collective agriculture. The government's objectives are broadly expressed in terms of Marxist-Leninist principles. Yet in practice there are conflicting interpretations of how to apply these principles.

The Congo is torn between the theoretical appeal of Marxist-Leninist ideology and the practical realities of economic development. There are signs that finally, pragmatism may emerge as a force which influences policies. The need for capital, entrepreneurial skills and technological know-how are not resolved by slogans or government intervention.

GEOGRAPHICAL ENVIRONMENT

With a total area of 342,000 square kilometers (or 132,000 square miles) the country extends for some 1,280 km. north and south of the equator between $3.6°$ N and $5°$ S latitude. At its maximum width, it is only about 480 km. and it has a coastline of only 160 km. About two-thirds of the country (65%) is covered with forest, the rest is savanna.

Total cultivable land is estimated at 115,000 square kilometers (44,500 square miles), of miles only 220,000 hectares or 2% are cultivated.

Major Geographical Regions

The main geographical division in the country is made by a line running northwest from Brazzaville, separating the north from the southwest. In the northeast, the <u>Congo Basin</u> extends from about $2°$ S to $5.6°$ N latitude, occupying some 150,000 km.^{2} It is in the form of a great amphitheater rising gradually from 280 to 370-380 meters. Covered to a large extent by flooded forests, the only means of access to most of the area is by the several rivers which drain into the Congo.

To the northwest the <u>Sangha region</u> is more elevated, from 400 to 900 meters with the Congo's highest peak, Nabemba, at 1,000 meters. The <u>Bateke region</u>, north of Brazzaville, is made up of a series of four plateaus between 600 and 860 meters in altitude. The landscape here is typically savanna. <u>The Pool</u> (also known as Plateau des Cataractes) is a hilly region west of Brazzaville with peaks reaching 600-680 meters. Northwest of the Pool is the <u>Massif of Chaillu</u>. Almost entirely forested, it consists largely of rounded hills with many streams and cataracts.

To the west of the Massif lie the <u>plains of the Niari river</u>, the most fertile region of the country. Separating these from the <u>coastal plain</u> are the <u>Mayombe mountains</u>, Appalachian in form, from 30 to 60 km. in width, and reaching a maximum height of 930 meters.

Administratively, the country is divided into nine regions which accord only in part with the geographical regions just described, Likouala, Sangaha, Cuvette, and Plateaux in the north; Pool, Bouenza, Lekoumou, Niari, and Kouilou in the southwest. (Map 1-1). Each region includes several districts, ranging from three (Kouilou and Likouala)

Map 1.1

Administrative Divisions

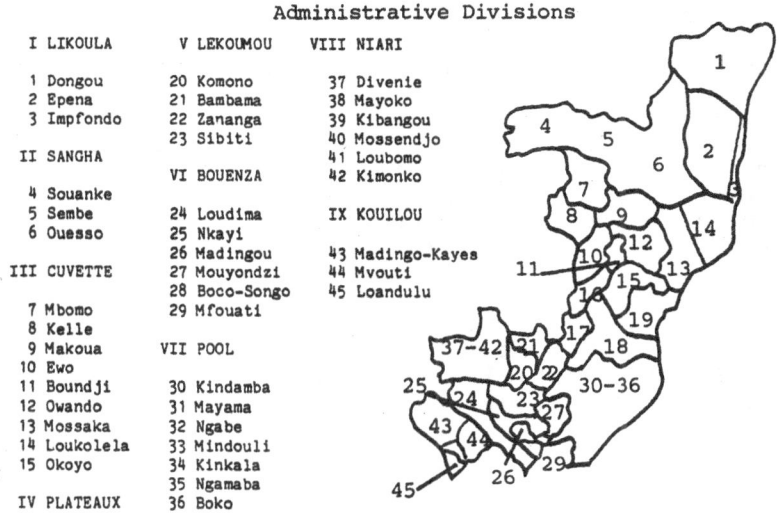

I LIKOULA	V LEKOUMOU	VIII NIARI
1 Dongou	20 Komono	37 Divenie
2 Epena	21 Bambama	38 Mayoko
3 Impfondo	22 Zananga	39 Kibangou
	23 Sibiti	40 Mossendjo
II SANGHA		41 Loubomo
	VI BOUENZA	42 Kimonko
4 Souanke		
5 Sembe	24 Loudima	IX KOUILOU
6 Ouesso	25 Nkayi	
	26 Madingou	43 Madingo-Kayes
III CUVETTE	27 Mouyondzi	44 Mvouti
	28 Boco-Songo	45 Loandulu
7 Mbomo	29 Mfouati	
8 Kelle		
9 Makoua	VII POOL	
10 Ewo		
11 Boundji	30 Kindamba	
12 Owando	31 Mayama	
13 Mossaka	32 Ngabe	
14 Loukolela	33 Mindouli	
15 Okoyo	34 Kinkala	
	35 Ngamaba	
IV PLATEAUX	36 Boko	
16 Abala		
17 Lekana		
18 Djambala		
19 Gamboma		

OLD AND NEW NAMES OF LOCATIONS			
Old Name	New Name	Old Name	New Name
BARATIER	KIBOUENDE	GUENA	BILALA
BRUSSEAUX	MASSENGO-LOUBAKI	HAMON	MADZIA
COMBA	KINGOYI	HOLLE	TCHITONDI
DE CHAVANNES	LOULOMBO	JACOB	NKAYI
DOLISIE	LOUBOMO	LE BRIZ	MOUKOUKOULOU
FAVRE	MOUMBOTSI	LES SARAS	MBOULOU
FORT-SOUFFLET	NGBALA	MARCHAND	MISSAFOU
FORT-ROUSSET	OWANDO	MARCHE	KINTEMBO
FOURASTIE	BILINGA	PATRA	NGONDJI
GARE THOMAS	TSIMBA	SAINT-PAUL	HINDA
GIRARD	MALEMBA	SIMON	KIELLE
		SITOU	MFOUBOU

Source: Jeune Afrique, 1977

to ten (Cuvette), and an administrative town, or chef-lieux. (Appendix 1.1).

Climate

The Congo has a typical Guinean forest climate, with an average annual temperature of close to 25°C. and precipitation generally above 1,200 mm. The southwest has from 1,200-1,700 mm of rain per year, a distinct dry season from May to September, and an annual variation in temperature of 4-6°. The central part of the country generally has a subequatorial climate with 1,600-1,800 mm of rain, a shorter dry season (1-3 months), and an annual variation in temperature of 1.5°. Within this general area, however, parts of the Bateke Plateaux receive 1,800-2,000 mm of rain, have a dry season of 2-3 months, and a greater temperature variation ($2.5-3^{\circ}$). The northern third of the country, from just south of the equator, has an equatorial climate characterized by 1,000-1,800 mm of rain, no dry season, and a temperature range of $2-2.5^{\circ}$.

A more detailed coverage of the geography and climate of the Congo will be found in Chapter 4 of this book.

GENERAL CHARACTERISTICS OF THE POPULATION

Size and Distribution

In 1986, the total population of the Congo is estimated to be 1,881,000 (Table 1.1) and growing at a rate of 2.7 percent per annum. According to a 1983 official estimate, the population was 1,675,067 persons. (Table 1.2 and Figure 1.1). This would mean an average population density of $4.9/Km^2$. It is a young population, with 60 percent of the total under 30 years of age.

For the country as a whole, a total female majority of 52% as compared to 48% for males. In 1977, an agricultural census was undertaken by FAO which provided a slightly different result: 54%, women and 46% men (See Appendix 1.2 and 1.3).

The population is very unevenly distributed over the country, 70% being concentrated in the southern 30% of the territory. Population densities (excluding Brazzaville) ranged from $0.43/km^2$ in the northern most region of Likoula to $9.43/km^2$ in Bouenza, to the

Table 1.2

The Congolese Population
by Age and Sex (1983)[1]

Age Group	Men	Women	Total
0 - 4	151,147	160,388	311,535
5 - 9	132,151	127,063	259,214
10 - 14	102,349	96,474	198,823
15 - 19	75,795	81,618	157,413
20 - 24	57,229	65,016	122,245
25 - 29	48,501	55,320	103,821
30 - 34	42,749	45,442	88,191
35 - 39	42,724	48,609	91,333
40 - 44	36,356	42,309	78,665
45 - 49	31,960	38,063	70,023
50 - 54	26,402	33,173	59,575
55 - 59	24,080	27,048	51,128
60 - 64	18,183	19,375	37,558
65 - 69	9,981	11,472	21,453
70 - 74	6,019	7,611	13,630
75 - 79	785	905	1,690
80 and above	922	1,111	2,033
N.D.	3,110	3,627	6,737
TOTAL	810,443	864,624	1,675,067

1. Estimated.
Source: CNSEE, Ammáire Statistique, 1982.

Figure 1.1
Population Pyramid

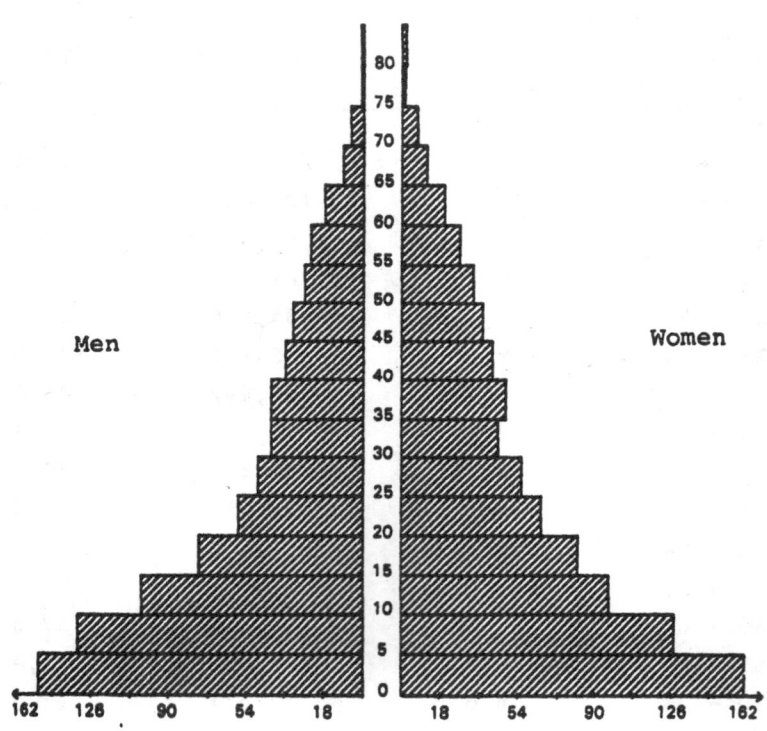

(Thousand persons)

Source: Table 1.2

west of Brazzaville, against an overal rural density of 2.55/km². The uneven distribution of population is due not only to soil conditions and climate, but to the means of communication available. The railroad and road between Brazzaville and Pointe Noire have brought about the heaviest concentration of population in the country. Elsewhere as well, population is distributed in linear fashion along either roads or waterways. There also appears to be a strong tendency of concentration in urban and larger rural centers. In 1986, the urban population (in agglomerations of more than 2,000) is estimated at 46% of the total; population in Brazzaville and Pointe Noire alone reached almost 700,000 or 38% of the total population. In recent years, the number of villages has declined steadily and the trend toward agglomeration has been intensified. This was in part a result of the government's effort to group the farmers together to improve their production and marketing. The government's pressure for grouping was based on its consideration of the size of the villages and the economic consequences which accompanied their smallness.

In order to help to enlarge the size of the villages, a program of establishing large and modern "Village Centers" (Village Centres) was launched in 1983 to induce the peasants to leave their small hamlets and to move into a more viable economic units. In the seventies, 58% of the villages had less than 100 inhabitants each, 39% from 101 to 500 inhabitants, and 4% from 501 to 2,000 inhabitants.

Ethnic Groups

An important aspect of the geographical distribution of the population is its division into a multitude of ethnic groups differing linguistically in varying degrees from each other. Jeune Afriques atlas of the Congo recognizes 74 such groups which it reduces to 13 whose distribution it maps (see Map 1.2). Of these, 97% of the population speak so-called Bantu languages, whereas Pygmies, Ubangies, and foreigners (mostly west Africans) constitute only about 1% each. The largest of these groups, the Bakongo (which the atlas subdivides into 12 smaller ones), constitutes 48% of the population and is found between Brazzaville and the coast, particularly in the southern half of that area. The next largest group is that of the Bateke (equally divided into 12 subgroups), who constitute 22% of the population. They are found principally north of Brazzaville in

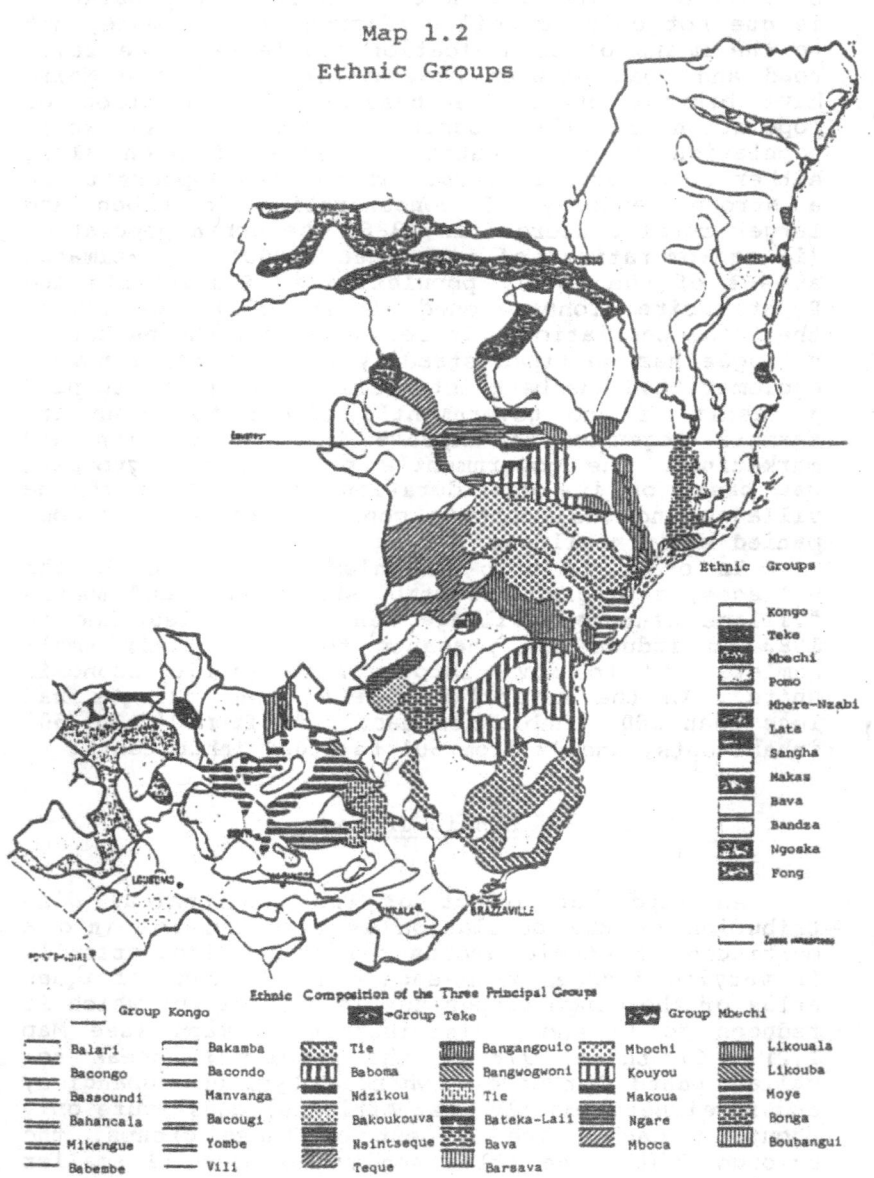

Map 1.2
Ethnic Groups

Source: Jeune Afrique, 1977.

the Plateaux region and the northern parts of the Pool, but also extend westward into Kekoumou. The Mboshi (subdivided into ten groups) makes up 13% and are found principally in the Cuvette.

French is the official language of the Congo, but in addition three <u>lingua franca</u> have developed in different regions of the country; <u>Lingala</u> for the Bateke and other Bantu peoples further north, <u>Munuku-tuba</u> for the Bakongo and other southern groups, and <u>Sangho</u> for those along the Ubangi river. The ethnic divisions within the country are reflected not only in the rural areas, but in the cities as well, where one tends to find distinct ethnic sections. Ethnic loyalties have important political ramifications, being clearly evident in the support for different political figures and factions since independence. The major division here has been that between the north and south, opposing essentially the Mboshi in the north to the Bakongo and Bateke in the south.

2

Economic and Financial Conditions Bearing on Agriculture, 1960–1985

BACKGROUND

At the dawn of independence in 1960, the Congolese economy was already burdened with an oversized service sector stemming from the fact that since 1905 Brazzaville had replaced Libreville (Gabon) as the administrative capital of the Federation of French Equatorial Africa (including in addition to the Congo, Cameroon, Central African Republic and Gabon). Much of the pre-independence economic activity in the urban area was, therefore, centered around the catering of services to the administrative sector of the French Federation. During most of the Colonial era Congo shared with the rest of the Federation investment funds appropriated annually by the French Treasury for public works. Since 1946 these funds were channelled through the French Investment Fund for Economic and Social Development (FIDES). The major portion of these funds were allocated for the construction of housing for civil servants, administrative buildings and infrastructure in the urban area with very little left for agricultural production and rural development.

The Sixties

The first task facing the Congolese economy after independence was to readjust the economy from being an administrative outpost of the French Federation into a fully independent economy with a development strategy more realistic and conducive to natural resources of the Congo. Subsequently, a Planning committee was established within the Ministry of Finance and Economic Planning in order to formulate policy and development programs. Because of the lack of data of basic information on the economy one of the first tasks of the new institutions was to make factual studies and gather the basic data necessary for future programming and development. As a result of these studies, a Five-Year Development Plan officially called "The Interim Plan" was formulated.

The first Five-year Plan (1964-1968) called for a total investment of CFAF 54.3 billion, of which 46% were allocated for industry and mining, 35% for economic and social infrastructure, and only 9% for agriculture (Appendix 2.1). The plan was based upon an optimistic assumption of the inflow of foreign public assistance. When it came to an end in 1968, public sector investment had fallen far behind targets. Several projects, therefore, remained uncompleted; in the agricultural sector actual investment amounted to only 5%, compared to 9% planned. As a consequence, agriculture remained stagnant. The end of the plan also coincided with the change of the government in 1968. The new government headed by President Marien Ngouabi declared its intention to follow the "Scientific Socialist" approach to economic development. The government also abandoned the second Five-Year Development Plan (1970-1974) which was to follow the Interim Plan.

The Seventies

During the seventies the government moved to take over most of the existing enterprises in transport, energy, water and agri-industry. It also established new ones in agriculture, especially state farms and ranches. The government also reinforced its control over the entire agricultural marketing system. At the end of the decade only some pockets of the modern sector remained in private hands. These pockets exist in forestry, petroleum, and manufacturing, which traditionally had been the activities of the French sector. Having abandoned the second Five-Year Plan, development efforts in the Congo during the early seventies have followed pretty much investment guidelines issued by the Congolese Labor Party. During this period two important developments took place which significantly brightened the prospects for the Congolese economy. First, the exploitations of the potash mine at Holle beginning in 1969, and second, the off-shore oil exploration which began in 1972. The prospect of fiscal revenues from oil and potash induced the government to embark upon ambitious development programs, and upon the expansion of the public sector. New enterprises, including the National Refinery and a system of state farms, were launched during the 1970-73 period.

In order to finance these projects the government resorted to increased foreign borrowing. External debts were doubled in 1972, amounting to CFAF 74 billion or 83% of that year's GNP.

During the seventies, both potash production and oil production reached their peaks in 1974 when 2.4 million metric tons of oil were produced and 475,000 tons of potash were extracted. The favorable outlook of oil and potash further induced the government to launch large investment programs. A Three-Year Development Plan (1975-1977) was promulgated calling for a total investment of CFAF 76 billion (Appendix 2.1). As soon as the plan was implemented, however, all the expectation of future revenues from the mining sector proved to be overly optimistic. After a boom of 1974 oil production declined significantly during the following two years, while the Holle potash mine had to be closed in 1977 due to severe flooding. As a consequence of heavy government borrowing abroad to finance development projects, the Congolese Treasury ran into a serious liquidity problem during 1975-77, and the Three-Year Plan had to be postponed.

First Half of the Eighties

The country began the third decade of independence with some favorable developments: dramatic increases in both oil production (reaching 4.1 million tons by 1981) and in oil prices. Receipts from oil exports which was quadrupled to CFAF 120 billion in 1980 ($53 million at 1980 exchange rate) continued to increase to CFAF 318 billion ($826 million at 1983 exchange rate) estimated for 1983. The oil boom brought unprecedented prosperity to the Congo which generated more optimism for the government's development outlook.

The 1982-1986 Five-Year Plan

An ambitious Five-Year Plan covering 1982-1986 was launched in December, 1981 calling for a total investment of CFAF 1,110 billion ($3,384 million in 1982 exchange rates). The plan was formulated with the objective to correcting the regional economic and population imbalance, putting heavy emphasis on

Table 2.1

The Five-Year Development Plan

1982 - 1986

Sector	Amount in CFAF millions	Percent
Agriculture	73,000	6.6
Forestry	194,826	17.6
Fishing	6,051	0.5
Mines & Energy	98,007	8.8
Manufacturing	95,554	8.7
Transportation	129,390	11.7
Construction & public works	195,753	17.6
Urban infrastructure & water	41,400	3.6
Trade & tourism	32,849	3.1
Information, telecommunications, arts, sciences	42,108	3.8
Education, health, social affairs, sports	60,994	5.5
Administrative investments	85,309	7.6
Other	54,759	5.0
Total	1,110,000	100.0

Source: Ministry of Planning, Plan Quinquenal, 1982-86.

physical infrastructure, especially roads, energy and water and on revitalization of the production sector (Table 2.1). The plan stipulated priority for redressing agriculture including forestry and fishing. Public investment going to this sector accounted for CFAF 73 billion ($222 million) or 6.6% of the total.

Within agriculture, the large share of the resource was budgeted for the state sector with relatively little left for the small farmers as discussed later in this book (See Chapters 5 and 10).

The favorable results of the oil sector performance in the late seventies and early eighties also induced the government to accelerate the speed of exploration of known deposits at Likalala, Libondo, Loango-south and Palakou.

STRUCTURAL DISEQUILIBRIUM

The year of 1986 marked the end of Congo's second Five-Year Development Plan during the post-independence era. During the first four years of the Plan, Brazzaville, the capital, shows signs of prosperity, while at Pointe Noire, the country's only sea port and second largest city, commerce is thriving. The prosperity stems from the remarkable performance of the oil sector which began in 1978. Beginning with 1985, however, the impact of sharp decline in oil price had become clearly visible with high unemployment and rising budgetary deficits, forcing the government to scale down to about a half of its development expenditures. The sudden deterioration of the economy dramatizes its vulnerability to one single factor: the receipts from oil. Whatever happens to the oil sector dictates nearly all other activities in the economy. For leaving oil aside, there is a serious weakness of the economy: the state of its imbalance which is imbedded in the development history of the country.

There are many factors which explain the imbalance. First, the oversized service sector in the economy which has already been explained in terms of the traditional role of Brazzaville as an administrative capital of the Federation of French Equatorial Africa. Second, the role of the transport sector which further enlarges activities. To a large extent, the Congolese transport development in the past was due to its location as a transport corridor for the neighboring countries, especially Gabon and Central African Republic, which ship timber, manganese, and other exported as well as imported products through the Congo. For this reason, an important part of income and employment were derived from transport services. Third, the emergence of the mining sectors. The oil and potash sector has not only provided direct services and related employment, but through its income generation effect, increased opportunities for services in Brazzaville and at Pointe Noire, especially in the catering services to the growing expatriate sector. Finally, the government's full employment policy. The rise in urban population has been too great to be absorbed by the private industrial and commercial sectors. To relieve the pressure the government has committed itself to guaranteeing full employment to all graduates from high school who cannot find work in the private sector, thus greatly enlarging its personnel. The expansion of the state enterprise system, both in manufacturing and agriculture, has also contributed to the enlargement of the service sector. As the oil sector grew in recent years so did the public sector which further exacerbated the economic disequilibrium.

BEHIND THE $1,000 PER CAPITA INCOME

One of the implications of the disequilibrium in the Congolese economy is its bearing on the per capita income. In 1983 the Congolese per capita income is estimated at CFAF 441,000 ($1,100). As such the Congolese income is generally considered as one of the highest income in tropical Africa. Nevertheless, looking through the structure of per capita income and against the background of the disequilibrium as described in the previous section, it is evident that careful attention must be paid when comparing the Congolese income with that of other countries. As illustrated in Table 2.2, the value of goods production, leaving oil aside, is exceptionally low, accounting for only 23% of the 1983 GNP. That leaves 77% to the production of services (excluding oil). The lopsided distribution of sectorial contributions to GNP in the Congo is unique among the West and Central African economies. Within the 23% of the goods production component of the GNP, agricultural production, including forestry, accounts for only 8.0%. If forestry is excluded (forestry being exploited by expatriates and state enterprise), the agricultural component would be only 7.0%. On the basis of agricultural production, per capita income in the rural sector is estimated at $150 or amounting

Table 2.2

Behind the High Per-Capita Income (1983)

Sector	CFAF (billions)	Percent of total	Observations
Agriculture and Forestry	64.2	8.0	
Mining (of which oil)	318.4	39.6	23% Goods component excluding oil (63% including oil)
Manufacturing & Construction	123.0	15.3	
Transport & Comm. Services	181.6	22.6	
Trade	84.4	10.5	77% Services component, excluding oil (37% including oil)
Import Taxes	33.0	4.0	
GDP (market price)	804.6	100.0	
Less Factor Services Payment	65.6		
GNP (market prices)	739.0		
Population (thousands)	1,675.0		
Per Capita GNP (in CFAF)	441,194.0		

1. 1983 Exchange rate: US $1=CFAF 385 (See Appendix 13).
Source: Table 2.3.

to only 13% of the national average. If the current trend is allowed to continue, the Congolese economy is likely to become more and more imbalanced in the years ahead, favoring the modern sector and leaving the traditional sector to become more and more depressed.

QUANTITATIVE TRENDS

Gross Domestic Product (GDP)

Official data on national income in the Congo are incomplete and are often estimates. As such they can only be interpreted as indicative of development trends. Because of the predominant role of oil, fluctuations in national income can be attributed directly to foreign exchange receipts from oil exports. Table 2.3, Figures 2.1 and 2.2 show the development of Gross Domestic Products (GDP), Gross National Products (GNP) and some major industry sectors in the 70's and early 80's. GDP growth rates average at 11.3% during 1970-73. It soared to a high of 33.5% in 1974, then slowed down considerably and steadily to 4.8% in 1977. Recovery took place in 1978 and growth rate again rose to 12.6% in that year. Another boom began in 1979 with a growth rate of 27.1%. It peaked at a record high of 50.2% in 1981. GDP growth rate averaged 40.7% during the 1980-82 period. Preliminary estimates for 1983 show a decline in the rate of growth to approximately 13.0%.

From 1970 to 1983 the least square estimate of the growth rate for GDP is 18.32% and for GNP is 17.82%. The estimated equations are as follows:

$$\log GDP = 3.9486 + 0.1832T \qquad R^2 = .956$$
$$(16.212)$$

and

$$\log GNP = 3.9264 + 0.1782T \qquad R^2 = .949$$
$$(14.975)$$

T stands for time trend. The coefficients of T stand for growth rate for GDP or GNP as specified in equations. Time trend explains the growth pattern for GDP up to 95.6% and for GNP up to 94.9%. The numbers in parenthesis are the t statistic associated with the coefficients (A coefficient is significant at 95% level if it is higher than 1.96.)

Table 2.3
Gross Domestic Product (GDP), Gross National Product (GNP) 1970-1983
(in billions of current CFAF)

	1970	1971	1972	1973	1974	1975	1976	1977	1978	1979	1980	1981	1982	1983
Agriculture and Forestry	12.1	12.5	14.1	14.2	15.0	18.1	19.4	22.9	25.6	29.0	42.0	42.7	60.7	64.2[1]
Mining (including oil)	1.5	1.9	3.8	9.5	32.6	25.8	31.0	27.3	33.8	71.0	121.0	212.7	274.8	318.4
Manufacturing and Construction	14.1	15.7	17.7	19.2	21.6	27.1	28.3	26.9	33.7	40.0	47.0	63.0	95.0	123.0
Trade	10.4	12.0	13.4	14.2	17.4	21.2	22.4	25.3	27.3	28.0	29.0	48.7	79.6	84.4
Transport, Communications and Services	30.3	33.0	36.1	38.7	42.7	55.0	55.5	62.3	66.4	74.0	104.0	152.6	171.2	181.6
Import Taxes	6.0	7.3	6.0	6.4	7.7	12.4	16.8	17.0	15.1	15.0	17.5	22.0	30.3	33.0
Gross Domestic Product (GDP) at Market Prices	74.4	82.4	91.1	102.6	137.0	159.6	173.4	181.7	202.2	257.0	360.6	541.7	711.6	804.6
Net Factor Services Payments	-1.7	-2.1	-1.8	-7.3	-5.2	-6.5	-9.7	-10.3	-17.7	-19.0	-32.6	-32.7	-59.6	-65.6
Gross National Product (GNP) at Market Prices	72.7	80.3	89.3	95.3	131.8	153.1	163.7	171.4	184.5	238.0	328.0	509.0	652.0	739.0

1. Preliminary data
Sources: Ministry of Planning, Centre National de la Statistique, et des Etudes Economiques, Annuaire Statistiques, 1982, 1983 and estimates by the author.

Sectorial Growth

Transport

Traditionally, the Congo has played an important role in the transequatorial transport system that linked Chad and the Central African Republic, and the interior of Gabon with the Atlantic Coast. Transequatorial system is comprised of a road, river and rail network with some 2,400 kilometers in length, linking Fort Archambault with Pointe Noire in Congo via Bangui on the Ubangi River and Brazzaville on the Congo River. The system was maintained by the Transequatorial Communications Agency (TCA). The TCA was a public interstate agency created in 1959 to serve the Central African Republic, Chad, Congo, and Gabon. All the rail portion and almost all the river portion of the system were within the Congo's frontiers. As such, an important part of import and export of the neighboring Chad, Gabon and Central African Republic had to go through the transport system of the Congo.

In 1970 the TCA was dissolved and Congo as well as Chad established its own transport agencies, the Agence Transcongolaise des Communications (ATC) and the Agence Centra-Africaine des Communications Fluviales (ACCF) for Congo and Chad, respectively.

At present the Congolese agency is comprised of a favorably located seaport at Pointe Noire, and river port facilities at Brazzaville, Mossaka, and Ouesso, some 500 kilometers of railway linking the main system with the Gabonese border. In 1970-73 the transport and communications sector accounted for about 25% of the GDP. In 1974, however, because of the substantial increase in oil and potash production, mining took over as the leading sector. Transport recovered its dominant role again in the following year continuing through 1978.

From 1970-83 the overall growth rate of this particular sector is estimated as 14.22%, which is obtained from the following growth function:

$$\log Y_1 = 3.1173 + 0.1422T \qquad R^2 = .949$$
$$(14.968)$$

Y_1 represents the GDP component of transport, communication and services. The numbers in parenthesis denote the t statistic. This equation has 94.9% of explanatory power.

Figure 2.1

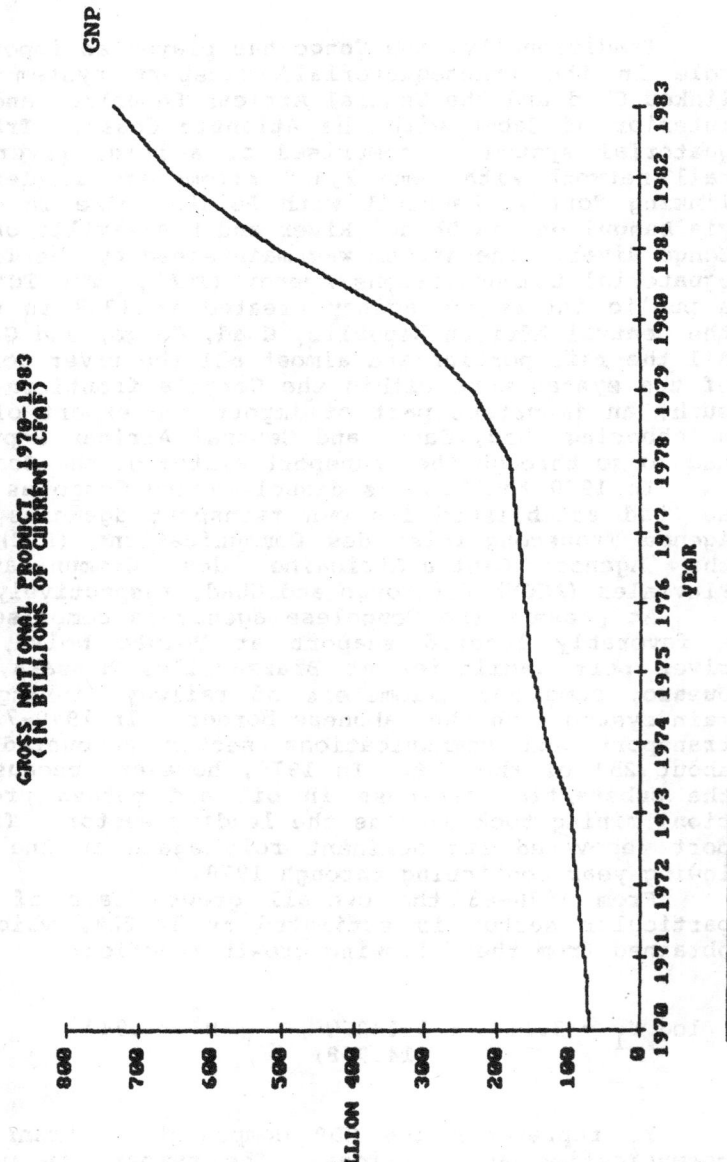

Source: Table 2.3.

Mining

Mining emerged as an important sector beginning in 1969 with the production of potash at the Holle mine by the Compagnie des Potasses du Congo (CPC). The role of mining became more and more important when in 1972 oil production started. The share of mining in the GDP which had been only 2% in 1970 rose to 27% in 1979 and 40% in 1983.

There are three main oil fields: the Emeraude, the Loango, and the Likouala. The Emeraude field started production in 1972; the Loango in 1977; and the Likoudla in 1980. Production carried out by two foreign companies (one French -- the ELF, and the other Italian -- the AGIP) on a 63:35% basis. Oil production reached 2.4 million metric tons in 1974, then declined to 1.8 million tons in 1975 and 1977 and 2 million tons in 1976. With the production of the Loango oil field, output again rose in 1978 to 2.4 million tons; in 1980 with the Likouala field, production reached 2.9 million tons. Oil output for 1984 was estimated at 5.9 million metric tons or 125,000 barrels a day.[1]

From 1970-83, the GDP growth rate of mining sector is 40.22% which is obtained from the following least square estimation of growth functions:

$$\log Y_2 = 0.3715 + 0.4022T \qquad R^2 = .938$$
$$(12.807)$$

where Y_2 represents mining sector of the GDP component. This equation has 93.8% of explanatory power.

In sum, the mining sector will continue to be the leading sector in the Congolese economy until the known reserves become depleted toward the end of the 80's.

Manufacturing

Manufacturing consists mainly of wood processing and the production of a small range of import substitutions such as sugar, flour milling, cement, textile, plastic, and cigarettes. With construction, manufacturing contributed 19% to the GDP in 1970,

---

1. U.S. Department of Commerce, <u>Foreign Economic Trends and their Implications for the United States/ Congo</u>, (Washington, 1985), p.2.

Figure 2.2

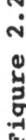

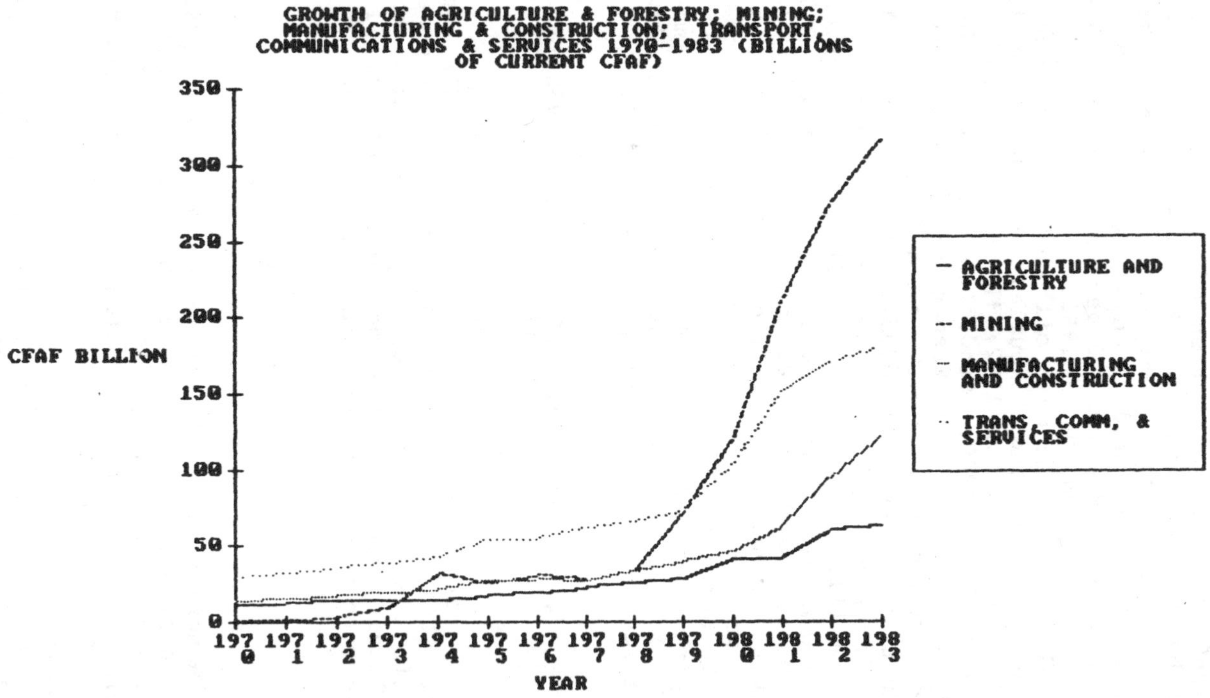
GROWTH OF AGRICULTURE & FORESTRY; MINING; MANUFACTURING & CONSTRUCTION; TRANSPORT, COMMUNICATIONS & SERVICES 1970-1983 (BILLIONS OF CURRENT CFAF)
CFAF BILLION
350
300
250
200
150
100
50
0
197 0
197 1
197 2
197 3
197 4
197 5
197 6
197 7
197 8
197 9
198 0
198 1
198 2
198 3
YEAR
AGRICULTURE AND FORESTRY
MINING
MANUFACTURING AND CONSTRUCTION
TRANS, COMM, & SERVICES

Source: Table 2.3.

then declined to 13% and 15% in 1982 and 1983, respectively, owing to the increased share of the mining sector.

During the seventies, manufacturing underwent important socialist transformation with the government taking over a major number of production facilities such as sugar, energy, wood processing, fishing and building new factories such as cement, textile, and plastic. The emerging of the public sector was also accompanied by a sharp decline in production and capacity utilization.

In 1976 a study by UNDP on the financial conditions of public enterprises shows that all public enterprises with the exception of two companies, the SOCOTON and the OCB, were in a financial deficit, requiring substantial government subsidies (see Appendix 2.2).

Manufacturing and construction have an average 15.24% growth rate during the period of 1970-83. This growth rate is obtained from the least square estimate of the following growth equation for this particular sector:

$$\log Y_3 = 2.3429 + 0.1524T \qquad R^2 = .932$$
$$(12.807)$$

Y_3 denotes the manufacturing and construction sector of the GDP components. The whole equation explains 93.2% of the growth pattern.

Agriculture

Agriculture plays a minor role in the economy. The share of agriculture including forestry which was 16% at the start of the 70's, declined steadily to 8% in 1983. In addition to the fact that transport and mining were the dominant sectors in the economy, there are other factors which have reduced the role of agriculture in the economy. Those factors will be analyzed in detail in later sections of this report.

The estimated growth rate of the agriculture and forestry sector was only 13.44% for 1970-83 period. This result is obtained from the following growth equation for agriculture and forestry sector:

$$\log Y_4 = 2.1627 + 0.1344T \qquad R^2 = .952$$
$$(15.448)$$

This equation explains 95.2% of the growth pattern of the agriculture and forestry GDP component.

Employment

The employment situation in the Congo reflects the structural imbalance of the economy itself; that is, the service sector stands out as the most important source of employment.

There is no current data on the actual labor force and employment. Fragmentary data and estimates of the labor force presented in Table 2.4 show that the Congolese labor force is estimated at 272,000 persons in 1964, and increased to 567,000 in 1983. During this period the employment situation is characterized by the fast growth of the cities and government as a source of employment, thus draining labor away from agriculture.

As a consequence, agriculture, which provided labor for 74% of the workforce in 1964 -- the major source of employment -- declined to 34% in 1983. Government, public enterprise, and private urban employment, which together accounted for only 26% in 1966, rose to 59% in 1983.

Table 2.5 shows the employment in the central government between 1971-1982; the number of employees was nearly doubled in the period. Since 1981, employment in the defense sector has been excluded from the data. It is evident that if the defense sector were included, total employment by the Central government would be much higher, in the years since 1981.

As was already explained elsewhere in this book, there are several factors explaining the fast growth of the public sector:

First, because of the traditional role of Brazzaville as the administrative capital of the former French Equatorial Africa, the government service sector has always been large;

Second, the role of the government as an employer has been more and more important in recent years due to the expansion of the public and semi-public enterprises and to the government's socialist full-employment policy;

Third, the deterioration of the agricultural sector itself has also been the prime motive behind the mass exodus from rural areas to the cities, especially to Brazzaville and Pointe Noire; and

Fourth, the educational system which provides high school education only in the cities and its vicinity; students who would like to pursue higher

Table 2.4

Labor and Employment in Selected Years
1964 - 1983 (In Thousands)

	1964[2]		1973		1977		1983	
	Number	Percent	Number	Percent	Number	Percent	Number	Percent
Agriculture[1]	202	74	226	48	215	45	193	34
Government			22	5	41	8	42[4]	7
Public Enterprises	70	26	22	5	29	6		
Private Urban[3]			198	42	197	41	332	59
Total Labor Force	272	100	468	100	481	100	567	100

1. Including forestry
2. Estimates for mid-sixties
3. Including urban underemployed
4. Excluding national defense sector

Sources: Bulletin Quotidien de l'ACI, May 5, 1966; 1974 Population Census; Ministere du Plan, Recencement Agricole 1972-73; Annuaire Statistique, 1982; I.B.R.D., Social Indicators Data Sheet P.R. of the Congo, 1985, and author's estimates.

Table 2.5

Employment in the Government Sector
1971 - 1982

Year	Civil Servant	Contractual	Other	Total
1971	14,545	3,513	3,638	21,696
1972	15,105	5,725	2,985	23,815
1973	15,715	7,875	1,390	24,980
1974	16,976	9,296	746	27,018
1975	17,533	11,231	391	29,155
1976	19,456	12,693	259	32,398
1977	21,647	13,810	429	35,886
1978	25,436	13,819	258	39,513
1979	27,403	13,711	248	41,362
1980	30,195	14,044	253	44,492
1981[1]	24,137	14,559	253	38,949
1982	26,198	15,061	250	41,509

1. Since 1981, employment in the National Defense sector is no longer included.

Source: *Annuaire Statistique*, 1980, 1981 and 1982.

education have had to go to the urban centers to do so and to search for employment upon graduation.

In addition to the problem of rural exodus, the history of migration in the Congo is marked by an important labor movement: more than 100,000 persons returned to the Congo after its independence in 1960. Some of these were voluntarily repatriated functionaries who had been working in the other countries of the French Union, but the majority were Congolese expelled by Gabon in 1963 and Zaire in 1966. On the other hand, independence also led to the departure from the Congo of several thousands of Europeans (particularly French government officials and military) as well as other non-Congolese Africans such as the Gabonese and the Togolese who had been working for the French in the Congo during the colonial era.

Fiscal Performance

The historical fiscal picture in the Congo is that of sharp fluctuations influenced by oil receipts and government's policy on expanding the public sector. The overall development of the budget is shown in Table 2.6. Fiscal stability, which had been reached in the late 60's, disappeared as the government opted for the socialist approach to economic development. Large socioeconomic programs, expansion of the state enterprise system, and a growing civil service sector have all contributed to the steady rise in public expenditures.

The seventies: In 1972, as oil production started, oil revenues began to flow into the treasury, reaching a peak of CFAF 16.7 billion in 1974, which represented 42% of that year's total revenues. The 1974 revenues were 81% higher than the 1973 level and 2.4 times the 1970 level. The spectacular rise in fiscal revenue fed expectations of future revenues and exerted strong pressure on government spending. There was, however, a sharp decline in oil production in the following two years due to geological problems at the oil fields,; oil revenue declined by 18% and 31% in 1975 and 1976, while current expenditures continued to rise at 11% and 19% over the 1974 level. Added to current expenditures were investment outlays, which more than quadrupled in 1975. In 1976 public investment was reduced substantially, but was still more than double the 1974 level. As a result of these large increases in government spending, the treasury ran a heavy overall deficit, reaching CFAF

Table 2.6

Fiscal Performance 1970 - 1983

(In Millions of CFAF)

	1970	1971	1972	1973	1974	1975	1976	1977	1978	1979	1980	1981	1982	1983
Current Revenues	16,687	17,902	18,927	22,128	40,068	44,278	47,793	50,421	51,700	55,412	99,000	209,000	249,000	282,000
of which, oil	---	---	250	1,238	16,716	13,759	11,604	14,137	12,846	13,491	62,000	126,000	152,000	163,000
Current Expenditures	16,214	17,826	20,466	22,873	39,340	46,603	48,497	57,484	52,059	55,410	87,000	95,000	155,000	180,000
Current Surplus (+) or Deficit (-)	+473	+76	-1,539	-745	+728	-2,325	-704	-7,063	-359	+2	+12,000	+114,000	+94,000	+102,000
Investment Expenditures	1,001	2,093	2,495	3,445	4,119	18,194	8,454	2,468	3,000	10,180	49,000	101,000	198,000	137,000
Other Accounts (net)	-574	-464	-22	-166	522	126	608	-762	---	---	---	---	---	---
Overall Deficits (-)	-1,102	-2,481	-4,057	-4,356	-5,869	-20,393	-8,550	-10,293	-3,359	-10,178	-37,000	+13,000	-104,000	-35,000

Source: Ministry of Finance; Loi de Finances, 1980-82; Annuaire Statistique, 1982 and estimates.

20.4 billion in 1975 or more than triple the 1973 level.

There is an institutional factor which characterizes fiscal development in the Congo and which has not been paid adequate attention by outside observers: that is the monetary and fiscal arrangement within the Central African Custom and Monetary Union under which each member government is allowed to borrow from the banking system under an annual credit ceiling. The modus operandi of borrowing is that the ceiling of the current year is fixed as equal to 20% of government revenues of the previous year. This means that if revenues in the preceding year is high, borrowing in the current year would also be high. For example, the 1974 oil boom boosted the Congo's budget revenues to CFAF 40 billion; this implied a ceiling of CFAF 8 billion for 1975. Table 2.6 shows that in 1975 deficit (and therefore borrowing) rose dramatically by 347%. The implication here is that high revenues of one year will automatically increase the government's capacity to borrow in the following year. In addition to domestic borrowing the government has also resorted to foreign borrowing to finance its growing deficit.

The large budget deficits in the period of 1975-1977 finally brought about the postponement of the Congo's Three-Year Development Plan; as a result, the budget picture improved substantially. The revised 1978 budget showed a deficit of only CFAF 3.4 billion as compared to CFAF 20.4 billion in 1975 and CFAF 10.2 billion in 1977.

The Early Eighties: Oil revenues increased dramatically in 1980, more than quadrupled the 1979 level, reaching CFAF 62 billion ($272 million). The increase continued through 1983 and into 1984, reaching the CFAF 200 billion level ($520 million in 1983 exchange rate). As revenues soared, the same process of revenue feeding expenditures and expectation was repeated: the government embarked on an ambitious development plan (1982-1986) while continuing to shoulder the burden of an enlarging public enterprise sector. As a consequence the overall budget situation deteriorated dramatically. With the exception of 1981 when a surplus of CFAF 13 billion was recorded, deficits in other years increased from CFAF 37 billion in 1980 to CFAF 104 billion in 1982. In 1983 the deficit was reduced to about a third of the 1982 level as the government undertook an austerity program and cut back development spending by about 31%. In spite of continued oil production increase, the soft world oil market in 1984, continuing into 1986, has exacerbated the fiscal pres-

Table 2.7

Commodity Exports, 1970-1982

(in millions of CFAF)

	1970	1974	1975	1976	1978	1979	1980	1981	1982
1. Agricultural Products	1,505	3,897	2,962	2,941	2,201	3,179	1,251	3,182	3,473
of which, Coffee	156	164	165	638	950	1,488	1,156	1,108	1,000
Cocoa	282	714	584	607	949	776	419	932	878
Sugar	710	2,628	1,323	1,106	--	657	131	014	547
2. Mineral Products	855	42,881	33,700	37,584		92,673	181,754	199,318	295,303
of which, Crude oil	60.5	38,499	27,904	31,003		92,259	181,513	198,722	295,058
Potassium	765.0	4,238	5,139	5,917					
3. Forestry Products	5,126	11,854	3,215	2,815		6,396	9,215	14,945	15,353
4. Other Products	5,065	3,905	5,391	6,778		6,085	9,871	2,947	11,903
Total	12,551	62,537	45,304	50,154		108,333	202,591	220,392	326,032

Source: CNSEE, Annuaire Statistisque, 1982, p. 178; La R.P. du Coryo, En Quelques Cliffres, 1983, p. 19, and author's estimator.

sure in the Congo leading to reorientation of government policy toward diversification of revenue resources as well as developmental policy.

International Trade and Finance

In recent years the Congolese foreign trade and finance has also been influenced by the petroleum sector.

International Trade

Exports. On the trade side, prior to potash and oil production, exports of forestry products, mainly logs, had been the most important source of foreign exchange earning, accounting for 40% of total exports in 1970. Following the exploitation of potash mining in 1969, potash became an increasingly important export, and in 1974 reached CFAF 4.2 billion (Table 2.7). However, after reaching a peak of nearly CFAF 6 billion in 1976, potash exports ceased totally as the mine was closed due to flooding.

Beginning with oil production in 1972, crude oil has been the single major source of exports reaching CFAF 38.5 billion in 1974 (2.4 million metric tons), and accounting for 62% of total exports. Due to technical and geological difficulties, however, oil exports declined to nearly CFAF 28 billion and CFAF 31 billion in 1975 and 1976, respectively, or by 28 and 19% (as compared to 1974). Owing to price rises and some production increases, oil export recovered in 1978. In 1979, oil production reached 2.7 million tons then increased to 4.6 million tons in 1982. Current level of production is estimated at 5.2 million tons per year with an annual production potential of 7 million tons for the next ten years.[1] Receipts from oil exports was nearly doubled to CFAF 182 million in 1980 and reached CFAF 295 billion in 1982. The increase continued into 1983 then began to level off in 1984 as oil price dropped on the world market.

Agricultural exports, which consist mainly of coffee, cacao, sugar, palm kernels and tobacco, accounted for only 12% of total exports in 1970.

---

1. U.S. Department of Commerce, Marketing in Congo, (Washington, D.C.: International Trade Administration, 1983), p. 7.

This share declined to 6% in 1974 and further to just over 1% in 1982.

Given the fact that agriculture is the main source of employment for almost half of the population, and that agricultural exports represent the main source of monetary income to the rural population area, it is clear that agriculture's share of the nation's income has deteriorated dramatically in recent years.

Imports. Oil revenues have generated large fiscal expenditures as well as private income and employment which were translated into a sharp rise in demand for imports; total imports reached CFAF 66 billion in 1979 or increased by 77% over the 1976 level (Table 2.8).

The oil boom of the early eighties induced another large jump and by 1982, imports reached CFAF 243 billion or nearly four times the 1979 level; machines and equipment imports increased significantly in 1981, by 74%. As the country embarked on its second Five-Year Plan, these imports rose sharply in 1982, to CFAF 68 billion, accounting for 28% of total imports. Imports of consumer goods, especially of foods and beverages, reflecting the rising demand of growing urban population also increased noticeably. In 1982, these imports amounted to CFAF 34 billion, more than doubled the 1979 level.

International Finance

The sharp rise in imports was only partially a result of the growing mining sector. In addition, mining induced large increases in the Congolese purchase of foreign technical and other services related to oil and its exploration. All together, these developments add heavily to the balance of payments pressure (Table 2.9). Thanks to the increase in oil receipts and a large inflow of foreign capital in 1974 the overall balance of payments recorded a surplus of CFAF 2.4 billion in that year in spite of the large rise in imports. In the years following 1974, however, the balance of payments situation deteriorated to an overall deficit averaging CFAF 4.3 billion during 1975 and 1976. In 1977 the deficit reached CFAF 10 billion, or more than doubled the 1976 level. Beginning with 1978, as oil export recovered, balance of payments improved and the 1978 deficit was reduced to CFAF 6 billion or by 40%. The oil boom in the early eighties brought about sizeable surplus in the trade balance.

Table 2.8

Commodity Imports 1976 - 1982

	1976	1979	1980	1981	1982
Foods and beverages	6,598.2	14,591.9	16,646.4	17,909.8	33,992.4
Mineral products	1,111.6	4,697.6	8,226.0	16,326.2	29,757.5
Chemical products	2,720.9	4,866.5	8,156.4	7,294.4	13,366.8
Paper products	1,558.6	1,431.9	2,523.4	2,206.6	11,016.6
Textile products	3,289.2	4,468.4	4,901.3	4,675.8	10,342.9
Metals	3,795.3	5,829.1	14,021.6	18,411.6	35,420.6
Glass products	782.7	720.8	995.8	1,491.1	3,019.5
Machines and equipment	8,046.2	17,548.1	11,020.4	19,151.3	68,339.5
Transport equipment	5,740.7	6,210.2	8,541.0	17,483.0	4,884.7
Optical instruments	599.4	814.2	1,200.3	1,543.0	4,884.7
Others	2,864.1	4,496.2	5,279.1	11,925.2	10,965.3
Total	37,106.8	65,675.9	81,502.5	118,418.3	242,940.0

Source: CNSEE, La R.P. du Congo En Quelques Cliffres, 1981, 1982 and 1983.

However, given the large deficit in the services account, the overall 1982 balance of payments recorded a large deficit (CFAF 21 billion). Since 1978, there have been two distinct developments: the fast growing services payment item in the balance of payments and the large increase in the inflow of foreign capital. Services payments, which increased from CFAF 42 billion in 1978 to CFAF 112 billion in 1980, nearly tripled to over CFAF 268 billion in 1982, have been the dominant factor responsible for the outcome of the balance of payments.

The Debt Burden

Development in the balance of payments situation has exacerbated the country's external debts burden, which has resulted mainly from foreign borrowing by the government to finance large capital projects throughout the seventies, and during the 1982-86 Plan. By the end of 1983, total external public debts stood at CFAF 572 billion as compared to CFAF 256 billion in 1980, or were more than doubled in three years (Table 2.10). On a per capital basis external debts in 1983 reached CFAF 341,492 or nearly 77% the size of per capital income.[1] The large amount of debts implies a heavy burden of debt servicing estimated to reach 23% of total export in 1983, a burden which appears to be very difficult for the Congolese economy to sustain.

The Other Side of Oil

In analyzing the economic development in the Congo, one factor stands out clearly: the dominant role of oil. By the summer of 1980, almost all economic indicators in the Congo appeared to be following the leading oil indicator, from government consumption to private consumption, from public programs to private investments, from money supply to prices, from exports to services and to balance of payments. The country counted on the rising revenues from oil to finance its growing budget and development projects. Nevertheless, there is another factor which must be taken into account in appraising the financial prospects of the Congo. It is the limited prospect of production. Oil reserves are not only limited but geological conditions severely restrict oil output. For example, it is estimated that there are 500 million tons of oil reserves at Emeraude, the

---

1. Estimated based on Tables 2.10 and 2.2.

Table 2.9

Balance of Payments 1970 - 1982

(In CFAF Billions)

	1970	1974	1975	1976	1977	1978	1980	1982
Exports, f.o.b.	17.1	63.5	49.5	52.9	61.5	69.5	192.0	364.0
Imports, c.i.f.	29.2	57.0	69.4	69.4	67.8	74.7	115.0	235.0
Trade Balance Surplus+ or Deficit-	-12.1	+6.5	-19.9	-16.5	-6.3	-5.2	77.0	129.0
Services (net)	-7.1	-20.6	-32.5	-40.4	-44.2	-42.0	-112.0	-268.0
Private Unrequited Transfers (net)	-1.4	-12.3	-5.3	-5.5	-6.7	-0.9	-14.0	-16.0
Current Account Balance Deficit	-20.6	-26.4	-57.7	-62.4	-57.2	-48.1	-49.0	-155.0
Public Unrequited Transfers (net)	2.5	4.5	7.4	8.8	5.4	8.7	13.0	8.0
Capital Movement	17.3	30.4	44.8	39.9	38.1	33.3	66.0	44.0
Errors and Ommissions	1.8	-6.1	1.7	8.9	3.9	0.2	-25.0	82.0
Overall Balance Surplus+ or Deficit-	+1.0	+2.4	-3.8	-4.8	-9.8	-5.9	5.0	-21.0

Source: Amaire Statistiques, 1982; IMF/International Financial Statistics, May 1975-85.

Table 2.10
External Public Debt, 1970-1983
(in billions of CFAF)

	1970-72	1973-74	1975-77	1978	1980	1983
Outstanding disbursed debt	39.2	49.0	95.4	152.0	256.0	572.0
Outstanding including undisbursed debt	63.5	91.6	152.9	196.6	--	--
Service payments as a percentage of scheduled debt service						
- Central Government	57.8	58.4	76.4	67.5	--	--
- Other public sector	99.2	100.0	96.2	62.8	--	--
Outstanding including undisbursed debt as a percentage of GNP	88.8	86.3	103.8	110.5	--	--

Source: IBRD.

first oil field, but only 15 million tons could be extracted during its lifetime. Most current estimates point to quick depletion of the oil fields by the end of this decade. The decline may take place as early as in the second half of the 1980's.

When oil production ceases to increase or when oil price declines as in recent years, the economic contraction which follows is certainly far reaching. The inevitable downward adjustment of everything from government payrolls to foodstuff imports is extremely painful. The economic crisis of 1977 following the decline of crude oil production in the two preceeding years and the contraction of 1984-86 following the decline in oil prices are illustrations of the effect of decline in oil revenues.

Some Indicators on the Effect of Oil

Table 2.11 illustrates "the other side of oil," showing that during the seventies when oil became more and more important as an economic sector, it dramatically changed the structure of the economy as well as the pattern of consumption in a way which could not be permanently supported by the Congolese economy. Though indicators in the Table are only estimates and all changes in the economy cannot be attributed to oil, the magnitude of economic changes during the seventies had certainly been dictated by the leading oil sector:

First, as a result of the oil related expansion of income and employment in the urban area, the rural exodus was greatly intensified. (As a result, urban population grew at between 3% to 4% annually (See Table 1.1 in Chapter 1).

Second, the Congolese traditional consumption pattern has quickly changed in the cities from manioc toward subsidized, imported bread and rice and from dried fish toward subsidized meat, calling for an increase in imports of foodstuffs averaging 27%, and of gasoline, 269% per annum during 1973-76.

Third, as it has already been discussed, oil revenues have also exerted heavy pressure on government spending. During the same period, current expenditures increased 37% per annum, while capital expenditures moved faster at an annual rate of 48%.

Fourth, the high level of government spending exerted inflationary pressure at the time when agriculture failed to produce more food to support the fast rising urban population. As a result, the price of manioc, the basic foodstuff, increased at an

Table 2.11

The Other Side of Oil: Some Rough Indicators
(1973-1980)

	1973	1976	1980	Average annual rate of change (%) 1973-76	1976-80
Draining Agricultural Labor Force:					
Agricultural Population (Thousand)	756	719	647[1]	-1.6	-2.5
Changing Consumption Pattern:					
Consumer Goods Imports (In million CFAF)	8,187	15,083		28	
of which, Foods and Beverages	3,063	5,585		27	
Gasoline Imports (In million CFAF)	13	118		269	
Fiscal Pressure:					
Current Expenditures	22,873	48,497	69,800[2]	37	11
Investment Expenditures	3,445	8,454	16,420[2]	48	24
Employment in Public Sector (Thousand)	44	70[3]		15	
Inflationary Pressure:					
General Price Index, City (1964=100)	145	201		13	
of which, Food Stuffs	148	199[3]		11	
Manioc (foufou) (CFAF/kg)	55	133[3]		35	
Maize	125	179[3]		11	
Meat (Smoked)	694	2,000[3]		47	

Balance of Payments Pressure:
Total Imports (In billion CFAF)	37	69	115	29	17
Services (NET)	12	40	112	18	20

Expectation: Rising Fast!

Source: Tables 2.3, 2.6, 2.8, 2.9 and estimates by author.
1. Estimated
2. Budgeted
3. 1977 Data

annual rate of 35% and meat at a rate of 47% during 1973 and 1976.

Fifth, an analysis of the balance of payments in a previous section shows that though receipts from oil exports have increased dramatically, expenditures by the oil companies on exploration together with profits and dividends paid abroad by petroleum companies operating in the Congo were mostly responsible for a dramatic rise in outward payments for services. Net services payment increase at an annual rate of 18% during 1973-76, and 20% in 1976-80. In 1980, services payment amounted to CFAF 112 million, equivalent to 55% of exports.

Sixth, the growing income and consumption induces rising expectations, which will inevitably render the call for austerity measures in the future more and more difficult.

In recent years, the government has turned attention to reorienting its policy in order to prepare the economy and the population to face the prospect of declining oil receipts by undertaking drastic measures to redress the situation. These measures called for substantial downward adjustments of both public as well as private consumption (and investment) and the revitalization of agriculture.

Planning for Development: Toward Agriculture

Many of the current fiscal and financial problems in the Congo have their roots in the policy of the country since it embarked upon the socialist path to development in the late sixties. During the seventies, agriculture was about completely neglected while public sector greatly expanded. Since 1980, there has been some change in the direction of the government's development strategy and more attention is now being given to agriculture. In that year, the government launched a "Supplementary Development Program" to follow the Two-Year Action Program (1978-79) with a planned investment of CFAF 72 billion ($318 million). In contrast to all previous programs and plans, in the complementary program the government accorded priority to the agricultural sector and allocated to it CFAF 9.4 billion or 13% of total investment (Table 2.12). The 1980 program calls for "dynamizing" the small holder sectors in order to restore its productivity, especially in food productions. The changing national priority in development policies reflects the government's grave concern about the continued deterioration of structural disequilibrium and depression in agriculture.

In the 1982-86 Plan, priority was given to agriculture, forestry and fishing, which was allocated CFAF 274 billion or 25% of total. Within this sector, agriculture, excluding forestry, shared only less than 7% (Tables 2.1 and 2.12). Nevertheless, in terms of total amount allocated (CFAF 73 billion), annual investment in agriculture during the Plan was to be higher than in any previous year. Details on the role of agriculture in the Plan is analyzed in the subsequent chapter.

Table 2.12

Planning for Development 1978 - 1986 (CFAF Billions)

	Two Year Action Program 1978-79		Supplementary Program 1980		Five Year[1] Plan 1982-86	
	Amount	Percent	Amount	Percent	Amount	Percent
Agriculture, forestry & fishing	18.4	14.0	9.4	13.0	273.8	25
Industry and mining	26.4	20.0	18.5	25.8	193.6	17
Economic infrastructure	57.4	44.0	26.0	36.0	366.6	33
Social infrastructure	5.8	5.0	8.7	12.1	103.1	9
Services	18.6	14.0	13.1		118.1	11
Others	3.9	3.1			54.8	5
Total	130.5	100.0	72.0	100.0	1,110.0	100
Financing by:						
Domestic resources	49.0	37.0	27.0	38.0	--	--
External resources	82.0	63.0	45.0	62.0	--	--

1. See Table 2.1 for details.
Source: Ministry of Planning: Programme Biennal d'Action Governmentale, 1978-79; Programme Complementaire, 1980; Plan Aninquenal, 1982-86

PART II
THE AGRICULTURAL SECTOR

3

Agriculture in the Congolese Economy

A Shrinking Sector

From the economic and financial analysis in the previous section, one conclusion may be drawn: agriculture is shrinking in the Congolese economy. Table 3.1 shows some rough indicators of a quickly declining agricultural sector.

Since independence in 1960, the Congolese population has been growing at an annual rate of between 2 and 2.7%. The rate of rural population growth, on the other hand, has lagged far behind that of urban population (See Table 1.1 in Chapter 1). Whereas the rural population constituted 79.2% of the total in 1960, it amounted to only 54% in 1986.

The decline in the rural population reflects an increasingly important trend in migration toward urban areas. Rural/urban migration has long been a feature of Congolese life, as indicated earlier in the historical introduction, but the movement accelerated between 1955 and 1965, when urban population increased at rate the rate of 10.6%. Migration appears to have slowed between 1965 and 1970, urban growth averaging only 6% annually. Since 1970, however, the annual rate jumped to 8.6% and has remained high ever since.

The rate of migration in this period can be explained in terms of the expansion of the public sector and the maintenance of socialist full employment policy. The government greatly increased its budget for education in the city schools while guaranteeing employment for high school graduates. As a result, young men left their villages for urban areas in search of employment and educational opportunities. Beginning with the 1974 oil boom, the modern sector in the cities grew rapidly, offering more service related opportunities for young workers. The rate of decline in the rural population was

Table 3.1

Agriculture: Indicators of a
Shrinking Sector (1960-1980)

	1960	1970	1974	1976	1977	1978	1979	1980
Agricultural Population								
Number (thousand)	767	797	756	737	719	698	674	647
Average annual growth rate (5)	0.4	-1.3	-1.3	-2.4	-2.9	-3.4	-4.0	
As Percent of total population	79	67	58	54	52	49	48	43
Agricultural Production[1]								
Value (CFAF billions)	8.0^6	12.1	15.0	19.4	22.9	25.6	--	--
As percent of gross domestic product	23	16	11	11	13	13	--	--
As a source of employment to labor force (%)	60	60^2	41^3	37	37	37^4	36^4	36^4
Agricultural Exports[5]								
Value (CFAF thousands)	851^6	1505	2897	2941	2540	5220	5465^7	7700^5
As percent of total exports	8^6	12	6	6	6	8	6	5
Agricultural Income								
Per capita income (CFAF thousands)	11	15	20	26	32	37	43	--
As percent of national per capita income	27	25	20	22	26	29	26	--
Agricultural Prices								
Cocoa producers price (CFAF/kg)	--	--	100	100	130	180	200	--
As percent of export price	--	--	34	30	27	24	29	--
Coffee producers price	--	--	60	70	90	120	150	--
As percent of coffee export price	--	--	19	19	10	20	27	--
Financial Inflow to Agriculture								
Government investment in agriculture[1] (CFAF millions)	--	667^9	781	595	142	9009^{10}	9009^{10}	9009^{11}
As percent of public investment budget	--	7^9	11	7	2	14	14	13
Agricultural banking credit[1]	--	188	489	942	692	787	1293	--
As percent of total development credit	--	2	3	5	3	4	6	--

1. Including forestry; separate data for forestry are not available. Investment shown here is actual which is different from that of Table 2.12.
2. Mid-1960's figure (average)
3. 1973 figure
4. Estimated rate of annual change: -1.1% (for 1977-80)
5. Excluding forestry
6. 1963 figures
7. Estimated
8. Estimated
9. 1968 planned investment
10. Average of planned investment for two-year program
11. Planned investment

Source: Estimates based on Tables 1.1, and 2.1 through 2.12.

estimated at 2.4% between 1976-1977, increasing steadily to reach an estimated 4% in 1980.

In the early eighties, as the mining sector continued to expand, the rate of migration became even higher. The evidence of migration can easily be found. In Brazzaville and the vicinity, one may find plenty of young men driving taxis, serving in hotels and restaurants; if one takes a short trip of about 20 miles beyond the city limits, it is difficult to find a single young man cultivating the land. As the rate of growth of the rural population declined, so did agricultural production. The most important part of the migrants were young persons, leaving behind a labor force averaging 40 years of age and comprising mainly women to engage in cultivating the land. Agricultural production, which accounted for 23% of GDP in 1963, declined to 16% in 1970 and 13% in 1980.

As a source of employment, agriculture which had provided jobs for 60% of the labor force during the 1960's, declined to about 41% in 1974 and 36% in 1979-80. In the same two years, agricultural exports amount to only between 5% and 6% of total exports compared to 8% in 1960 and 12% in 1970. The marginal contribution of agriculture to exports explains the widening gap of income and welfare between the rural and the urban population.

The Socialist Option

Agricultural Transformation

The agricultural sector has undergone a profound socialist transformation since the late sixties. Parallel with the emergence and growth of public and semi-public enterprise in the manufacturing and transport sectors, the growth of government intervention in agriculture has gone unchecked. By 1980, the government had taken over the marketing of all cash crops such as cocoa, coffee, maize, tobacco, and all agro-industries such as wood processing, palm oil processing, and sugar refinery.

On the production front, some 25 state farms of all sizes were established, covering nearly all agricultural production from the growing of fruit trees to the raising of cattle and chickens. The state also has a monopoly in forestry and ocean fishing. Table 3.2 shows the locations, activities, and production of the 25 major state farms and ranches. Appendix 3.1 shows a financial accounting of the state farms and enterprises. All of them, with the exception of the SOCOTON, were in deficit,

Table 3.2

Major State Farms: Locations and Products

Farm or Ranch	Locations	Products
Loudima Fruit Station	Loudima	Fruits
		Fruit plants
SOCOTON	Nkenke	Maize
	(Bouenza)	Paddy
		Cotton
Makoua manioc farm	Madingou	Manioc
Mantsoumba manioc farm	(Bouenza)	Manioc
		Maize
		Paddy
SONEL	Gamaba	Pigs
	Kombe	Pigs
	U.A.B.	Pork
	Loubomo	Pork
	Mssangui	Cattle
	Louamba	Cattle
F.E.D. Ranch	Louboulou	Cattle
	(Bouenza)	
	Louila	Beef
	(Pool)	
R.N.C.P.	Mokeko	Palm oils
	(Ouesso)	
	Kunda	Palm oils
	Sibiti	Palm oils
	Komono	Palm oils
Dihesse Ranch or O.R.D.	Loudima	Beef
Poultry farm	Pointe Noire	Chickens/eggs
Owando farm	Cuvette	Pork/chickens
SONAVI (with Cuba)	Mossendjo (Niari)	Chickens
	Loubomo	Chicks
	Loandjili (Kouilou)	Eggs
	Mafouta (Pool)	
	Ouesso	
Milk farm	Gamaba (Pool)	Milk

Source: Ministry of Rural Economy.

requiring financial subsidies from the state budget. The item "transfers to public enterprises" in the Central Government budget shows an increase from CFAF 1.6 billion in 1973 to CFAF 6.5 billion in 1977, or a threefold increase.

The result of the greatly enlarged state sector in agriculture is the declining role of the farmers in the national economy. Due to lack of incentives to produce a surplus, the farmers concentrate mainly on the growing of food crops for their own consumption. Cooperatives and pre-cooperatives are the socialist institutions by means of which the government has endeavored to transform the peasant sector in order to minimize the adverse impacts on agricultural development of the highly dispersed population (see Chapter 9 on Cooperatives).

Up until 1980, government policy toward agriculture was formulated and implemented by the Ministry of Rural Economy. Agronomic research was the responsibility of the Ministry of Youth and Culture and Science, while agricultural training was that of the Ministry of National Education. The Ministry of Rural Economy (MER) comprised four main departments: Agriculture and Husbandry (DAE), Water and Forestry (DEF), Research and Planning (DEP), and Administration and Financing (DAF). During 1980-1985, the Ministry of Rural Economy were split twice into four ministries: Agriculture and Livestock, Rural Equipment and Cooperatives, Fishing and Aquaculture, and Forestry.

The government institutions in charge of marketing agricultural products are: The Food and Crops Marketing Office (Office des Cultures Vivrieres, or the OCV, see Appendix 3.2). The Cacao and Coffee Office (Office du Cacao et du Cafe, or the OCC, see Appendix 3.3), the Congolese Tobacco Office (Office Congolais des Tabacs, or the OCT), and the Agriculture and Forestry Stabilization Fund (Caisse de Stabilisation des Prix de Produits Agricoles et Forestiers, or the CSPAF). The OCV and OCC were officially established in 1979 to take over the operation of the former Office National Pour la Commercialisation des Produits Agricoles (ONCPA).

The government's policy for the creation of these offices was based on its intention to bypass its own bureaucracy in implementing agricultural policy. The OCV is entrusted with the function of marketing all food crops. In practice, however, it is concerned mainly with the marketing of maize, ground nuts and rice, leaving other subsistence crops such as manioc, yams, and plantain bananas to private traders. The OCV is also involved in the distribution to farmers of such items as seeds and fertilizers. The OCC and OCT have overall responsibility in marketing and increasing production of the major cash crops: coffee, cocoa, and tobacco.

The Agriculture and Forestry Stabilization Fund (CSPAF) was created in 1979 to undertake the stabilization function of agricultural producers' prices; it is the successor of the former Caisse de Soutien a la Production Rurale.

The operations of the OCV and OCT will be discussed in some detail in Chapter 6.

Land Utilization

In 1982, a "mini-census" on agriculture was undertaken providing the most recent data on land utilization. Nevertheless, because of the fact that the "mini-census" is limited in scope, the 1972-73 agricultural census undertaken by FAO, together with its 1977 analysis of the census, is still being used officially to present the agricultural picture of the Congo. This section is based on data of that census.

Of the total area of 132,000 square miles in the Congo, there are 44,500 square miles, or 33% considered cultivable. Of these, only about 200,000 hectares, of 2%, which are under cultivation. Of the cultivated land, 30% is in monoculture and 70% is under mixed cultivation.

Most of the land in monoculture (62.7%) is for the cultivation of manioc. The amount of area in monoculture varies considerably according to the region. In Likouala, for example, only 14.1% of the farmland is in monoculture, while in the Plateaux, it is 36%. In the Sangha region, cocoa is the most common monoculture, while in Lekoumou, one-fourth of the area is devoted to rice. On the average, there are three crops which are grown in association with each other. Again, there is regional variation. For example, the average is 2.9 crops for Sangha and 3.8 for Lekoumou.

On the national level, the distribution of land for various crops is as follows: tubers, 43.9%; other food crops, 22.7%; cereals, 11.7%; oil crops, 7.7%; and others, 14.0%. Among the tubers, manioc is the dominant crop; among other food crops it is plantains; in the cereal group, maize; and among oil crops, peanuts. On the regional level, land utilization patterns vary greatly. The most important agricultural region is the Pool; 22% of all the land cultivated in the Congo is found here, as is 20% of all the farms (Table 7.1 in Chapter 7). The least important region agriculturally is Likouala with only

3.3% of the cultivated land and 2.8% of the farms. The differences between the two regions are great. Pool has seven times the amount of land under cultivation and the number of farms as Likouala.

The percentage distribution of land for various crops in each of the regions is shown in Table 3.3. According to the FAO census, the characteristics of each region are summarized as follows:

Kouilou (8% of the total number of farms, 9% of the total developed land area) (See Table 7.1 in Chapter 7). As in many other regions, manioc is the dominant crop representing about 17% of the area cultivated. It is also the second largest producer of pimento and the most important sweet banana producing region in the country.

Niari (18% of the total number of farms, 16% of the developed land area). Niari is the most important maize producing area in the country with 20% of the national crop. Taro and another root crop, known as macabo, represent 37% of the national total. Other major crops of the area are peanuts (25% of the national production), plantains (20%), and beans (47%). Given the number of farms and the area under cultivation, the Niari is the second most important agricultural region in the country.

Lekoumou (7% of the total number of farms, 7% of the developed land area). Lekoumou has about the same area under cultivation as Kouilou. Manioc is again the principal crop, but the proportion of land devoted to yams is the highest in the country.

Bouenza (15% of the total number of farms, 14% of the developed land area). The leading producer of tuber crops other than manioc, such as white potatoes (25% of the national total) and peas (54% of the national total). Although manioc is the dominant crop, maize covers a higher proportion of land (14%) than in any other region. A higher proportion of peanuts is produced in this area than anywhere else in the Congo.

Pool (20% of the total number of farms, 22% of the developed land area). Pool is the most important agricultural region in the Congo. It is not surprising that of the 28 crops listed, the Pool area is first in production of 13 of them. Among them, rice is 41% of the national harvest, okra 64%, tomatoes 48%, and pineapple 32%. The proportion of land devoted to the last three crops is the highest in the country.

Plateaux (14% of the total number of farms, 10% of the developed land area). The amount of cultivalble land here is only slightly higher than in the Pool; the area cultivated, however, is substantially smaller. This region is characterized by a

Table 3.3

Land Utilization by Regions (in percentage)

Crops	Kouilou	Niari	Lekoumou	Bouenza	Pool	Plateaux	Cuvette	Sangha	Likouala	Congo
Maize	10.4	12.5	11.1	14.8	9.7	9.2	7.6	9.0	6.1	10.6
Rice	0.0	0.9	2.4	0.9	2.0		1.4			1.1
Other cereals	0.0	0.0		0.0	0.0		0.0	0.1		0.0
Yams	7.4	9.1	12.2	8.6	9.5	4.6	8.1	4.1	2.0	8.1
Taro and Macabo	5.3	4.9	2.0	0.2	0.8	0.3	1.9	2.0	5.2	2.3
Manioc (less than 1 year old)	17.1	15.7	11.4	14.0	19.0	19.8	14.8	12.2	13.5	15.9
Other Tubers	3.2	1.2	2.1	3.1	1.9	1.7	1.4	0.3	1.0	1.7
Peanuts	2.7	7.4	6.1	8.9	4.8	5.0	2.1	1.6	0.2	5.1
Gourd seeds	1.5	2.3	4.1	2.5	3.8	2.0	1.5	0.2	1.0	2.4
Other oil crops		0.0	0.4	0.3	0.0		1.1			0.2
Plantains	7.9	9.8	8.1	6.7	3.8	6.3	9.7	22.9	18.5	8.4
Beans	1.7	3.4	0.7	2.1	0.5	0.6			0.0	1.2
Peas	0.1	1.7		5.0	0.7	0.2				1.1
Okra	0.1	0.0	0.0	0.2	0.9	0.0	0.0	0.9		0.3
Pimento	3.1	1.3	1.9	0.5	2.2	0.2	0.5	3.1	1.7	1.5
Tomatoes	1.0	0.4	0.9	0.6	1.5	0.3	0.1	0.1	0.0	0.7
Sugar Cane	2.0	2.4	2.8	0.5	0.4	3.1	5.4	2.7	7.7	2.3
Other food crops	8.0	7.3	10.1	5.4	7.4	8.9	7.9	3.6	4.4	7.2
Pineapple	4.6	1.4	4.4	7.2	8.3	6.8	7.6	0.9	6.2	5.5
Oil palm	0.1	0.1	0.8	0.5	1.8	1.1	2.2	0.3	6.5	1.2
Avocados	0.4	0.3	0.2	0.3	0.4	0.3	0.4	0.9	1.6	0.4
Sapoutier	0.4	0.5	0.8	0.6	0.6	0.7	1.1	0.2	1.9	0.7
Sweet Bananas	4.2	0.6	0.7	1.0	1.7	1.5	1.6	0.4	1.3	1.4
Cocoa	0.1	0.1	0.0		0.0		1.0	20.2	3.9	1.6
Coffee	0.1	0.3	1.7	0.6	0.0	2.3	2.5	1.0	0.9	0.8
Tobacco	0.1	0.9	1.3	0.2	0.9	5.2	2.8		0.0	1.3
Other crops	0.8	0.5	0.9	1.1	0.7	1.0	0.9	0.7	3.8	0.9
Total	100.0	100.0	100.0	100.0	100.0	100.0	100.0	100.0	100.0	100.0

Source: F.A.O., Recensement Agricole, 1972-73.

larger proportion of manioc than elsewhere. It is the same for tobacco which makes this region the largest producer of this crop, with 35% of the national total.

Cuvette (10% of the total number of farms, 10% of the developed area). Cash crops are important in this region. One-fourth of the area cultivated in sugar cane and one-third of the area in coffee are found here, making the Cuvette the most important producer of these crops. The actual land area devoted to these crops is small: 5.4% of all of the land area developed is in sugar cane, 2.5% for coffee.

Sangha (4% of the total number of farms, 7% of the developed land area). This is the only region where three crops, manioc, plantain, and cocoa cover two-thirds of the land area developed. Although cocoa is only third in importance, the region is the largest producer of this crop (81.7% of the national harvest). Cacao is the only crop in the Congo that is so concentrated in one area. Plantains are more important here than in the other regions.

Likouala (3% of the total number of farms, 3% of the developed land area). This is the least populated region of the country and shares with Lekoumou the privilege of not being first in the production of any crop. The percentage of area planted in sugar cane, oil palm, and avocado is among the highest in the country, but in production those crops would be ranked third, second, and fourth, respectively. In contrast, with only 0.9% of the developed area in cocoa it is the second largest producer in the country.

Agriculture Research

Basic agronomic research in the Congo has been limited in scope. During 1964-1975, it was almost completely abandoned. Currently, agricultural research is the responsibility of the Agronomic Research Center of Loudima, the Tropical Forestry Center and by the French Office for Overseas Scientific and Technical Research (ORSTOM).

In 1975, working with the Ministry of Culture, Sports and Science, which supervised these centers, the French government began a program to assist the Congolese in reestablishing its agricultural research facilities. Activities have centered on the agronomic station in Loudima. The station, which served the large French farms during the colonial period, was closed in 1964.

Since 1975, research was aimed at providing assistance to the state farms; in recent years, however, a new emphasis has been placed on research that would benefit the small farmers. Until the 1977-78 season, Loudima research publications were of low quality. Since then, there has been a marked improvement in the quality of work published. Recent reports include a number of valuable studies which, if properly disseminated, would have important impact on the small farmers' production.

Starting with <u>manioc</u>, the country's staple crop, the Loudima laboratory has begun a program of selection for resistance to the most serious disease problems, cassava bacterial blight (<u>Xanthomonas manihotis</u>) and anthracnose (<u>Glometella manihotis</u>), in collaboration with the ORSTOM office in Brazzaville. In addition, work is being done to improve genetic resistance to mealy bug, another common problem of the small farmer. Improved germplasm from the International Institute for Tropical Agriculture in Ibadan, Nigeria, has been introduced for testing, although initial results seem disappointing. Of 14 disease resistant varieties introduced from Nigeria, only three proved to have any resistance to Congolese types of the pathogens. Another 1,500 genotypes from Nigeria are being multipled for further testing, and a collection of 83 Congolese varieties has been made to help in the search for genetic disease resistance.

Other research includes a <u>maize</u> improvement program, again in collaboration with Ibadan. One of the problems of the maize program is that farmers grow maize first to eat fresh as a vegetable, with use as an animal feed being a secondary consideration. Improved types that have been introduced such as ZM 76 have been found unsuitable for human consumption, in spite of higher yields, and, therefore, have encountered resistance by farmers.

Other programs at Loudima include a <u>peanut</u> improvement program that is looking for higher yielding alternatives to the Rouge du Congo types that were originally developed in the Congo and then reintroduced in the sixties. The station is also attempting the difficult task of simultaneously raising both oil and dry weight yields through selection. These two traits frequently have negative correlations with each other.

Loudima has also begun to undertake some research on <u>rice</u> of both medium and short-term varieties. The short season types introduced were Durado, Precose, and IRAT 10 (95 days to maturity). Medium types introduced were Moroberekan (140 days) and Ignape Catato.

Other activities at Loudima include a small scale <u>mechanization</u> program attempting to see if maintenance and cost problems can be overcome at the village level to improve cultural practices, and a very well done soil mineral deficiency study. There is also a small soybean introduction and adaption program which is being tested against the odds that soybeans do not do well in areas with high night time temperatures, friable, infertile soils, or low light intensities, the conditions which exist in the Congo. Furthermore, soybean seed does not store well at high temperatures. Data from the Loudima station indicates that the best germination rates obtained for soybean seed, stored the required five months from one growing season to another without refrigeration, is somewhat less than 50%. In the United States, varieties with germination rates of less than 95% are considered uneconomical.

Research at ORSTOM has been criticized for lack of scientific quality in the collection of research samples, especially the germplasm collection for manioc and peanuts research.[1] This can be attributed to dependence on local peasants for help in collection and a lack of biochemical assays in distinguishing types. Currently, only phenotypic traits such as leaf shape, petiole and stem color, and tuber irregularities are used. Facilities for the more common biochemical tests (protein analysis, lipids, etc.) are not yet available. Other facilities include a small laboratory, five irrigated hectares to make up for the station's somewhat typically dry location, and a cold storage area. Plans include opening additional testing centers in Odziba and other locations to obtain tests results that take into consideration the variation in climate from one part of the country to another.

Agricultural research activities in the Congo encounter a major problem, that of dissemination of information to the small farmers on the improved selections for plantation. Published reports often go unread, partly because of lack of staff directly responsible for dissemination of research results.

In addition to research centers, some of the research work is being done at the state farms. For example, a program of extensive manioc research was conducted at the state farm at Mantsoumba in the seventies. This joint effort by the then Ministry of Agriculture and Animal Husbandry and the French Bureau pour le Developpement de la Production Agri-

---

1. The administration of the station is refreshingly simple. The Congolese director is a soils agriculturalist. He supervises five Congolese agriculturalists, each assigned to a different crop or technical area, and two French agronomists.

cole (BDPA) produced a valuable technical report that in the most part, centered around economic aspects of the state farm, such as man hours required, and the profitability of certain crops. Mantsoumba also produced useful agronomic studies on manioc and corn grown on the farm. Nevertheless, the results of this work were not available to the farmers; emphasis was placed on industrial manioc and corn production methods, more suited to the state farms than to the small scale production at the village level.

4

Agronomic and Engineering Aspects

Climatic Resources

The People's Republic of the Congo has a forest type Guinean climate characterized by higher precipitation and temperatures during the months of October through April. Weather variations throughout the year are affected mainly by the movement of air masses surrounding the country. Two centers of high pressure, the Saharan and South-African, are formed as a result of dry and warm air masses moving, in general, toward the west (see Figure 4.1). A high pressure center originating in the Atlantic (the Saint Helena), carries moist warm air north and eastward onto the continent between the two other high pressure centers. The contact of these air masses produces the Northern and Southern Intertropical fronts. In between these, a monsoon front is formed by the contact of the Atlantic air, and air coming from the Indian Ocean, which is equally warm but dried in part by its passage over the continent from east to west.

Seasons

The southern winter occurs during the months of June through September. During this period the monsoon front covers the entire country extending into Africa, while the Northern Intertropical front recedes as far as $20°N$ (see Figure 4.1a). Along the Atlantic coast, an upwelling of cold waters from the depths cools the advancing air, which is then reheated over land and absorbs great quantities of water vapor. The outcome is a stable atmosphere with scarce precipitation. This results, for most of the country, in dry seasons, characterized by dew and

Figure 4.1

Position of Air Masses During Southern Winter and Summer

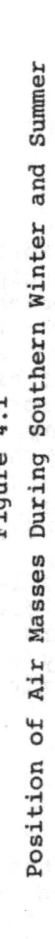

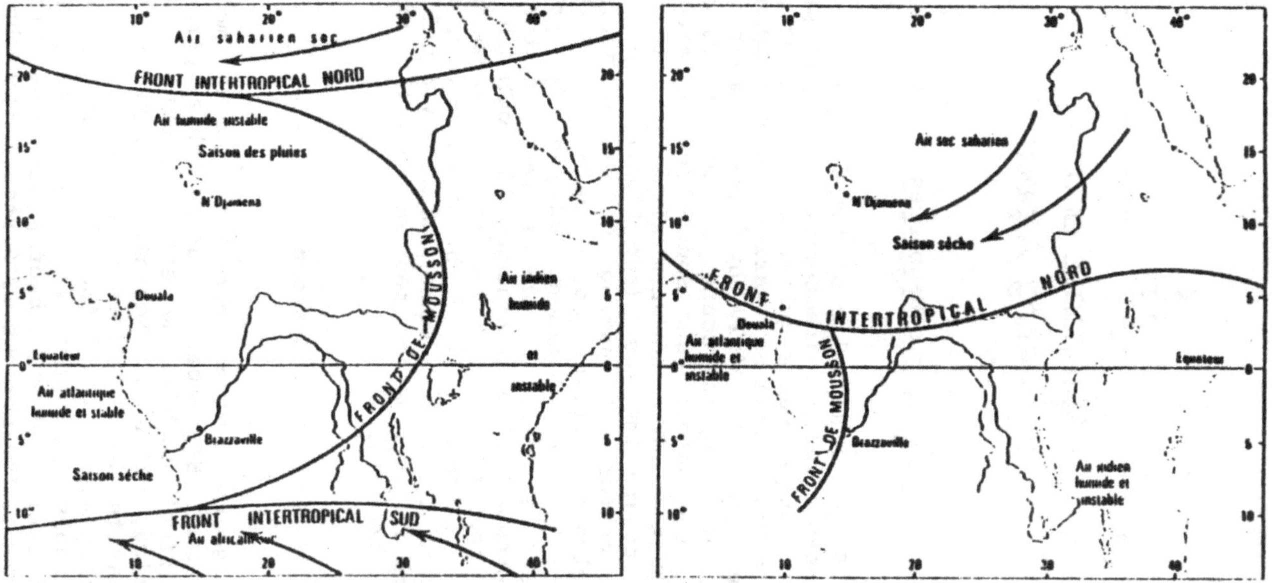

(a) Winter   (b) Summer

Source: Jeune Afrique, 1977.

morning mists, minimum temperatures below 20°C, and a low ceiling of gray clouds most of the day. Figure 4.2 shows the duration of the long dry season, in days, which occurs between the months of June and September. For the extreme northern part of the country, however, this is the rainy season.

Following the dry months, the dry Saharan air masses push the Intertropical Northern front towards the equator. Rains move progressively southward, covering central and southern portions of the country. The temperatures are high. This is the beginning of the rainy season, with storms, showers, sudden tornados, interspersed with hot days. The rains cover the entire country with more than 100 millimeters per month.

In the month of December, the Equatorial African Monsoon front is in its extreme western position, and the Atlantic winds reach only a small portion of the continent (see Figure 4.1b). At this time the rains are less frequent and less intense, with interruptions which might last several months, producing the so-called short dry season. Figure 4.3 shows the duration in days of the short dry season in the northern portion of the country together with the dates at which this dry season ends. The Intertropical Northern front advances to a position near the equator. Saharan dry winds then invade the northern portion of the country, where precipitation reaches its annual low point.

In January, as the monsoon front moves towards Central Africa, the rains increase, covering the whole country, and the temperatures are high. This corresponds to the long rainy season in which rainfall levels of over 200 millimeters are registered during some months.

Rainfall

The Congo has a variable rainy season throughout the year. The pluviometric regime always shows two distinct peaks, the first one occurring between March and May, and the other one between September and December. There are never more than four absolutely dry months between these peaks. Data on the evolution of rainfall from 1979 to 1983 is shown in Appendix 4.1.

Although precipitation generally exceeds 1,200 millimeters per year, there are local factors such as altitude, latitude, and orientation of slopes, which affect the general precipitation patterns. For example, the valley of the Niari, perhaps the most

Figure 4.2

DURATION OF LONG DRY SEASON IN DAYS

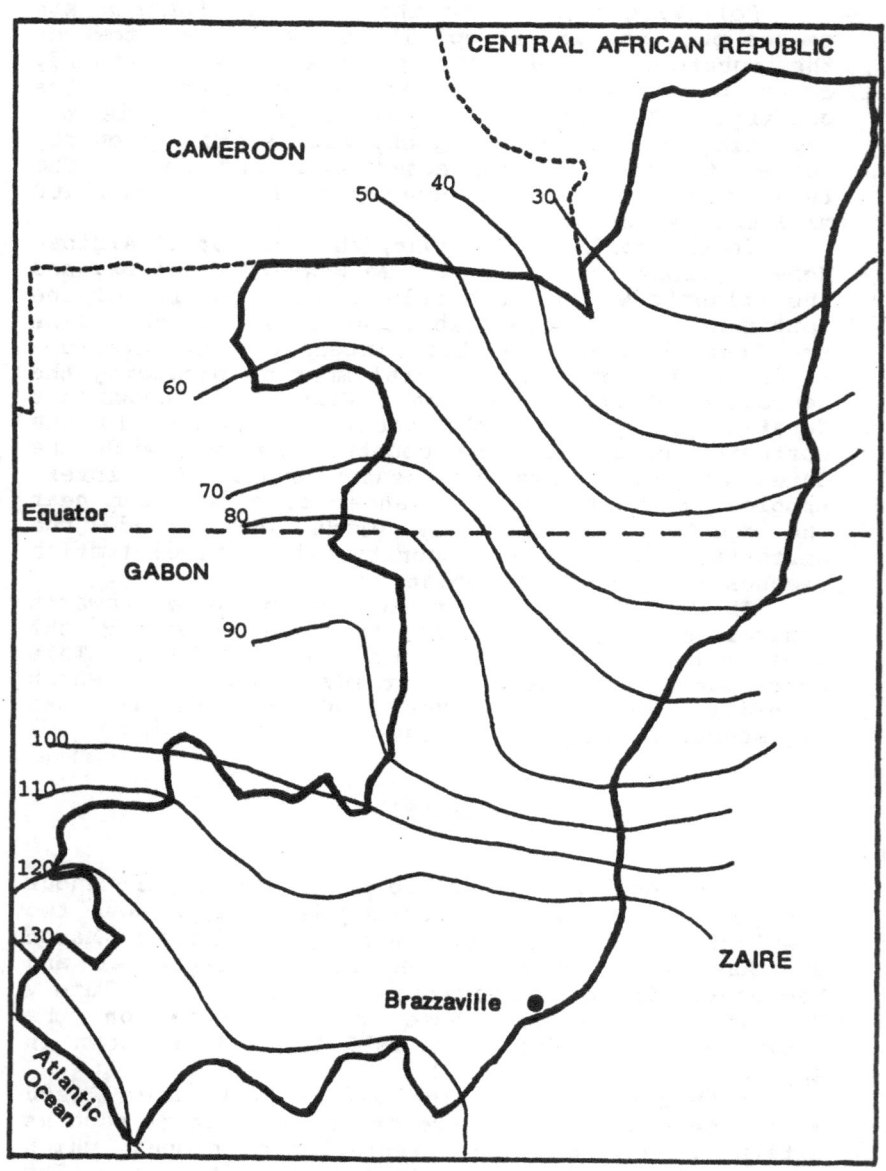

Source: Jeune Afrique, 1977.

Figure 4.3

DURATION IN DAYS AND ENDING DATES OF SHORT DRY SEASON

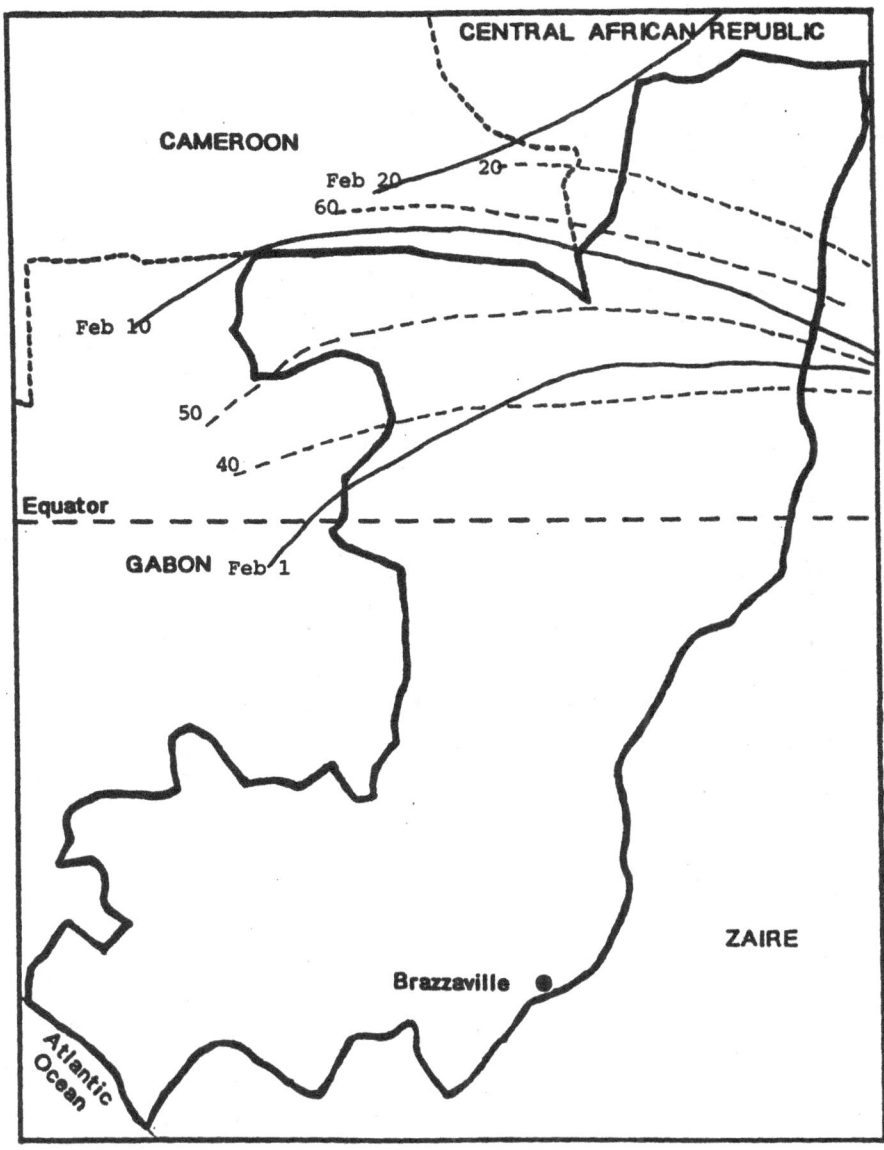

Source: Jeune Afrique, 1977.

fertile and potentially the most productive valley agriculturally, has a relatively dry zone (less than 1,200 millimeters per year) west of the Mayombe mountains, while the Mayombe mountains themselves, the Chaillu massif, and the Plateaux of Bateke, receive from 1,200 to 2,000 millimeters of rain a year.

Yearly variations in precipitation are also observed in the Congo. They are especially noticeable in the west and northwest of the country. In 1958, the area around Pointe Noire received only 299 millimeters of rain instead of the usual 1,300 millimeters. During the same year, Boko, southwest of Brazzaville, received 826 millimeters rather than the expected 1,290. In the northern portion of the Congo, annual variability is less important, showing a steadier pluviometric regime. Here, unusually long dry periods are less common, On the other hand, this area has experienced uninterrupted diluvial rains which have caused famine at times when they should normally have been more spaced.

The annual rainfall at the coastal city of Pointe Noire is depicted in Figure 4.4. The long term mean rainfall of 1,238 millimeters is also included for comparison. This figure shows the variability of the annual rainfall with the minimum value of 299 millimeters corresponding to the drought of 1958, and the maximum of 2,048 millimeters in 1961. Out of the 25 years shown, 14 years fell under the mean or "normal" rainfall. Annual precipitation at Loubomo in the Niari Valley is shown in Figure 4.5. Here the variability over the years is less than that shown for Pointe Noire. The mean annual precipitation is also 1,238 millimeters, but the minimum, which occurred in 1958 and 1971, was 801 millimeters, and the maximum was 1,666 millimeters. In the north, the rains are, in general, more uniform from year to year, as is shown by the records for Impfondo on the northwest edge of the Congo (Figure 4.6).

The annual rainfall distribution within the country is depicted in the map of isohyets, Figure 4.7, showing equal mean annual precipitation values. Although the Congo seems to have sufficient water for agriculture, with lower values in the southwest, an analysis of the monthly rain distribution shows a distinct dry season occurring from June to September.

Figure 4.8 shows the mean monthly rainfall for a 25-year period for Loubomo, Mouyondzi, and Brazzaville, representing the rainfall variability for the Southern Congo.

Figure 4.9 shows the monthly variability for Mpouya, Owando-Makoua, and Ouesso. The appropriate

FIGURE 4.4
ANNUAL RAINFALL VARIABILITY
AT POINTE NOIRE
1950-1975

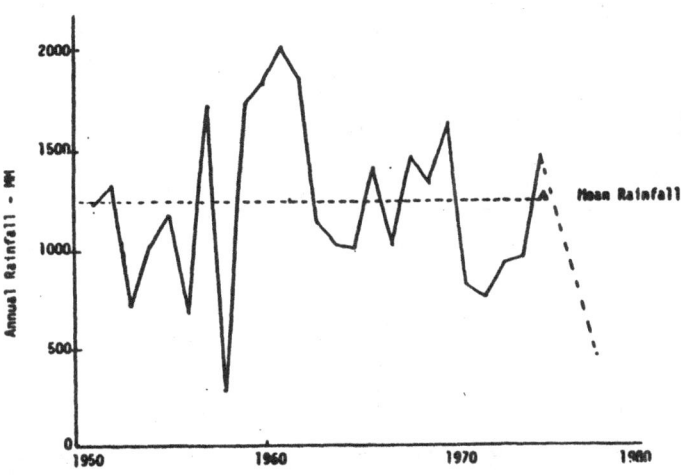

Source: Moliniere, M. and B. Thebe, Donneé Hydrologique en Republique Populaire du Congo, ORSTOM, Brazaville, 1977; DA Mission.

Figure 4.5
ANNUAL RAINFALL AT LOUBOMO
1950-1980

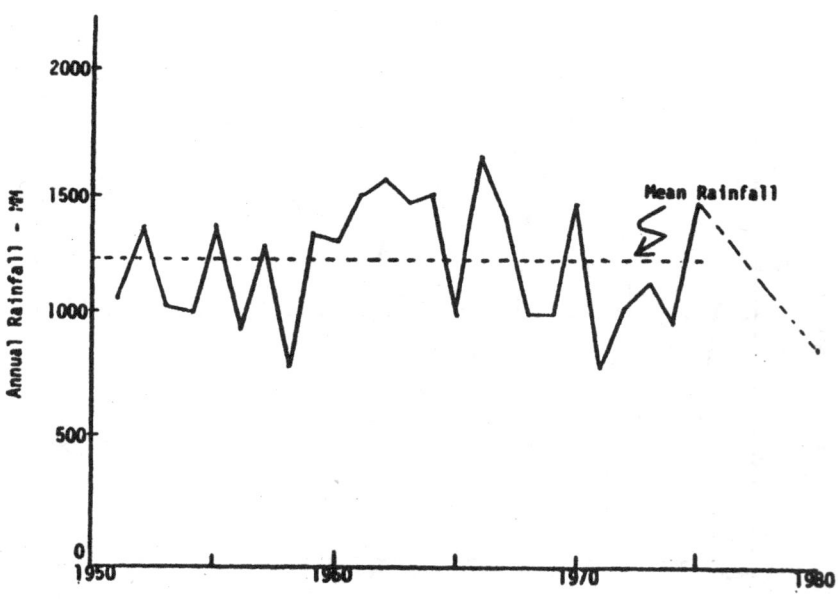

Source: Same as Figure 4.4.

locations of these stations are depicted in Figure 4.10. Examining Figures 4.8 and 4.9, it can be seen that the length of the dry season increases as one moves north, where the dry season is shifted to the months of December and January with a minimum precipitation never below 50 millimeters.

Evapotranspiration

Evapotranspiration is the quantity of water used consumptively by the growing vegetation. This includes the water utilized in the process of transpiration and the evaporation of free water from the surrounding soil and plant leaves. When the ground is completely covered by a green short-growing crop, such as grass, ad has a continuous supply of water, the evapotranspiration is said to be Potential (ETP). Real or actual evapotranspiration (ETA), on the other hand, represents the amount of water used by a crop which might be growing under conditions different from the potential. Usually actual evapotranspiration is less than the potential transpiration.

A study on the subject for the region was undertaken by C. Riou of the Office for Overseas Scientific and Technical Research.[1] Riou studied the actual evapotranspiration in Central Africa at several locations, taking into consideration the precipitation, water storage in the soils, and the ETP. This study indicated that between the lattitude of $4°N$ and $2°S$, the actual and potential evapotranspirational are quite similar. In another study, the same author concluded that the ETP might be considered as a fraction of the solar radiation. Therefore, for the Congo (between $4°N$ and $5°S$), the two evapotranspirations might be considered equal, except in the southern part of the country (south of Gambona) where the ETP is somewhat greater than the ETA.

Data for the lines of equal annual evapotranspiration shown in Figure 4.11 were obtained by the inflow-outflow method for which the precipitation over a given watershed and the resulting runoff were measured. According to a study by Molinier and Thebe it was assumed that over the long term, the soil-water storage remained constant.[2]

---

1. C. Riou, *Etude de L'Evaporation en Afrique Centrale*, *Contribution a la Connaissance de Climats*, (Paris; O.R.S.T.O.M., 1972).

2. Lee M. Molinier and Thebe B., *Donnes Hydrologiques en Republique du Congo*, (Brazzaville: O.R.S.T.O.M. 1977).

Figure 4.6
ANNUAL RAINFALL AT IMPFONDO
1950-1980

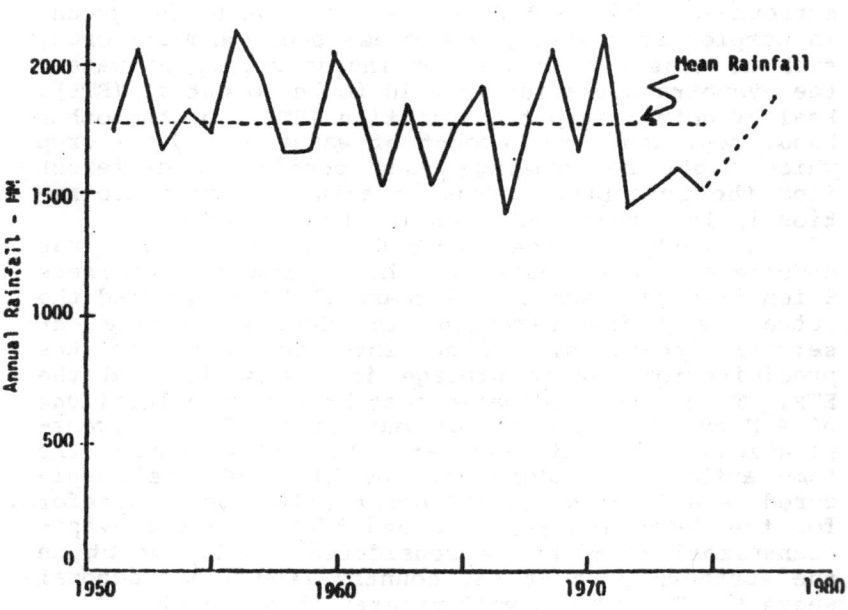

Source: Same as Figure 4.4.

FIGURE 4.7
MEAN ANNUAL PRECIPITATION IN MM (1951-1975)

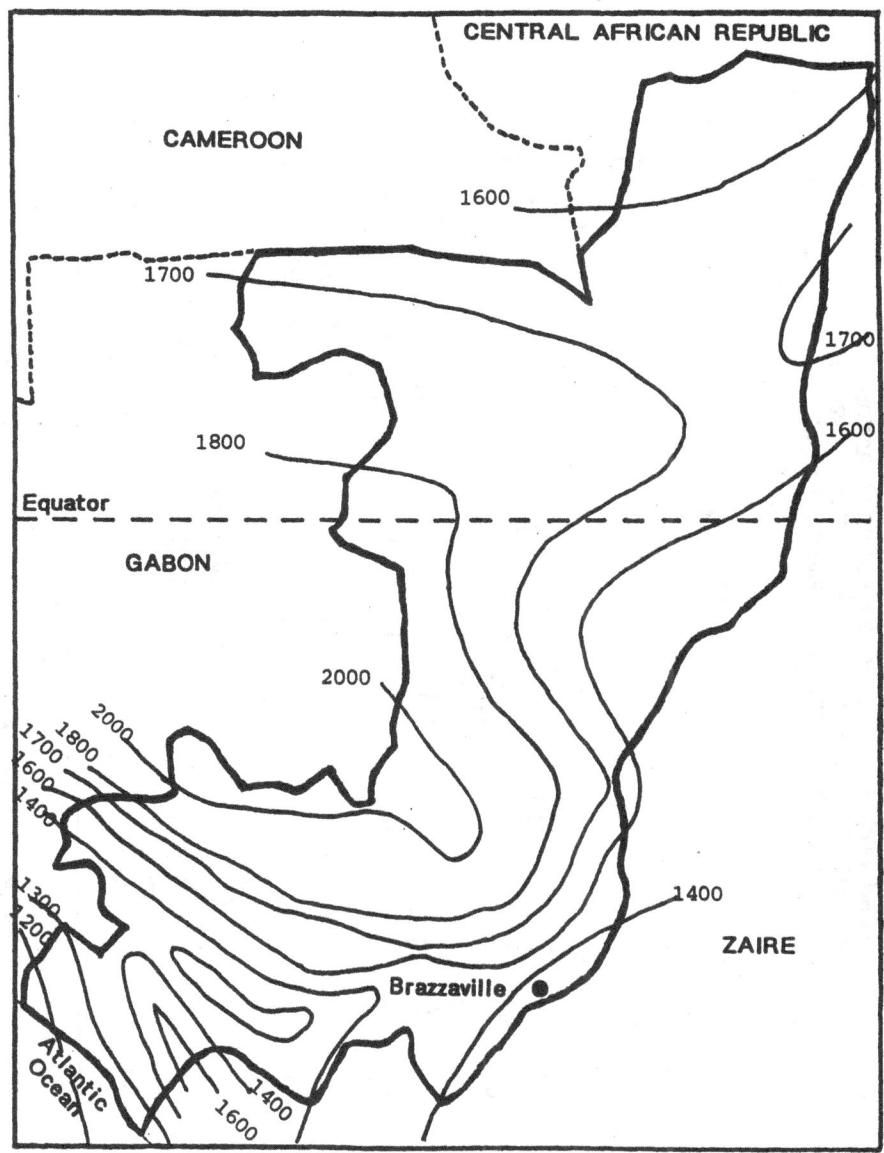

Source: Same as Figure 4.4

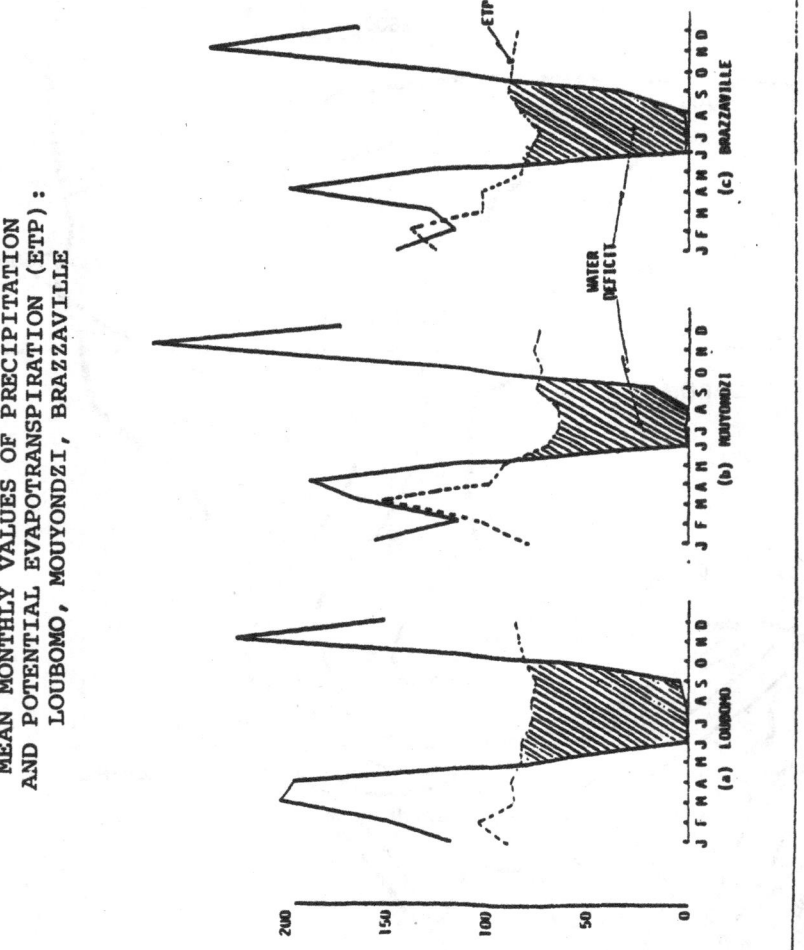

FIGURE 4.8
MEAN MONTHLY VALUES OF PRECIPITATION
AND POTENTIAL EVAPOTRANSPIRATION (ETP):
LOUBOMO, MOUYONDZI, BRAZZAVILLE

Source: Same as Figure 4.4.

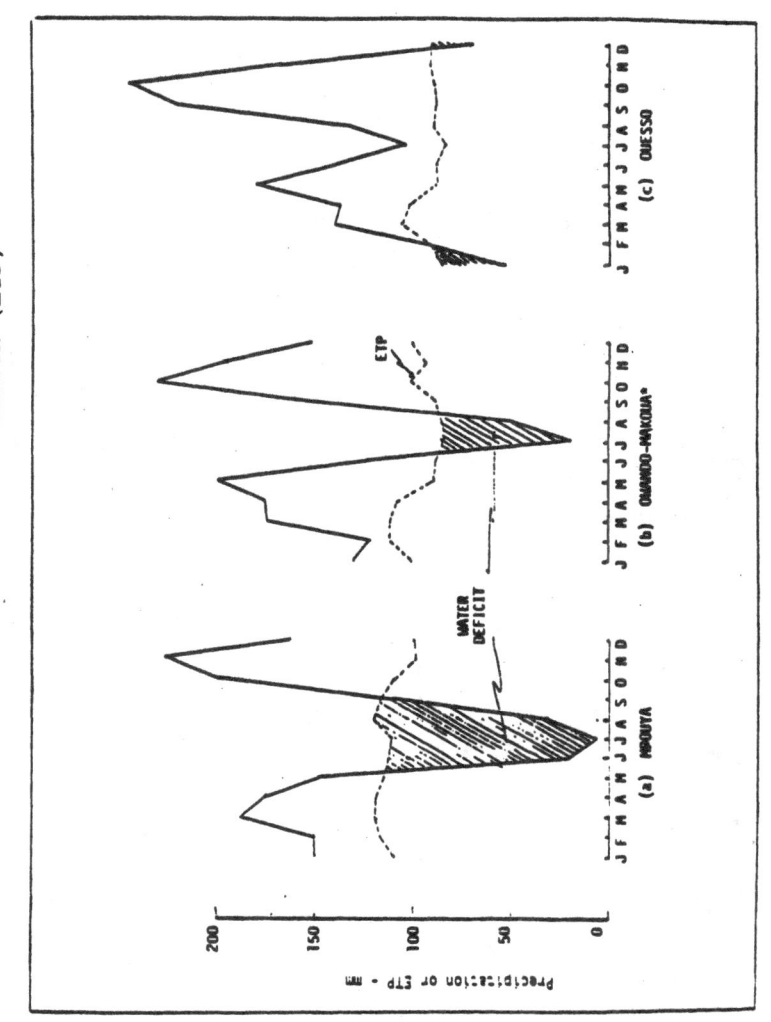

FIGURE 4.9
MEAN MONTHLY VALUES OF PRECIPITATION
AND POTENTIAL EVAPOTRANSPIRATION (ETP)

Source: Reference 2 and 4. Same as Figure 4.4.

FIGURE 4.10

DISTRIBUTION OF STATIONS WITHIN THE CONGO

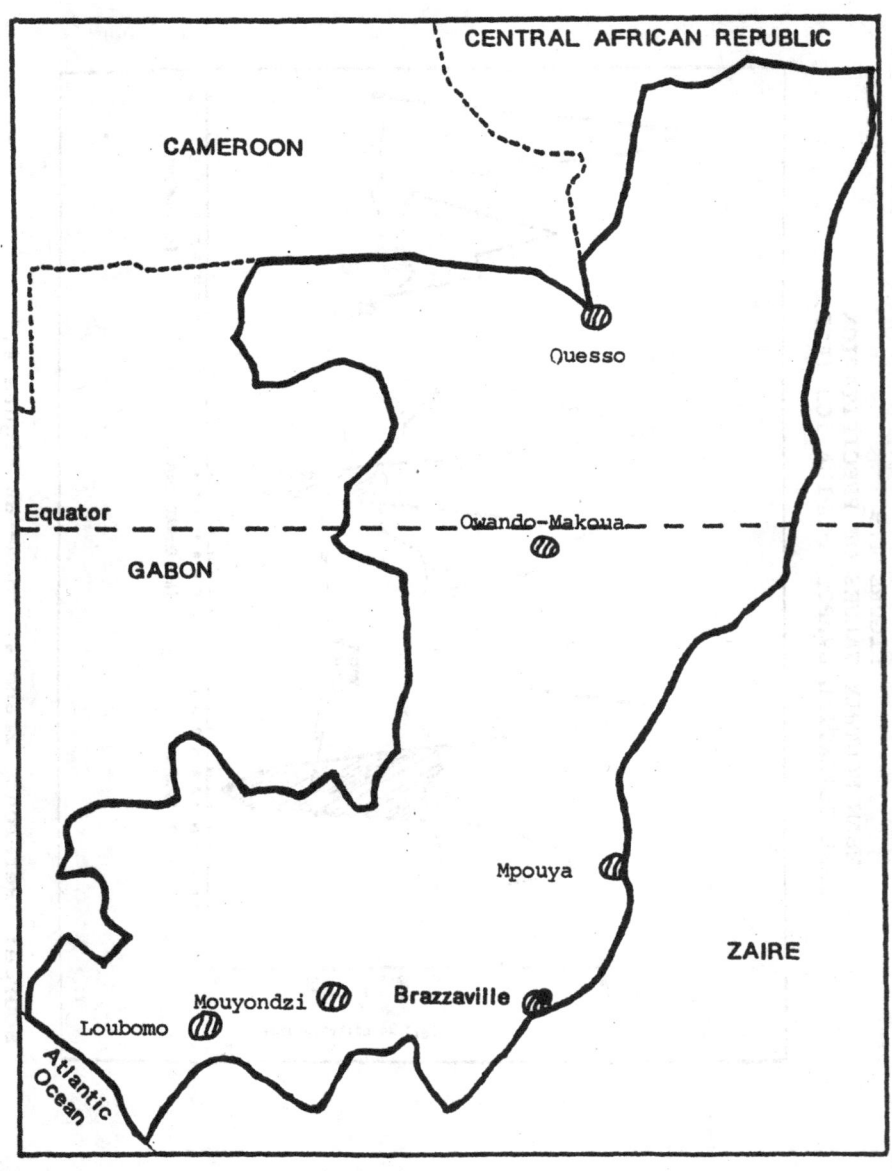

Source: Same as Figure 4.4.

An interesting observation is that for the northern part of the Congo, covered with equatorial forest, the maximum values of ETA are higher than than those of ETP. The annual evapotranspiration varies within the country from about 1,200 millimeters to 900 millimeters in the Southern Congo. Although the annual precipitation values shown by the isohyets in Figure 4.7 exceed those of total annual evapotranspiration, the water actually retained within the root zone and available for plant growth might not be sufficient during some months and at certain locations.

Potential evapotranspiration values, computed by the method of Turc, were plotted in Figures 4.8 and 4.9 to compare them with the mean monthly values of precipitations. The shaded area shown on these graphs represents the water deficits for plant growth. The water deficit during the months of June through September is most acute in the south, and decreases as one goes north, becoming almost negligible at Ouesso. It is necessary to emphasize that the water deficit might be even more severe, since the comparison of evapotranspiration is made with the average total monthly precipitation and not with the effective precipitation. Effective precipitation is that portion of the total rainfall that is stored within the root zone and, therefore, is available to the plants. It varies with soil profile characteristics, terrain topography, vegetative cover, and other factors.

Temperature and Solar Radiation

Incoming solar radiation or insolation is one of the most important climatic elements affecting plant growth. Temperature, radiation and day length determine crop adaptability to a region and crop phenology, the relation between the crops' biological phenomena and climate. The upper limits of production can be estimated utilizing data concerning the mean radiation during the growing season, the mean day time temperatures and the mean seasonal temperatures for crops meeting the phenological requirements and climatic adaptability.

Water requirements of crops can be accurately estimated from climatic data. The most important weather elements influencing potential water use are ambient air temperature and solar radiation. Average daily solar radiation for the Congo ranges from about 380 to 440 cal cm^{-2} day^{-1} or 140 to 160 kcal cm^{-2} $year^{-1}$. The average duration of sunshine ranges from

117 to 167 hours per month or 1400 to 2000 hours per year. No reliable records for directly measured incident solar radiation were found. However, this can be calculated from theoretical values of extraterrestrial radiation and the percentage of possible sunshine. The percentage of possible sunshine, S, is determined from the ratio of actual duration of sunshine, K, in hours to the day length, dL.

Figures 4.12 and 4.13 were constructed from data of actual hours of sunshine and of temperature in degree Celsius[1] for the stations as shown in Figure 4.10. The sunshine in the southern portion of the country (Figure 4.12) is relatively low with mean temperatures around $25°C$. The months of lower sunshine coincide with the occurrence of the long dry season with cloudy and overcast days.

Crops that might adapt better to these conditions are those requiring a radiation intensity of 1.0 to 1.5 $calories/cm^2/min.$ and a rate of photosynthesis of about 20 to 100 milligrams of $CO_2/dm^2/hour^{-1}$. These include sorghum, corn, some vegetables, and for the warmer zones, sugar can and cassava.

In the northern portion of the country (Figure 4.13), the more hours of sunshine are registered. The temperatures are more uniform with averages around $25°C$. The northern portion of the country would lend itself to more photosynthetically efficient crops.

Management of Climatic Resources

To take advantage of the climatic resources, it is necessary to consider the biological requirements of the crops to be grown and their adaptability to the climate and physical environment. From this point of view, the major consideration of the crops' biological requirements in the Congo are (1) crop life; (2) photosynthetic crop requirement; and (3) phenologic crop requirements.

With respect to crop life, crops should be grown in a zone with a growing season long enough to allow for the completion of the crops's life. Crops having life cycles which do not correspond to the length of the growing period will not produce good yields and will be more susceptible to insects and diseases.

The photosynthetic requirements of a crop are dictated by its physiological processes; physiological reverses will occur at optimum rates only

---

1. Based on data from Molinier and Thebe.

FIGURE 4.11

MEAN ANNUAL ACTUAL EVAPOTRANSPIRATION
IN MILLIMETERS (1951-1975)

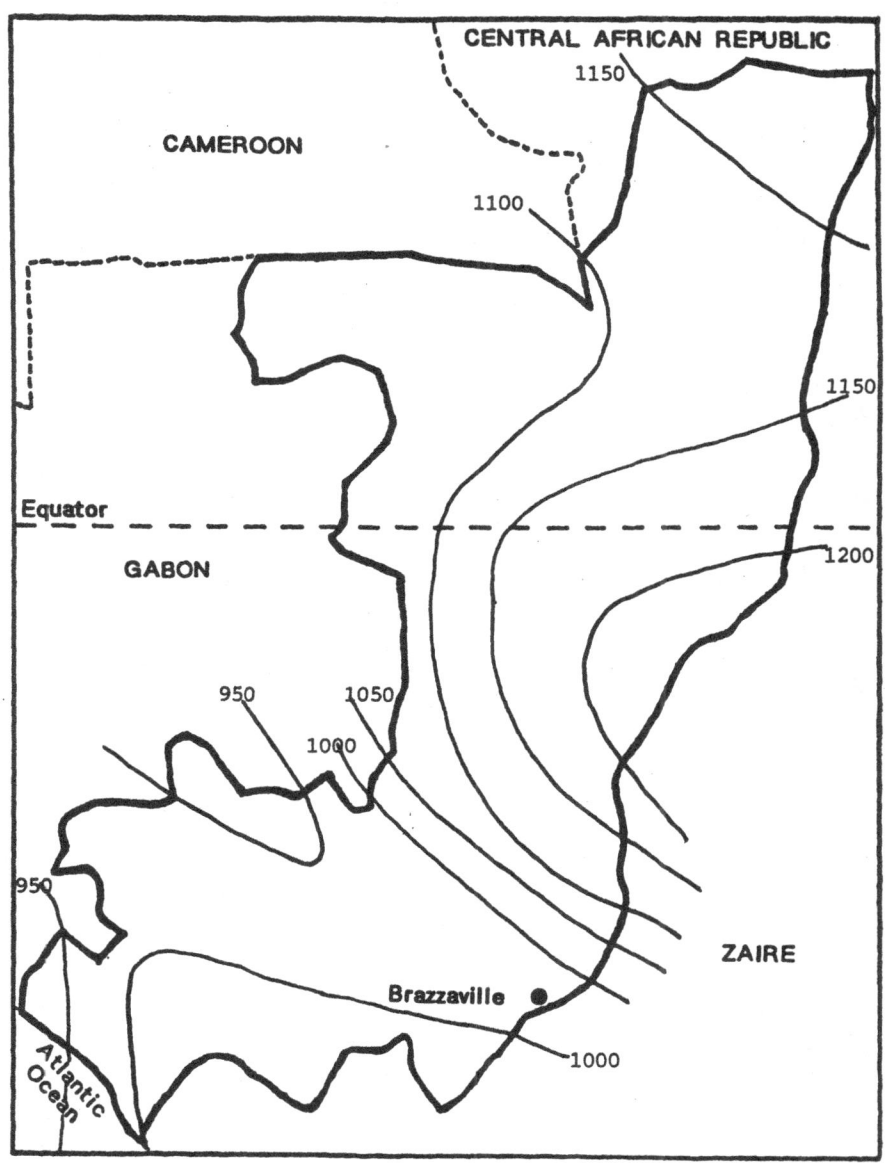

Source: Same as Figure 4.4.

FIGURE 4.12
MEAN MONTHLY SUNSHINE
AND TEMPERATURES (1951-1975)

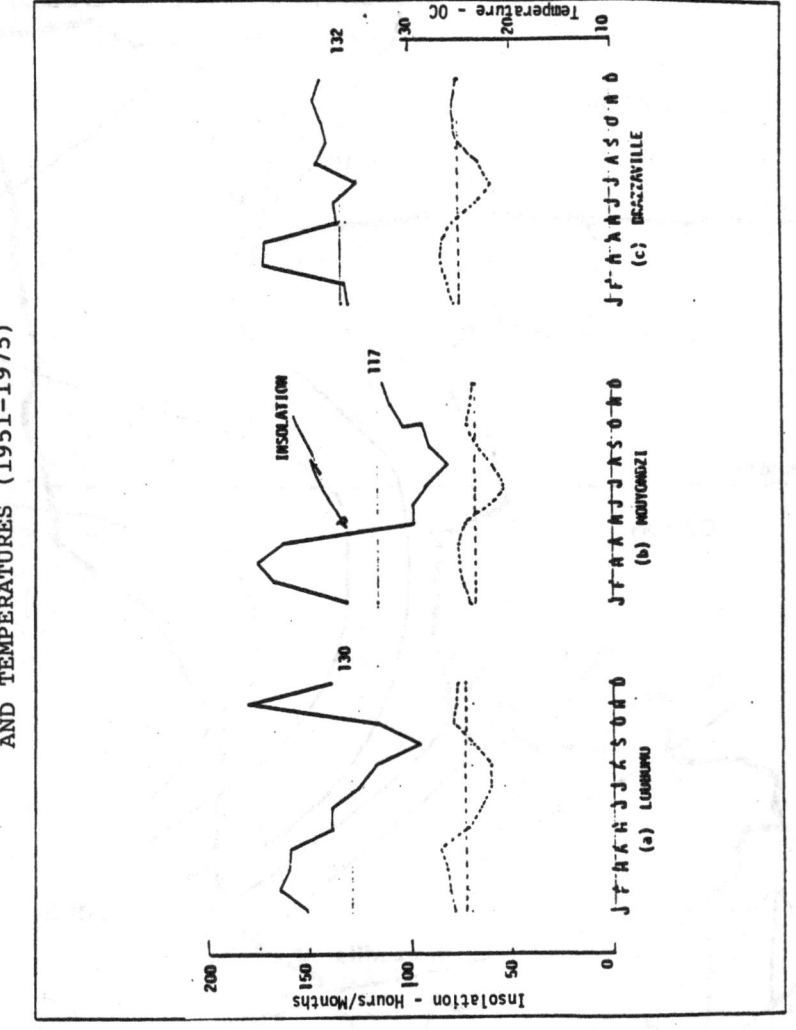

Source: Same as Figure 4.4.

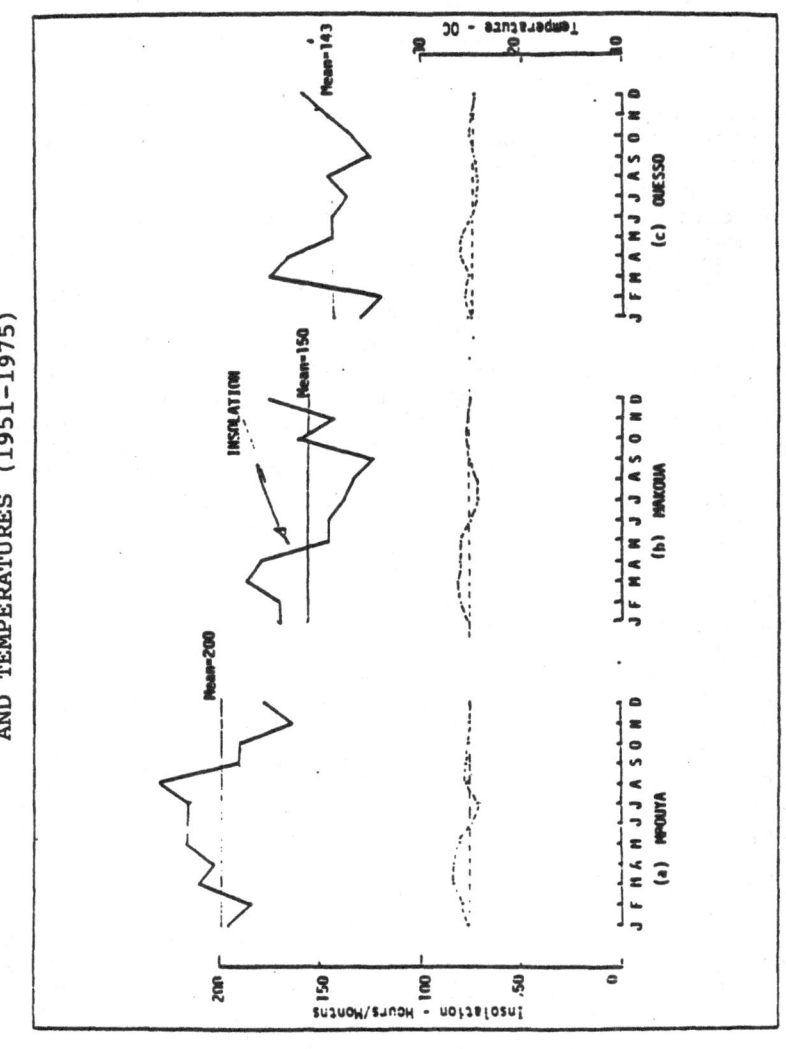

FIGURE 4.13
MEAN MONTHLY SUNSHINE
AND TEMPERATURES (1951-1975)

Source: Same as Figure 4.4.

within certain ranges of temperature and radiation. Therefore, it is possible to study the temperatures and solar radiation regimes of an area and to match the crops' photosynthetic requirements to assure high productivity.

Crop phenology refers to the developmental sequence of crop growth in relation to the growing season. The sequential growth pattern of crops, such as length of vegetative growth, flowering time, seed or fruit setting, leaf shedding, etc., is biologically determined. Timing of these phenological characteristics, however, is controlled mainly by length of day and temperature.

In order to determine the climatic adaptability of crops, it is necessary to know their specific climatic requirements (day length for yield quality, in addition to those of photosynthesis.

The growing period in the tropics can be assumed to be a continuous length of time during the year when the precipitation is greater than half the rate of evapotranspiration (P = 9.5 ET). In addition, the growing period must have a humid stage in which the precipitation exceeds the evapotranspiration demands of the crop and replenishes the water deficit within the root zone. Locations without this humid period are not suitable for crop production under normal dry land farming.

The effective rainy season is the number of days between the beginning of the rains and their end. The first 10-day period during the year when precipitation is equal or greater than one-half the evapotranspiration marks the beginning. Likewise, the end of the rainy season is considered as the last 10-day period of the season during which the precipitation is less than one-half the evapotranspiration.

For most crops, the growing period extends beyond the rainy season and they mature on water reserves stored in the soil. This amount of water will depend, of course, on the soil's physical characteristics, water holding capacity, depth of the root zone, root pattern, and the soil water potential characteristics of the soil.

The growing period for the Congo might vary from seven to ten months (Figures 4.8 and 4.9) with yearly insolation from 1,400 hours at Mouyondzi (Figure 4.12) to 2,400 hours in Mpouya (Figure 4.13). This, of course, is a very rough estimate, but it gives an idea of the climatic resources available for crop production. A good management of these resources will require an in-depth study of the climatic characteristics, perhaps by regions, together with experimental research, to select the cultivars which will adapt phenologically to the existing climate.

It is recognized that there is some need for supplemental irrigation during the dry seasons. At the farmers' level, the existence of some rudimentary irrigation has been observed, in the area around Loubomo. Additional information indicates that this might be the case in other parts of the country; Niari, Pool, and the Plateaux regions.

Water and Land Resources

The surface water resources of the Congo have been extensively studied by the Office for Overseas Scientific and Technical Research (ORSTOM). Detailed hydrographic studies are available at this institution, and only a brief summary will be included here. Unfortunately, the data is not complete since most of the work stopped with the departure of the French at the time of Congolese independence. Nevertheless, efforts are being made to resume research at ORSTOM.

The number of ground water investigations and relevant data are minimal. The only report found is that of the ground water investigation sponsored by the FAO and executed by l'Enterprise de Forage Marconi of Rome[1] between November of 1965 and April 1966.

The People's Republic of the Congo has considerable surface water resources. To describe and evaluate them, the country has been divided into three zones according to their climatic and physical characteristics. Each of these zones is subdivided into subregions representing areas which are hydrologically homogeneous (Figure 4.14). Zone A corresponds to the Niari river basin with the plateau, the Chaillu mountains, and a coastal plain. This zone includes the sub-zones 1 to 5. Zone B, or sub-zone 6, corresponds to the Bateke Plateaux, with undulating surfaces, eroded hills, and large expanses of sandy soils. This zone includes the Lefini, Nkeni, and Alima river basins. Zone C corresponds to the Cuvette, Sangha and Likouala regions (sub-zones 7, 8 and 9), containing the Ivindo, Djoua, Likoula, Sangha, and Lilouala and Herbes basins.

Table 4.1 is a resume of the hydrological characteristics of the nine sub-zones. Basic data include precipitation, river discharges, and runoff. The method utilized was that of inflow-outflow, with an assumption that changes in subsurface water

---

1. FAO Microfiche of Documentary Unit, Co. 1-25566-F1.

Figure 4.14
Hydrologically Homogeneous Sub-Zones and Drainage Areas

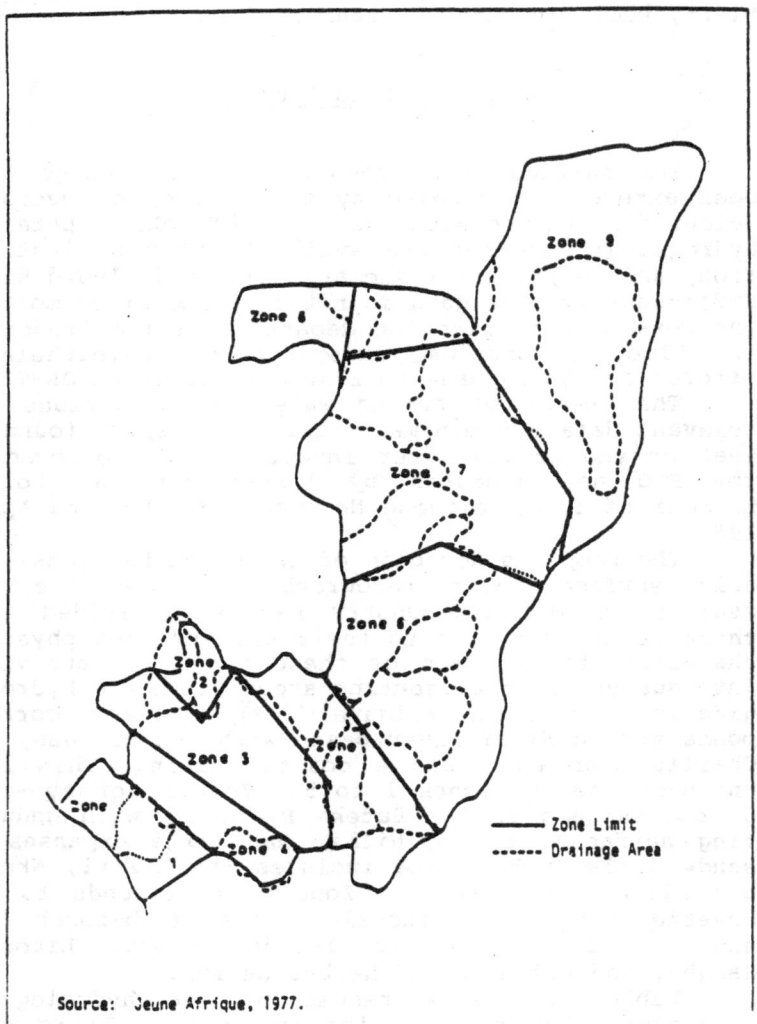

Source: Jeune Afrique, 1977.

Table 4.1

Annual Surface Water Hydrological Balance
for the Nine Sub-Zones of Congo

Zone No.	Area Km^2	Discharge M^3/S	Specific Runoff	Precip mm	Runoff mm	% Runoff Co-efficient
1	14,100	160	11.3	1,335	358	26.8
2	5,500	170	30.9	1,920	975	50.8
3	28,500	510	17.9	1,525	564	37.0
4	15,200	120	7.9	1,255	249	19.8
5	28,000	610	21.8	1,645	687	41.8
A	91,300	1,570	17.2	1,510	542	35.9
B	62,500	1,685	27.0	1,800	850	47.2
7	73,600	1,290	17.5	1,735	553	31.9
8	14,400	260	18.1	1,700	569	33.5
9	100,200	1,395	13.9	1,635	439	26.9
C	188,200	2,945	15.6	1,680	493	29.4
TOTAL	342,000	6,200	18.1	1,655	572	34.6

Source: Moliniere, M. and B. Thebe, Donnees Hydrologiques en Republique Populaire du Congo. Brazzaville: O.R.S.T.O.M., April, 1977.

storage over a long period were minimal and, therefore, negligible.

Total runoff for the country is 572 millimeters, which corresponds to an average flow of 6,300 cubic centimeters per second (cms), with a total yearly flow of 195.5 billion cubic meters. The region most able to contribute to the surface waters, besides the region of the Chaillu mountains in sub-zone 2, is the Bateke Plateaux. Rains in this zone are quite strong and a large portion of them is absorbed by the sands, thus contributing to the groundwaters.

The Niari basin is an important system, since it covers one of the most productive areas of the Congo. Studies regarding the surface water resources of the Niari Valley were first started in 1928, and continued in 1947-48, sponsored by Electricite de France in collaboration with ORSTOM.

The first period of high waters in the Niari begins in October, becomes more acute in November, and ends in December. In March, the second peak period begins reaching the maximum in April or May.

The low waters in the Upper Niari also show two distinct periods. The first one is very irregular in duration and intensity from year to year. It can occur in the month of February, but it can extend from January to March. This is followed by a second period of low flows which is more serene and longer than the first one, lasting from the end of May to the beginning of October. During this period, the water level declines continuously until the end of September.

Geology and Ground Water Resources

Geology

Although topography and climate constitute primary factors governing the infiltration of water to deeper ground layers, geology is the paramount factor which determines the occurrence, distribution, movement, and quality of groundwater. In addition, the geological nature of the terrain influences the relief forms which in turn have an important impact on the climate. Subsurface geology determines not only the location of groundwater reservoirs but also their ability to store and transmit water. Therefore, it is important to study further, check, and update the available geological information for possible future groundwater exploitation.

In the southwest, extreme north, and northwest portions of the country, the very ancient basement of rocks comes to the surface almost everywhere. Elsewhere, it is covered by thick blankets of sedimentary materials. The most extensive are those of the tertiary terrains of the Bateke region and the alluvial ones of the Congo basin ("Cuvette Congolaise").

The Precambrian basement complex originated from the consolidation of magma and has undergone a long tectonic evolution from remote geological times. This basement complex is more or less covered by sedimentary deposits and covers vast areas in many parts of Africa. Tectonic movements have provoked deposits of schists, limestone, and sandstone.

In the Congo, three main formations can be found:

1. **Extensive massifs of granite and gneiss**, which constitute the metamorphic complex of the low Precambrian, such as those of Chaillu and western Sangha (basin of the upper Ivindo, west of Souanke).

2. **Appalachian chains** (belonging to the middle Precambrian) like the Mayombe range running generally southeast to northwest, or that between Ouesso, Kelle, and Souanke running southwest to northeast. Here schists and quarzites are found in tight, strongly tilted folds, and, therefore, have poor groundwater potential, but at the same time they show weathering and fracturing which given them some water conducting properties. Rivers carve deep valleys and narrow gorges. Gold and cassiterite are found in some of their alluvial deposits.

3. A vast synclinorium between Chaillu and Mayombe, where sedimentary layers over 3,000 M. deep were laid down during the Upper Precambrian. This western Congo system consists of tillites, Bouenza sandstone, calcareous and sandstone schists which have been deformed by folds and faults.

The more recent formations have more or less completely covered the basement rock. West of the Mayombe range this basement is found at depths of over 3,500 meters. On the surface a series of Cirques (probably of Tertiary origin) appears, formed of sand, gravel, and yellow, purplish-blue, and especially red clays. It is deposited on cretaceous formations which contain important beds of salts (rock salt and potash), phosphatic deposits, and occasionally oil.

In the Bateke region is found the so-called series of the Bateke Plateaux covering secondary sandstones only visible at the bottom of certain valleys. It consists of white, pink, or mauve sandstones, which form the "Cliffs of Dover" on the banks of Stanley Pool, and sandy silts deposited by wind during the Miocene and Pilocene. These formations continue irregularly until Ouesso and reappear to the north near the border with the Central African Republic, where they partially cover formation of sandstone and argilites.

The rest of the Congo basin (La Cuvette) is covered with recent deposits of alluvial clays or sand to depths which are not well known but reach at least several tens of meters.

Groundwater

As mentioned, earlier, very little work has been done in investigating the groundwater resources. In 1965 the FAO contracted the Entreprise de Forage Marconi to carry out a well drilling program to study the groundwater resources in the Niari Valley. This project was finished in April 1966.

The project consisted of drilling seven piezometric wells and three testing wells. A total of 379.40 meters were drilled in the alluvial terrain and 208.5 meters in the rock underneath.

The area studied was the southern part of the Niari Valley between Mandingou and Loudima. It is a flat terrain under cultivation, limited by a series of hills to the left and the river to the right. The profile characteristics of the area are (a) 0-30 meters: Alluvial blanket made up of sandy-clay soils of variable depth; and (b) over 30 meters: Basement of the schist and limestone type which comes to surface at low points, particularly along the rivers.

Preliminary pumping tests gave results varying from very little to a discharge of 30 Lt/Sec. The water level was found in the piexometric wells at 35-48 meters. The presence of clay made the pumping more difficult, sealing the cracks and, therefore, reducing the hydraulic conductivity of the material. Precambrian dolomite made up the basement complex which offered great resistance to drilling. It was recommended that future exploration should be made by reverse rotation equipment or a combination of percussion with rotation with possibilities of various well diameters.

In the calcareous formations in the Niari Valley, water flows through cracks causing dissolutions which result in connecting subterranian cavities. On the surface, large depressions without natural drainage, sudden disappearances, and surfacing of rivers can be found. These phenomena associated with the calcareous materials are very important in the general utilization of the groundwater and deserve further study.

In 1956 and 1957 ORSTOM collected information on the groundwater hydrology of the Loudima, Loubetsi, and Vougou basins, and in particular on the intercommunication between these basins. In 1961, near the Agronomic Station in Loudima, a well of 63 meters depth was pumped for three days with a discharge of 10 to 16 m^3/hr at pumping levels between 44 and 48 meters. The flow obtained was attributed to the interconnecting cracks in the calcareous zone. In another test in the Telemina plateau, in 1961, large depressions in the upper level of the calcareous zone were observed, which could correspond to areas of intense cracking and would, therefore, be apt for well drilling.

The importance of future studies in the Niari region is evident, since it is in this area that greatest agricultural activity is concentrated. As the rains are not sufficient for certain crops, and the dry season lasts sometimes five months, supplemental irrigation would be necessary.

Land Resources

The soils of the Congo may be classified in general as ferralitic soils. These soils are formed by the leaching of silica and bases by midly acidic or neutral solutions and characterized by a large content of iron oxide. Various types have resulted from differences in climate, the nature of the original rock, topography, exposure, natural vegetation, and human interventions, all of which influence the pedogenetic process.

The atlas distinguishes <u>hydromorphic soils</u> from <u>ferralitic soils</u>, the latter category being subdivided into <u>impoverished soils</u> and <u>altered soils</u> which are in turn divided into <u>red</u> and <u>yellow soils</u>. <u>Hydromorphic soils</u> are found in large expanses of flooded forest in the Cuvette Congolaise, along swampy tributary valleys, in the depression at the foot of the Mayombe mountains south of the Niari, and in littoral lagoons. They are characterized by profiles completely charged with water, high peat content and black color, and a low pH which reduces fertility. Included in this group are ferralitic soils which are flooded more or less completely each year. They are acid, low in bases, and are also found in the Cuvette, the Niari Valley, and along the coast.

More important from the agricultural point of view are the ferralitic soils. The impoverished soils, belonging to the class of desaturated soils, are derived from sandstones, sandy clays or sands, particularly of quartz type. These soils are found in 50% of the country, both in forests and savannas. They are chemically poor, lack coherence, and are not well suited to agriculture.

Altered ferralitic soils cover 30% of the country, with the red soils in the north and yellow soils in the south (for soil classification see Appendix 4.2). The red soils owe their coloration to advanced ferralization resulting from abundant rainfall, constant high temperatures, and a high iron and magnesium content of the parental rocks. They are deep soils, low in bases, with a pH of four to five and a clay content of 40%. They are found overlying the granitic rocks of the Sembe-Kelle region and on the quartzite and basic rocks of the Sembe-Ouesso series.

The yellow soils are characterized by three distinct horizons: an upper one of loose, fine-textured soil, a middle one of hardened soil, frequently with a stone lime; and a lower mottled one corresponding to altered parental rock. These soils include (according to their derivation):

- Argillic, thick, heavy soils of good physical structure derived from calcareous schists with a pH of six to seven;

- Soils formed on the series of Bouenza (marl limestone, argillites, sandstone);

- Soils of sandstone schist, very argillic and susceptible to deep ravinement; and

- Soils of Mayombe and Chaillu, derived from quartzitic schists and granites, which are argillic, thick and with a pH of five.

The soils of the Congo are old, highly weathered, and generally infertile. This infertility is attributable to a lack of essential minerals for plant nutrition. Recent work by the agronomic research station at Loudima shows that even virgin soils that can be found in that area are highly deficient in calcium, phosphorous, potassium, and magnesium. Available nitrogen levels are low throughout the country. Not only are essential minerals lacking, but these soils are of a type that cannot hold plant nutrients for long periods. Agriculturally this means that chemical or natural fertilizers are quickly leached out of the plant root zone, making plant response to such treatment poor, and fertility maintenance difficult. As a consequence, these soils are fragile and easily disrupted by modern agricultural techniques. Their deficiencies must be remedied, permanent vegetable ground cover must be maintained to protect them from severe erosion, and all modifications must be undertaken with great prudence. (See Appendix 4.2 for further details in soil classification).

Natural Vegetation

The natural vegetation of the Congo falls into two basic categories, the forest and the savanna. The forested area, which covers about two-thirds of the surface area of the country, can be divided into at least five different types, classified according to the soil and atmospheric water requirements of the dominant species. The savanna regions are classified into seven types according to their vegetative cover. Smaller areas are covered swamps and steppes.

The Forest

A great classical rain forest is found in the upper Sangha region, the Mayombe Mountains and Chaillu massif. There is a variety of large ombrophilous (water loving) trees. A number of them have large buttresses at their base, such as the stately Klainedoxa gabonensis. Trees of the Leguminosaw and Meliaceae families are most common. The former, like their smaller relatives, are pod-bearing, nitrogen-fixing trees, most of which have compound leaves that give them a graceful feathery appearance. In some local areas resinous conifers such as Terminalia superba or Gilbertiodendron dewevrei dominate. There is little underbrush in the forest except when land is cleared. In this case, when cultivated trees are abandoned secondary species such as the Umbrella tree (Musanga cecropioides) appear rapidly.
Within the Sangha area, however, there are forests where thin stands of fully mature trees tower over a dense underbrush. The flooded forests that are found in the Cuvette are also ombrophilous

formations, less dense than those found on dry land. Medium size trees with gnarled buttresses grow out of a jumble of roots in a dark mire. Dense thickets of raphanus palms are found here and there.

In the Mesophile (moderate water need) forests found in the sandy Bateke soils. a mosaic of forest and savanna vegetation is the natural cover. These are, for the most part, gallery forests extending 20 or 30 kilometers along each bank of the Lefini, Nkeni, Alima, Mpama, and lower Congo rivers. The typical deciduous vegetation is neither dense nor continuous. Frequently degraded by man, these forests are hence often colonized by young arborescent species and the oil palm, Elaeis guineensis. The coastal forests are found in small residual groups on the low plateaux of the Pointe Noire region, in semi-marsh formations, and in mangroves (Rizophora racemosa) bordering the lagoons.

The Savannas

The savannas are covered with a number of different types of grass species. On the sandy soil of the Bateke Plateaux one finds a sparse cover of Loudetia demeusii, along with scattered bushes, usually Hymenocardia acida. On soils that are more heavily leached, another grass species, Trachypogon thollonii, is more common.

The savanna of the Niari valley is tall with grass types reaching between two and five meters in their natural state. (Hyparrhenia, Andropogon, and Panicum). Scrub bushes include Annona arenaria, Bridelia ferruginea and especially Himenocardia acida, which grows only on soils that were formed from calcareous schists.

A third type of savanna is confined to the plateau area near the Congo river cataracts. They are distinguished by a rather sparse cover of the grass Aristida deweldemanii, accompanied by Hymenocardia and Annona type bushes.

In the Likouala area, a sort of forest-savanna area is found, dominated by the Andropogon grasses. Trachypogon thollonii is absent.

Other Formations

Two types of steppes are distinguished, the so-called lousseke type of the Cuvette and Bateke Plateaux, and those of coastal region, sometimes

known as pseudo steppes. Both are dominated by
Loudetia simplex.
Semi-swampy areas are found in the southern
Kouilou-Niari region and the coastal lagoons with
papyrus (Cyperus papyrus). The floating prairies of
the rivers of the Cuvette are associations of aquatic
grasses and other waterborn plants that form into
natural rafts. The marshes and marshy prairies of
the Alima and Likouala rivers combine aquatic grasses
and papyruses in a landscape of forests, savannas,
and low steppes.

Rural Roads

Another engineering aspect of agriculture is the
question of the road network, especially rural roads.
The Regie Nationale des Transports et des Travaux
Publics (R.N.T.P.), under the Ministry of Public
Works, Construction and Housing (M.T.P.C.), is the
state organization in charge of the planning,
control, and execution of the road network in the
People's Republic of the Congo. Its most important
task is the upgrading an maintenance of all the roads
in the country.

The organization at the national level of the
R.N.T.P. is depicted in Appendix 4.3. In addition,
in each of the nine regions of the country there is a
"Direction Regionale." The Directorate of Road
Maintenance (Direction de l"Entretien Routier) also
has regional directorates in each of the regions.

In theory, the R.N.T.P. is in charge of the main
road network (4,519 km). The network of secondary
roads is the responsibility of each Direction
Regionale. In practice the road maintenance has been
minimal and they have suffered rapid deterioration.
Secondary roads are not maintained mainly because of
lack of equipment and financial means.

The available credit for the maintenance of the
main roads is always insufficient. The equipment
available is old and much of it is not operating.

The personnel available to the Directorate of
Road Maintenance consist of 1,168 men of which ten
are engineers (the Central director and nine regional
directors). The region of Niari has the most (175
men) and Bouenza the least (65 men).

Road Classification

Of the total of 10,818 km road network, only
3,300 or 31% are all-weather service; of these only

600 km are paved. The road network in the Congo may be classified into three categories: administrative, economic and technical.

Administratively, the roads are classified as:

```
National (RN) roads . . . . . . . . . . . . . 1,933 km
Prefectural (RP) roads  . . . . . . . . . . . 3,950 km
Roads of Local Interest (RIL) . . . . . . . . 2,723 km
Non-classified roads  . . . . . . . . . . . . 2,572 km
       Total . . . . . . . . . . . . . . .   10,818 km
```

Economically, the roads may be divided into (a) main road networks of 4,519 km under the responsibility of the R.N.T.P.; and (b) second road networks of 3,727 km under the responsibility of each region with technical assistance of the R.N.T.P.

Technically, there are four categories: (a) permanent roads built with an underlayer of 15 cm and a double layer of asphalt of 6 to 7 cm; (b) well-graded roads with selected natural materials (laterite and gravel); (c) permanent roads poorly defined which might be closed during the rainy season; and (d) non-permanent roads with poor access during the rains. These are the roads which are used to transport the agricultural produce of the small farmers. According to this classification, the following is the theoretical inventory of the road network in the Congo:

```
Category A . . . . . . . . . . . . . . .   535 km
Category B . . . . . . . . . . . . . . .   868 km
Category C . . . . . . . . . . . . . . . 1,623 km
Category D . . . . . . . . . . . . . . . 1,493 km
       Total . . . . . . . . . . . . . . 4,519 km
```

In reality, because of the lack of maintenance, many of the C category roads should be classified as D. The category B roads do not exist any longer; they now belong to the C group.

The Farm-to-Market Roads

The Seventies: the 1978 and 1979 Proposals. Although all the roads are important and necessary to transport the agricultural products to the markets, the small roads -- Class D -- are the ones which are mainly utilized by the small farmers and the ones which are not receiving any maintenance.

In order to remove some of the marketing bottlenecks, the Ministry of Rural Economy prepared a detailed plan of work in 1978 for the maintenance of the roads throughout the country in order to move agricultural products to the urban markets. The plan was given to the Ministry of Public Works, which was to be in charge of construction, upgrading, and maintenance work. The plan included the following tasks: (a) <u>Maintenance Work</u> -- which included mechanical and manual work. The mechanical work required the use of equipment such as land planes, loaders, bull dozers and trucks for road surfacing improvement, compacting, etc. The manual work required men with simple hand tools such as machetes, shovels, axes, picks, etc., for clearing the land, and building small wood or concrete bridges or culverts. In addition to the labor, this work called for the acquisition of such materials as wood, cement, and wire (gabions). (b) <u>Road Opening</u> -- this work consisted of constructing new roads, which require heavy machines and both skilled and unskilled labor. The unskilled labor was to be obtained locally from the nearby villages. Two years of work were estimated to complete the road plan. Table 4.2 gives the numbers of kilometers per region and the estimated cost per region.

This work was estimated to be the minimum needed to transport the agricultural produce of each region. The investment was expected to bring in high returns to the country via an increase in the agricultural production. Because of the lack of financing resources, the rural road program was slow to start and was not completed.

In 1979, the Regie Nationale des Transports et des Traveaux Publiques also prepared a proposal requesting financing for the upgrading and maintenance of the national road system. The proposal was submitted to the African Development Bank of Financing. Under this program, a total of 1,054 km would be upgraded. Of this total, 434 km was to be from main roads, 167 km from secondary roads, and 453 km from rural access roads.

The total time to complete the work was estimated to be 5 years. The cost of the equipment is shown in Table 4.3.

Most of the road structures, such as small bridges, are in very bad condition and need to be replaced by new ones. In total, about ten small concrete culverts need to be built in addition to bridges and other semi-permanent structures.

Table 4.2

Roads Needed and Estimated Cost:
The 1978 Program

Region	Road Length (Kilometers)	Cost (US Dollars)
Kouilou	290	580,000
Niari	712	1,424,000
Lekoumou	319	638,000
Bouenza	686	17,595,000
Pool	535	1,070,000
Plateaux	667	1,734,000
Cuvette	512	1,024,000
Sangha	332	1,049,000
Likouala	164	328,000

Source: <u>Etude des Possibilities de Refection des Principales Voles d'Evacuation de la Production Agricole En Republic Populaire du Congo</u>, Ministere de L'Economie Rurale, Ministere des Travaux Pubbliques et des Transports, Brazzaville, 1978.

Table 4.3

Equipment Needed and Cost:
The 1979 Program

	Cost per Unit (US Dollars)	Quantity Needed	Cost (US Dollars)
Equipment			
Land plane, 125 HP	84,265.00	3	252,795.00
Truck	84,925.00	1	84,925.00
Dump truck (6 M^3)	65,000.00	4	260,00.00
Roller	8,000.00	1	8,000.00
Tractor	27,500.00	1	24,500.00
Water truck	53,000.00	1	53,000.00
Fuel truck	67,000.00	1	67,000.00
Maintenance truck	120,000.00	1	120,000.00
Total equipment cost			873,220.00

Construction: Replacement parts and engines: 30% of total = $261,966.00.

The total fuel consumption was estimated to be 442,500 liters per year at a total cost of $221,250.

The construction of road structures and cost of materials was estimated to be $192,500.00.

Source: RNTP.

The roads which need to be improved are:

Ngo-Djambala-Kejana	180 km
Roads in the Koukouya Plateaux	130 km
Djambala-Mbon-Akou-Ossele	145 km
Ossele-Abala	27 km
Ossele-Gambona	86 km

The equipment needed to do the road work in the Plateaux region is presented in Appendix 4.4 and the cost to improve the road network, including the cost of the equipment, is shown in Appendix 4.3.

The Eighties: the 1982-86 Program. Several components of the 1978 and 1979 road upgrading and maintenance proposals were integrated into the 1982-86 Five-Year Plan. Under the Plan, the government gave priority to investment in transportation. A total of CFAF 129 billion ($307 million) was allocated for transportation, including the construction of new roads as well as paving old roads, accounting to 12% of total investment in the Plan. The length of the road considered was 1,329 km in all the regions with concentration on the northern part of the country (Cuvette, Sangha, Likouala). The most important sections were the Etsouali-Obouya road (256 km) connecting the Plateaux and Cuvette region and the Owando-Ouesso section (316 km), linking Cuvette and Sangha.

Thanks to sizeable oil revenues during the early years of the Plan, good progress has been made and by 1985 the Etsouali-Obouya section was nearly completed. However, Because of the sharp reduction of oil prices since 1985, it is not certain that all the road sections envisioned in the Plan could be completed.

5

Agricultural Performance

Agricultural performance since independence has been disappointing and agriculture remains the most depressed and backward sector in the economy. Very little information on agricultural production is available. The main source of information is the agricultural census of 1972-73 carried out with the aid of FAO There are also some data available from the recent population mini-census of 1982 (published in 1984). Agricultural statistics in this section are derived from these two sources together with data collected from the Ministry of Rural Economy and the Ministry of Planning.

The Three Sectors

Under the socialist framework, agricultural production is undertaken by three sectors: the small farmer, the cooperatives and pre-cooperatives, and the state sectors.

The Small Farmer Sector

Table 5.1 shows estimated production by the three sectors. The small farmers cultivate around 140,000 hectares and concentrate mainly on the food crops such as manioc (99% of the total), rice (67% in 1977 and 77% in 1982), ground nuts (68%), and the production of a few cash crops for monetary income such as coffee (100%), cocoa (100%), oil palm (100%), and tobacco (100%).

Table 5.1

Share of Agricultural Production by Sectors[1]
(In Percentage)

	State Sector		Small Farmers Sector		Cooperative Sector	Total
Manioc	0.79		99.20		0.01	100
Rice	27.32	(1982:17.30)[2]	66.83	(1982:76.83)	5.86	100
Corn	73.56	(1982:7.10)[2]	6.44	(1982:74.90)		100
Groundnuts	1.50		68.02		30.48	100
Coffee			100			100
Cacao			100			100
Oil Palms			100			100
Tobacco			100			100
Potatoes			21.43		78.57	100
Vegetables	68.84				31.16	100

1. Data for 1977.
2. By 1982, rice and corn production from the state sector was sharply reduced in favor of the small farmers and cooperatives sector.

Source: Ministry of Rural Economy.

The Cooperative and Pre-cooperative Sector

The cooperatives and pre-cooperatives, altogether including 1,305 units, and operate on the principle of the collective. The bigger ones are concentrated in the Pool region. These cooperatives have been the beneficiary of several assistance programs from the Ministry of Rural Economy in recent years. The Congolese cooperative model resembles the Chinese "work-exchange-team" arrangement, a first degree of communal cooperation. Each farmer works for his cooperative a certain number of days, the rest, on his own plot. Most of the cooperatives produce food crops and cash crops (about 85%); the rest produce vegetables, fruits, raise cattle, fish and produce handicrafts.

The overall production of the cooperatives and pre-cooperatives remains small compared to that of small farmers and state farms, with the exception of ground nuts (30%), vegetables (31%), and potatoes (79%).

The State Sector

In 1982, the state sector produced 17.3% rice and 7.1% corn, as compared to 27% and 74% respectively in 1977. State farms also play a dominant role in the production of meat (100% beef and 59% pork). The state sector includes some 25 state farms and ranches which may be classified into five categories:

(1) Small farms, ranging between 10-20 hectares, devoted to multiagricultural activities such as cattle raising, agriculture and fish culture. These small farms are being transformed into cooperatives.

(2) Large farms, operating hundreds of hectares, especially the three farms under the management of the OCV (the Mbe, Mantsoumba, and the food station at Loudima).

(3) A large state plantation, the SOCOTO, which specializes in the production of rice and corn.

(4) The so-called "Party Farms" (Champs du Parti) which produce manioc, corn, rice and ground nuts, such as the Makoua, the Odziba, and the Malela farms. These "Party Farms" are also being integrated into the OCV.

(5) Agricultural processing outlets such as the rice processing plants at Mossendjo, Kimtoumba and Ewo and two processing plants for corn in Brazzaville and Nkayi to supply animal feeds.

Agricultural Production

Structure

Currently, there are only 200,000 hectares of land or about 2% of the total area of the Congo under cultivation. There are a number of reasons for the small amount of cultivated land.

First, much of the north is covered with marshlands of dense forest, not unlike the cypress swamps of southern Florida in the United States, except that the tree species are different;

Second, all of the northwest and much of the southwest are covered with dense tropical forests which are not easy to clear and cultivate;

Third, the central and the southeastern savannas are too hilly to permit the cultivation of large tracts of land;

Fourth, where the land is flat enough for large scale cultivation, as it is north of Brazzaville, the long dry season would not permit intensive cropping, nor are water resources adequate for irrigating the drylands;

Fifth, land potentially suitable for plantation agriculture in Sangha and Cuvette regions are currently inaccessible for lack of rural infrastructure;

Sixth, there are not enough peasants to cultivate the available arable land at the present level of farming technolgy.

While the dense forest of the Congo would not permit bringing much of the country's potential arable land under cultivation, the forest is, however, a source of valuable hardwood. Before off-shore oil production became important, tropical hardwood had been the major source of the Congo's export receipts. Forestry is the second most important source of exports. In 1980, timber and other hardwood products provided 10% of the country's export earnings; agricultural products, on the other hand, account for only 5% of the total. Because of the dominant role of oil exports, receipts from timber exports has been reduced to only 4% of total in 1983.

Until recently, the government has not placed much emphasis on the contributions that Congolese small farmers could make toward the country's agricultural production. Consequently, farmers have not received adequate assistance in terms of agricultural extension service, inputs and marketing services. The quest for increased agricultural production had been targeted to be accomplished through large-scale mechanized state farms, but so far the state farms have not performed as expected. Since 1977, however, increasing attention has been given to the small farmers sector as the government begins to push for increased agricultural production and national self-sufficiency in basic foodstuffs.

In order to increase productivity, the strategy was to group farmers into cooperative production units; nevertheless, the government has adopted a cautious approach to carrying out the cooperative program because previous attempts to organize peasants into collectivism in the Congo, as well as experiences in other developing countries, have proved to be unproductive. In addition to the cooperative movement, the government has also launched a program to create modern villages with adequate infrastructure such as water supply, roads, and hospitals, to provide incentives in order to reverse the rural migration process. These villages are called "Village Centers." At present, the program is still in the experimentation stage.

Essential to the goal of increasing production is the question of price incentive. As discussed later in this book (see Chapter 6), the farmers have received low prices for their crops. Since 1977, one of the government policies has been to establish a level of producer prices that would elicit increased farmers' production of such key cash crops as cocoa, coffee, and tobacco. Late in 1978, a Stabilization Fund (Caisse de Stabilisation des Prix des Produits Agricoles et Foresteriers) was formed to consolidate the operational accounts of the government marketing organizations, the OCC, OCT and OCB, so that the funds could be used to stabilize producer prices in the event that world prices for cocoa, coffee, tobacco and timber should decline sharply.

A price commission appointed by the government in 1980 made an investigation into producer prices to see how they could be administered to induce increased agricultural production. As a result of the commission's study, the government has decided to fix producer prices which would be more in line with cost and would be remunerative in order to improve performance in the agricultural sector. In order to support the government's effort, the United Nations Development Program (UNDP) undertook a thorough "Study on the Problems of Food Self-Sufficiency"[1] in 1982. The study has resulted in some increase in farmers' prices for most crops.

Production of Food Crops

The production of food crops has been essentially a small farmer endeavor until recently when state farms were instituted. While the state farms grow some of the basic foodstuffs, 99% of manioc and 77% of rice and 75% of corn (in 1982) were supplied by small farmers (see Table 5.1). The rural areas are self-sufficient in their supply of the basic food crops, and peasants market whatever surplus they may have after meeting their own subsistence needs. Figures are, therefore, not available for total food crop production in the country. The Office of Agricultural Statistics of the Ministry of Rural Economy, however, maintains estimates of the volume of the basic food crops sold in the urban centers.

The basic food crops grown in the Congo include manioc (cassava), plantains, bananas, yams, sweet potatoes, rice, beans, fruits and vegetables. Manioc, the basic foodstuff of much of the Congo, is grown in all the regions. Cultivation of Cassava dominates the local food crop activity in all regions except the extreme northwest, where plantain is the favorite food crop. Bananas grow in all the regions to some extent, but do better in the forests than in the dry savannas. Yams (water yam and cocoyam) are also widely grown, but not the taro of the Pacific islands. Some rice is grown around Mossendjo in Niari, Kindamba in Pool, Ewo and Boundji in the Cuvette region. Sweet potatoes are also widely grown. Fruits, including papaya, sour sop, mangoes, citrus fruits and avocados are also widely grown in the wet valley of the savanna and in the forest areas. All types of vegetables, including cabbages, spinach, carrots, radishes, onions, tomatoes, okra and peppers are also grown in the wet valleys and by rivers near urban areas.

Total areas under cultivation are also difficult to come by, although the FAO made some estimates during a survey conducted between 1975 and 1977 (Table 5.3). It gave 63,600 hectares (ha) as area

---

1. UNDP, *Etude de la Problematique de l'Autosuffisance Alimentaire*, Congo, (Rome: 1982).

Table 5.2

Food Crops: Estimated Area Under Cultivation Production and Yields[1]

Crops	Area (Hectares)	Share (Percent)	Production (Metric Tons)	Yields (Metric Tons)
CEREALS				
Maize	21,200	10.6	4-5	0.2-0.3
Rice	2,200	1.1	3-4	1.4-1.8
Subtotal	23,400	11.7	---	---
TUBERS				
Yams	16,200	8.1	100	4.8
Cocoyams	4.600	2.3		
Cassava	63,600	31.8	500-600	7.9-9.5
Other tubers	3,400	1.8	---	---
Subtotal	87,800	43.9	---	---
SEEDS				
Groundnuts	10,200	5.1	15-20	1.5-2.0
Gourd seeds	4,800	2.4	---	---
Other oil seeds	400	0.2	---	---
Subtotal	15,400	7.7	---	---
FRUITS AND VEGETABLES				
Plantain bananas	16,800	8.4	30-40	1.8-2.4
Vegetables	4,600	2.3	---	---
Other food crops	19,400	9.7	25-30	1.3-1.5
Subtotal	40,800	20.4	---	---
OTHER CROPS				
Grand total	200,000	100	---	---

1. For 1975-1977 average
Source: FAO, Centre d'Investinement, Mission d'Identification Agricole Generale, Rapport 47/49 PRC-4.

under cassava cultivation, 23,400 under maize and rice, 20,800 ha under yams and cocoyams combined, 16,800 ha under plantain bananas, 10,200 ha under groundnuts, and 4,600 ha under vegetables. All other crops occupy 60,600 ha, giving the total area of the country under cultivation at the time of the survey to be 200,000 ha. Yields are also relatively low. From the FAO survey under reference, only 7.9 - 9.4 metric tons of cassava could be harvested on a hectare; for yams, the yield was 4.8 metric tons per hectare; for rice, 1.4 - 1.8 metric tons per ha, and for groundnuts, 1.5 - 2.0 metric tons per ha.

The output of locally produced foodstuffs has for some time now been unable to meet the total demand. The marketed portion of production of major food crops is shown in Table 5.3. During nearly a decade, most output of these crops were rather stationary. The shortage is reflected by the increases in the prices of locally produced food. A Noticeable development is the change in the diet of the urban population from the locally produced food to imported items. For instance, there is an appreciable shift to wheat bread away from the manioc <u>foufou</u> in the urban centers. The shift is being exacerbated by government intervention which has kept the prices of imported food low relative to that of locally produced food in an effort to hold down urban living costs. The situation raises a policy issue for the government to resolve, i.e., whether it would prefer to subsidize increased food production by assisting peasants with higher prices, agricultural extensions, marketing and credit services, or to continue subsidizing imported food. While the former line of action would be more difficult and would probably cost more initially than the latter, the former offers an attractive long-term benefit of strengthening the country's capacity to feed itself.

The Food Balance

Given the fact that agricultural production has not increased to keep pace with the growing population in recent years and given the rapid rate of urbanization, the supply and demand situation of food in the Congo has been out of balance.
There is, of course, no major problem in meeting rural consumption, since rural populations live at a subsistence level. However, with population in the urban areas keeps on rising fast, the food surplus from the rural area has not been

Table 5.3

Marketed Production of Food Crops

1973 - 1982

(Thousands Metric Tons)

Period	Cassava	Bananas	Peanuts	Yams
1973-74	574.2	33.5	16.3	11.1
1974-75	553.2	33.8	16.5	11.2
1975-76	559.3	34.8	16.7	11.4
1976-77	565.5	34.2	16.9	11.5
1977-78	571.7	34.6	17.1	11.6
1978-79	650.0	32.0	15.6	9.0
1979-80	580.0	29.5	13.9	6.4
1980-81	628.0	30.0	14.4	6.8
1981-82	678.0	32.0	15.0	7.4

Source: Office of Agricultural Statistics, Ministry of rural Economy; U.S. Department of Commerce, *Marketing in Congo*, Washington, D.C. October, 1983.

adequate to meet urban consumption. The urban demand for food in recent years has been met, to a large extent, by importation of foodstuff especially wheat flour (for bread), cooking oil, meat, and rice. For example, between 1975 and 1981 the importation of wheat increased from CFAF 238 billion, a threefold increase,[2] resulting in dramatic changes in the consumption pattern. At the current rate of consumption, local rice production meets only between 30% to 40% of the total urban consumption. Annual meat imports have also increased significantly, from CFAF 327 million in 1975 to CFAF 1.5 billion in 1981, or nearly a fourfold increase. In 1979-80, Brazzaville alone consumed 5,500 tons of beef, a per capita consumption of 13.5 kilograms, of which 5,200 tons or 95% were imported. In order to assure a regular flow of imported foodstuff, the government created two important offices: the Office National de Commercialisation (OFNACOM) which imports rice, salt, salted fish, sugar and the ONIVEG, which imports meats.

In 1983-1984 the total meat consumption in the urban area is estimated to reach nearly 30,000 tons per annum, of which only a little over 2,000 tons could be produced domestically, leaving nearly 28,000 tons of meat in deficit. The government has tried to solve the food deficit problem in the cities by creating state farms and state ranches; however, these ventures have not been successful, as these farms have operated in heavy deficits from year to year.

Production of Cash Crops

Historically, the production of <u>sugar cane</u>, <u>palm fruits</u> and <u>tobacco</u>, the former major cash crops of the Congo, was the preserve of plantation owners, mostly Europeans. With the fading away of their presence in the Congo, the output of these cash crops, particularly those of raw sugar and palm oil, declined precipitously. For example, the export of raw sugar was recorded by the Customs Service in 1967 to be as much as 90,689 metric tons. The figure declined to 17,836 metric tons in 1976 and to a negligible level in recent years (about 14,000 metric tons). Production of major cash crops is presented in Table 5.4.

The production of both <u>palm kernels</u> and <u>tobacco</u> has declined by 37% during 1977-78 and 1981-82. The

---

2. For 1975-77 average.

    Total areas under cultivation are also difficult to come by, although the FAO made some estimates during a survey conducted between 1975 and 1977 (Table 5.3). It gave 63,600 hectares (ha) as area under cassava cultivation, 23,400 under maize and rice, 20,800 ha under yams and cocoyams combined, 16,800 ha under plantain bananas, 10,200 ha under groundnuts, and 4,600 ha under vegetables. All other crops occupy 60,600 ha, giving the total area of the country under cultivation at the time of the survey to be 200,000 ha. Yields are also relatively low. From the FAO survey under reference, only 7.9 - 9.4 metric tons of cassava could be harvested on a hectare; for yams, the yield was 4.8 metric tons per hectare; for rice, 1.4 - 1.8 metric tons per ha, and for groundnuts, 1.5 - 2.0 metric tons per ha.

    The output of locally produced foodstuffs has for some time now been unable to meet the total demand. The marketed portion of production of major food crops is shown in Table 5.4. During nearly a decade, most output of these crops were rather stationary. The shortage is reflected by the increases in the prices of locally produced food. A Noticeable development is the change in the diet of the urban population from the locally produced food to imported items. For instance, there is an appreciable shift to wheat bread away from the manioc foufou in the urban centers. The shift is being exacerbated by government intervention which has kept the prices of imported food low relative to that of locally produced food in an effort to hold down urban living costs. The situation raises a policy issue for the government to resolve, i.e., whether it would prefer to subsidize increased food production by assisting peasants with higher prices, agricultural extensions, marketing and credit services, or to continue subsidizing imported food. While the former line of action would be more difficult and would probably cost more initially than the latter, the former offers an attractive long-term benefit of strengthening the country's capacity to feed itself.

The Food Balance

    Given the fact that agricultural production has not increased to keep pace with the growing population in recent years and given the rapid rate of urbanization, the supply and demand situation of food in the Congo has been out of balance.

Table 5.4

Marketed Production of Cash Crops

(Metric Ton)

Commodity	1977-78	1978-79	1979-80	1980-81	1981-82
Cocoa	2,275	2,339	2,113	1,900	2,000
Coffee	684	750	550	1,070	1,000
Tobacco	656	434	553	410	415
Palm kernels	712	373	624	550	450

Source: OCC, OCV, OCT; U.S. Department of Commerce, **Marketing in Congo**, Washington, Oct. 1982.

The Cocoa Research Institute of Ghana, which has been doing research work on cocoa since the 1920's, developed new varieties of cocoa trees which are not only disease resistant, but also have larger pods and beans, and mature within five and seven years. The Ministry of rural Economy is looking into obtaining the seedlings of the new cocoa tree varieties from Ghana, and to test them.

The coffee growing regions in the Congo are Cuvette, Likouala, Bouenza, Lekoumou and Niari. Local coffee production fluctuated between 550 to 1,070 tons during the period 1977-78 through 1981-82. However, the export volume of coffee rose sharply from 778 tons in 1975 to 2,172 tons in 1981. This increase was due to the fact that the Congo agreed to market for Angola some of that country's coffee. Small quantities of coffee produced in Zaire also found their way into the Congo through border trade.

Most of the coffee grown in the Congo is of the Robusta variety. In recent years, seedlings of improved Robusta and Arabica coffees have been distributed to the farmers. While Arabica beans sell for more in the international coffee market, the demand for Robusta coffee is increasing faster than that for Arabica due to the popularization of instant coffee, which is usually ground from Robusta beans.

As part of the cash crop rehabilitation program, the government has been preparing to regenerate 3,750 ha of coffee plantations and to undertake new plantings on 3,000 ha with foreign financial assistance. Producer prices paid by O.C.C. to peasants, though still very low, have been in the increase from CFAF 70 per kilogram during 1975-1976 season to CFAF 150 per kilogram during 1978-1979 crop season, an increase of 114.3% over the three crop seasons (Tables 6.1 and 6.2).

Livestock

Different from the neighboring country, the Central African Republic, where cattle raising is a thriving business, cattle production in the Congo has not proven to be very successful for both technical and economic reasons. One aspect of the problem is a disease caused by tsetse which has been somewhat solved by the introduction of the tsetse resistant N'dama breed of cattle; other problems involved is the poor management and lack of technical personnel to adequately run the state ranches where the bulk of cattle were raised. The capital costs of the state ranches run very high, as the operating costs relative to revenues. The unprofitable operations are partly attributed to government policy which controlled meat prices at an uneconomic level to the farmers in order to hold down urban living costs.

In 1980 the **cattle** population of the Congo was estimated at 94,000 heads (Table 5.5). Of these, nearly two-thirds were raised in the state ranches. The various government owned ranches of the Congo were developed with financing from the World Bank and the European Economic Development Fund. The latter organization continues to provide technical assistance for running the ranches. The production of beef is still limited in quantity, accounting for only a fraction of the local requirement (about 7%). Imports make up for the short fall.

Small farmer involvement in cattle raising is small but has begun to become more and more important as the state ranches have proven to be unsuccessful. The farmers have also started to keep their animals in fenced enclosures at night in order to provide some manure to enrich the soil of their gardens and farms. The sedentary pastoralists in West Africa used similar enclosures constructed with bamboo and palm branches to herd their livestock at night. In the morning they sprinkled ashes on the droppings and collect them as manure to fertilize the land.

The **sheep** and **goat** populations are estimated at 220,000 heads in 1980. Their raising is part of the economic activities of the small farmers. At present, there is no special program to improve the small farmers' production of sheep and goats. The government has launched a project to encourage the raising of swine. The project is sponsored by ODE (Office de Developpement de l'Elevage), a government agency formed in 1978 to oversee the country's livestock development program, and to serve as the buying and marketing organization for livestock and meat products. The cooperation between the government and the farmers works in this way: cooperatives buy piglets from a government breeding farm, raise the piglets to maturity and sell them back to the government, in this case, ODE. ODE in turn has the animals slaughtered and distributes the meat to retailers. The government, through OCV (Office des Cultures Vivrieres), supplies the farmers with animal feeds. The government's credit agency, the Commercial Bank of the Congo (BCC) pays the feed and piglets suppliers directly for their products.

By mutual agreement, BCC could serve ODE with copies of bills outstanding against each debtor participating in the project. ODE would pay indivi-

Table 5.5
Livestock Population
(Heads)

	1976	1978	1979	1980
Cattle	32,624	85,475	95,045	94,383
Sheep	49,826	443	25,100	60,657
Goats	97,970	--	--	159,410
Swine	36,404	19,289	25,173	20,465
Poultry	680,816	840,000	1,120,000	1,632,400

Source: Direction de l'Elevage; Annuaire Statistique, 1982.

dual peasants for their finished hogs, less the amount each peasant is owing BCC The arrangement is explained in advance to all peasants participating in the project. This is one of the situations where a small farm credit was successfully implemented in the Congo. Effort is being made to extend the same arrangement to all farmers who could raise the swine. The project is to be expanded to poultry and to sheep and goat production.

There are two relatively large municipal abattoirs at Loubomo and Nkayi. While the output of beef and pork from the abattoirs represented almost all the local output of the two meat products, the sheep and goats slaughtered represented only a miniscule amount of mutton consumed in the country, since most of the sheep and goats are raised and slaughtered for consumption in the subsistence sector of the economy.

<u>Chicken</u>, <u>ducks</u> and limited numbers of guinea fowls (<u>Numida meleagris</u>) are raised in the Congo. The country meets its requirements of poultry products from local production. The relatively high prices charged for poultry products indicate the production can be increased beyond existing levels. In 1980, poultry population was estimated at 1.6 million. Since much of the output of poultry and poultry products are by small farmers who also sell the bulk of the output as live chickens and eggs, there is no reliable estimate of the poultry population, nor of the total annual production of poultry products.

Fishing

One national resource which the Congo has in abundant supply is water in the form of rivers and the sea. The potential for salt-water and freshwater fishery development is great. This potential has yet to be tapped. A basic constraint on the development of the fisheries potential of the country can be attributed to lack of keen government interest and coherent policy on how to go about the development. In addition to the policy vacuum there are other constraints such as limited landing facilities to handle modern vessels at Pointe Noire and to accommodate small vessels and canoes at the various inland ports. Furthermore, there is a complete lack of incentive for and assistance to small fishermen to improve their catch; large quantities of fish which are being consumed each year in the Congo have to be imported; in 1982, fish import reached CFAF 4 billion.

Currently one public and three private enterprises carry out coastal and deep sea fishing from Pointe Noire on a commercial scale. The largest of the four operators is SICAPE (Societe Italienne-Congolaise d'Armement et de Peche), a joint venture in which the Congolese government holds the majority interest. The charter for SICAPE called of the establishment of a fish canning factory, construction of a deep freeze plant in Pointe Noire and a network of small cold stores in the interior, the manufacture of fish meal in addition to coastal and deep sea fishing. SICAPE was established in 1974, but to date, all of its catch is sold to foreign buyers. It has yet to commence on any of its other intended activities besides fishing. SICAPE and the other three commercial fishing firms, one of which is owned by a Congolese national and the other two by expatriates, account for much of Congo's saltwater fish harvests. Nationals from other countries on the western coast of Africa operate within the territorial waters of the Congo. The catch of the traditional Congolese fishermen operating from Pointe Noire and along the coast are very small. Estimates of the catch are usually sold in heaps to dealers without the benefit of any weighing. The annual volumes of the catch by the commercial fishermen operating from Pointe Noire between 1970 and 1979 are shown in Table 5.6.

Freshwater fishing is carried out by small-scale fishermen operating in the various rivers of the country, particularly in the Congo river near Brazzaville and the upper reaches of the Congo and Ubangi rivers. Estimates for freshwater catches of fish range from 13,500 metric tons in 1971 to 15,000 tons in 1978. These estimates are not reliable, since the traditional fishermen, who account for all the freshwater catch, neither weigh their catch, nor is there any system to record their landings. Judging by experience with the operation of traditional fishermen in other African countries, the estimates are only a fraction of the actual catch by the fishermen, since much of the catch is usually consumed in the villages along the river, with only a small surplus smoked for marketing. Fish is a very perishable commodity and deteriorates rapidly in tropical villages without refrigeration to preserve it; consequently, there is a high rate of spoilage in traditional fishing. There used to be a fish drying facility at Mossaka in Cuvette region. The closure of this facility has seriously affected the supply of dried and smoked fish in Brazzaville.

Table 5.6

The Volume of Fish Landed at Pointe-Noire by Commercial Fishermen, 1970-1980

(in metric tons)

1970	1971	1972	1973	1974	1975	1975	1976	1978	1979	1980
9,445	7,119	13,850	12,310	11,691	14,318	12,623	10,357	14,117	13,450	12,730

Source: Bulletin de l'Afrique Noire, No. 1057 du 23 juillet, 1980.

There was a thriving aquaculture endeavor in the Congo during the 1950's, when an estimated 4,000 metric tons of pond-raised fish, mostly tilapia, were harvested. The harvest is now estimated at only five metric tons a year. The government has been trying to organize peasants into cooperatives to raise pond fish. In order for these cooperatives to be successful, however, a great deal of technical assistance in the design of the ponds and in the care of the fish is needed to turn the ponds into profitable enterprises. (For value of annual fish products and of other agro-industrial products, see Appendix 5.1.).

6

Agricultural Marketing

The Markets

Agricultural marketing includes moving of surplus foods from the rural to the urban markets and of exporting the various cash crops.

Traditionally, the majority of the rural population cultivating the land to provide for their own subsistence needs, and marketed a small surplus. This pattern has been changing rather rapidly with the continuing wave of migration from the rural areas to the major urban centers of Brazzaville, Pointe Noire, Loubomo, Nkayi and other secondary urban areas. The Congo is one of the few urbanized countries in Africa. Nearly half of the total population now live in the primary and secondary urban areas of the country as compared to only about 15% in 1950. The rapid urbanization has led to a rising demand for foods while at the same time to stagnant production. As such, the supply of locally produced food is not adequate to support the total population. The short-fall has been covered by increasing quantities of imported food and meat products (valued at CFAF 18 billion in 1981). Inadequate local food production to meet the rising demand has also resulted in a rapid rate of increase in the consumer price for food items. Between 1980 and 1982, the consumer price index for food items in Brazzaville rose by an annual average rate of 54.5% (Table 6.1). In recent years, the government has attempted to impose a freeze in prices while introducing subsidies on certain items such as meat and wheat flour.

The local food processing industry constitutes another segment of the domestic market for agricultural produce. The local food processing facilities include the sugar refinery, palm oil and peanut oil presses, a soap and a cigarette factory, and fish

Table 6.1
Composition of Coffee Prices and Marketing Costs, 1973-1979
(prices in CFAF per kilogram)

	1973-74		1974-75		1975-76		1976-77		1977-78		1978-79*		Average 1973-74–1978-79	
	Amt.	%	Amt.	%	Amt.	%	Amt.	%	Amt.	%	Amt.	%		%
Producer Price	60	18.8	70	30.8	70	11.0	90	10.1	120	20.3	150	27.3		21.1
Collection	18	5.6	21	9.3	25	6.8	28	3.2	31	5.3	36	6.6		6.1
Transportation	49	15.3	46	20.3	47	12.7	58	6.5	77	13.0	99	18.0		14.3
Export Tax	22	6.9	22	9.7	22	5.9	22	2.5	25	4.2	25	4.5		5.6
OCC Margin	171	53.4	68	29.9	205	55.6	691	77.7	338	57.2	246	43.6		52.9
Average Export Price	320	100.0	227	100.0	369	100.0	889	100.0	591	100.0	550	100.0		100.0

* 1978-79 estimated from prevailing world prices.
Source: OCC.

drying and processing facilities. Other newer agro-industrial processing facilities include rice mills, manioc flour mills and animal feed blending plants. The output data for the new agro-industrial plants are not available.

Cocoa, coffee and palm products (palm oil and palm kernel) constitute the agricultural export commodities of the Congo. While there is great international market for these commodities, their current output and export earnings are limited. In 1981, the export value of coffee and cocoa amounted to CFAF 2 billion, or 6.4% of total agricultural and timber exports.

The entire output of Congo's commercial deep sea fishing is now exported; the SICAPE now runs three ocean-going fishing boats. However, no figures are available on the financial outcome of the venture. Three other privately owned ocean fishery companies operate from fish processing and refrigeration facilities located in Pointe Noire. The output of traditional fishing operations are not exported.

The Marketing System

At present, there are three agricultural marketing systems in the Congo. A large state marketing channel operated by five organizations, a parallel channel, consisting of small-scale Congolese food crop dealers and a few European farmers who export their limited amount of special fruits (such as mangoes), and an uncontrolled channel under which the farmers sell the crops themselves.

The public marketing organizations have the statutory authority to buy and sell agricultural produce within their crop or group of crops division. They act both as monopolies and monopsonies.

The public marketing organizations include the following:

Office de Cultures Vivrieres (OCV).

The office was established in 1978 to be responsible for the marketing of all food crops, as well as to run the food producing state farms. To date, however, OCV handles only a few commodities such as maize, peanut and rice, which have relatively short and well-established marketing chains. The peanut oil presses, which now operate under capacity take nearly all the peanut OCV supplies. The nascent animal feed blending industry also buys the locally produced maize that OCV sells. The market for rice is concentrated in the urban areas with well-established wholesale and retail outlets. OCV has prudently kept away from handling manioc and plantain, the basic staple foods produced by the farmers.

In recent years, OCV has been ridden with management as well as financial problems; its capability to collect the crops has also been hampered by the limited number of vehicles it operates.

The average Congolese urban dweller has to spend the bulk of his income (51%) on food items. Efficient marketing could significantly lower the cost of food to the urban population, in this case the majority (57%) of the total population. The manufacturing industries in the country, including sugar refining, oil pressing and soap manufacturing, cigarette manufacturing, animal feed blending, etc., depend on locally produced raw materials. Inefficiency in the marketing system for agricultural products which feed the industries will adversely affect the performance of the industries. Worse still, should the marketing system for the raw materials break down, the whole economy will be directly affected, since the large service sector of the economy cannot thrive for long without the agricultural and industrial base to support it. In a country, such as Congo, where the state dominates agricultural marketing activity, close attention needs to be paid to marketing than in countries where the self-correcting forces of the market work to set fairly competitive prices without any state intervention.

Office de Cacao et du Cafe (OCC), is another parastatal marketing organization, having the responsibility for buying and marketing the peasants output of cocoa and coffee. OCC has been doing a relatively more profitable marketing operation for the government than OCV. Between the 1973-74 and 1978-79 crop seasons, OCC cleared on the average an operating margin of 52.9% of total revenues on its coffee operation and 39.7% on its cocoa operation. Nevertheless, some of these revenues were obtained at the expense of the farmers. The corresponding percentages paid to farmers as producer prices were very low, accounting for only 21.1% of export prices for coffee and 30.4% for cocoa. Because of poor roads and inadequate transportation equipment, collection and transportation costs were also high. For coffee, the costs of moving the output to point of sale were as high as 20.4% of the sale price. The corresponding costs for moving cocoa during the same period were 26.2%.

Tables 6.1 and 6.2 show the composition of prices and marketing costs for coffee and cocoa.

RNPC <u>Regie Nationale des Palmeraies du Congo</u> and <u>Office Congolais du Tabac</u> (OCT) are the other two state marketing organizations. RNPC handles the marketing of palm products and OCT that of tobacco. The fifth state marketing organization is <u>Office Congolais du Bois</u> (OCB) which handles the marketing of timber and wood products.

Table 6.2

Composition of Cocoa Prices and Marketing Costs, 1973-1979
(prices in CFAF per kilogram)

	1973-74		1974-75		1975-76		1976-77		1977-78		1978-79*		Average % 1973-74—1978-79
	Amt.	%	Amt.	%	Amt.	%	Amt.	%	Amt.	%	Amt.	%	
Producer Price	100	38.8	100	38.5	100	38.5	130	26.9	180	23.7	200	29.2	30.4
Collection	27	9.0	31	9.4	41	15.8	45	9.3	54	7.1	54	7.9	9.7
Transportation	49	16.6	54	16.4	62	23.8	72	14.9	97	12.8	97	14.2	16.5
Export Tax	15	5.1	15	4.5	14	5.4	14	2.9	16	2.1	16	2.3	3.7
Margin	105	35.5	130	39.4	43	16.5	223	46.0	413	54.3	318	46.4	39.7
Average Export Price	296	100.0	330	100.0	260	100.0	484	100.0	760	100.0	685	100.0	100.0

* 1978-79 estimated from prevailing world prices.
Source: OCC.

7

The Rural Milieu

The Small Farmers

According to a minicensus taken in 1982, the small farmer population is estimated at 503,000 persons as compared to 798,000 persons when a complete agricultural census was taken in 1973, a decrease of 37%. Analysis in this chapter is based on the 1973 census because of the scope and depth of its coverage. (Table 7.1 and Appendix 7.1).

Of the 748,000 total, the number of farmers active in agriculture amounted to only 369,000 or 49%. The small farmers lived in and near villages of less than 300 inhabitants each. They comprised the private sector of agriculture, cultivated 196,810 ha of land and operated 143,485 small holdings of 1.37 hectares average (Table 7.1). The holdings in the Niari region are larger than the national average while those in the Lekoumou, Pool, Cuvette, and Likouala regions are slightly smaller. Each active person in the rural area cultivated an average of 0.53 hectares. On a family basis, the cultivated area per family member actively engaged in farming is about 0.68 hectares for farms operated by only one person, and 0.53 hectares or less for farms operated by four or more family members (see Table 8.2 in Chapter 8). Each small holding comprises on the average 5.6 persons of which only 2.58 persons, or less than a half, are active in agriculture (Appendix 7.1).

The farmer's population was characterized by the predominance of women in farming. As Table 7.2 shows, of the 369,000 active members, 236,000 or 64% were women and 134,000 or 36% were men. Males between the ages of 12-24 years old comprise only 2% of the total active population, while females in the same age bracket comprised 12%. The majority of both men and women (69%) are between the age of 25 and 54.

Table 7.1

Distribution of Rural Population, Number of Holdings and Area Under Cultivation by Regions

	Kouilou	Niari	Lekoumou	Bouenza	Pool	Plateaux	Cuvette	Sangha	Likouala	Total Congo
Total Cultivatable land (km²)	13,660	25,930	20,950	12,260	34,000	38,400	74,850	55,800	66,044	341,894
Area under Cultivation (ha)	16,901	32,299	13,819	27,088	44,254	20,603	20,040	14,492	6,314	196,810
Number of Holdings	13,001	23,256	10,452	18,012	34,698	15,088	16,726	7,230	5,022	143,485
Average size per Holding (ha)	1.30	1.43	1.32	1.50	1.28	1.37	1.20	2.00	1.26	1.37
Number of Farms	51,340	116,483	43,340	95,349	127,630	89,768	64,002	25,224	17,380	630,516
Number of Parcels	54,688	122,799	44,593	113,325	148,195	99,644	73,802	30,842	21,175	708,063
Agricultural Population	66,834	129,966	58,845	102,066	183,502	98,696	88,894	40,115	19,114	798,032
Number of Active Farmers	32,164	58,093	28,838	46,366	81,998	44,373	42,677	20,918	14,061	369,485

Source: Service Statistique Agricole (Recensement agricole 1972-73); Annuaire Statistique, 1982.

125

Table 7.2

Distribution of Active Farm Family Members
By Age, Sex and Region

	Niari		Lekoumou		Pool		Congo	
	No.	%	No.	%	No.	%	No.	%
MEN								
12-14 yrs.	78	0.1	-	-	69	0.1	168	0.1
15-24 yrs.	1,175	2.0	688	2.4	878	1.1	7,864	2.1
25-34 yrs.	4,036	6.9	1,560	5.4	3,660	4.5	21,856	5.9
35-44 yrs.	4,445	7.7	2,579	9.0	5,562	6.8	31,370	8.5
45-54 yrs.	6,426	11.1	2,294	8.0	9,831	12.0	39,270	10.6
55-64 yrs.	4,420	7.6	1,692	5.9	6,756	8.2	25,825	7.0
65 and over yrs.	1,071	1.8	997	3.5	1,914	2.3	7,161	1.8
Total	21,651	37.3	9,810	34.1	28,670	35.0	133,517	36.2
WOMEN								
12-14 yrs.	441	0.8	-	-	701	0.9	3,099	0.8
15-24 yrs.	5,866	10.1	3,156	11.0	9,310	11.4	40,361	10.9
25-34 yrs.	10,754	18.5	4,415	15.3	9,450	11.5	55,361	15.1
35-44 yrs.	8,642	14.9	3,976	13.8	16,069	19.6	60,746	16.5
45-54 yrs.	5,823	10.0	4,374	15.2	12,588	15.4	46,951	12.7
55-64 yrs.	4,221	7.3	2,280	7.9	4,724	5.8	24,025	6.5
65 and over yrs.	695	1.2	783	2.7	486	0.6	4,970	1.4
Total	36,442	62.7	18,984	65.9	53,328	65.0	235,815	63.8
Grand Total	58,093	100.0	28,794	100.0	81,998	100.0	369,332	100.0

Source: Recensement Agricole 1972-73; FAO, Centre d'Investinement, Rapport 47/49, PRC-4.

Cultural and Social Characteristics

As noted in Chapter 1, the rural population densities are low, though there is a general tendency to agglomeration in larger villages. There is a considerable regional variation in population densities with 70% in subsistence population living in the southern 30% of the country (Map 7.1) and in subsistence patterns as determined by ecological conditions and cultural preferences as well as in the social institutions associated with the different ethnic groups.

Because of this diversity and of inadequate literature (especially concerning the peoples of the north), no attempt is made to present a comprehensive picture of the small farmers throughout the Congo. Only some of the most salient features of the two largest ethnic groups (the Bakongo and the Bateke) is analyzed here in order to highlight factors relevant to economic development and planning of the rural sector and to give some indication of the complexity of the issues involved. The analysis in each will focus on four interrelated aspects: lineage structure, authority relationships between generations, the sexual division of labor, and rules governing the access to and the ownership of land. This is to be followed by a general discussion of the rural exodus and a summary view of the well-being condition of the rural farmers.

The Bakongo

As a rule, lineages (unilineal descent groups) are matrilineal among the Bateke and Bakongo of the south and patrilineal among the Mboshi and Sangha peoples of the north. Among the Bakongo, the lineages, which are ranked according to the seniority of their founding ancestors, have traditionally been grouped into named, exogamous clans. Sexual intercourse between clan members was regarded as incestuous and was formerly punishable by burning alive. Each clan had its own food tabu, land was property of the clan, and and all clan villages before the arrival of the Europeans were supposed to support each other in times of war. Clan members include, moreover, not only the living, but the ancestors as well. During the colonial period, however, it would seem that the clans lost much of their earlier importance, leaving control of village life largely in the hands of their constituent lineages. The head of a lineage is the oldest male member, and his

Map 7.1
Rural Density

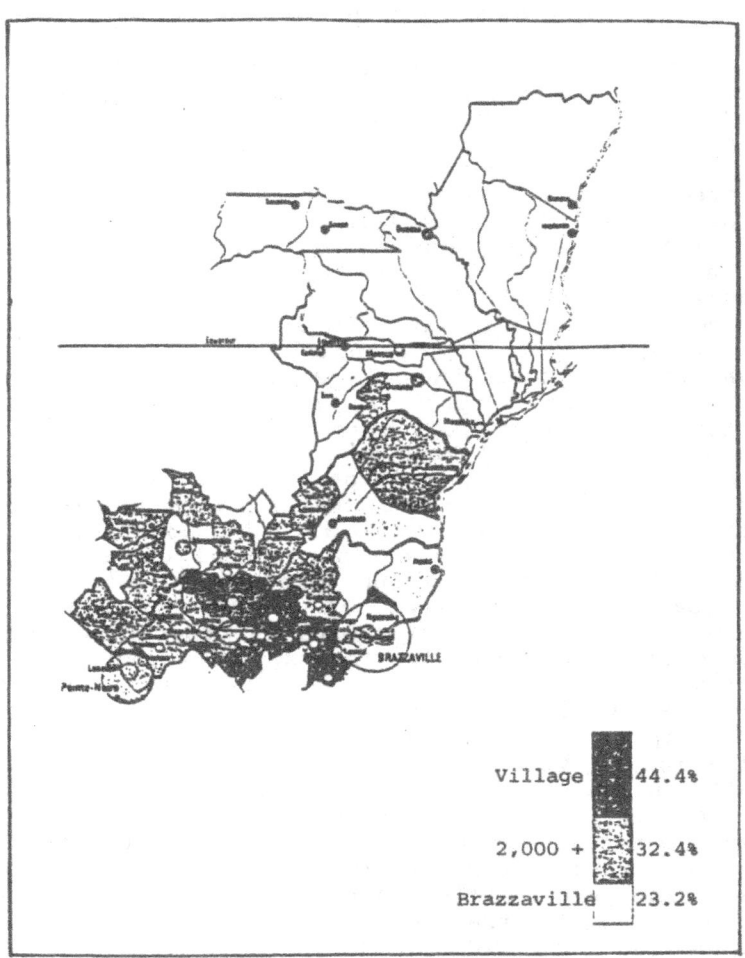

Source: Jeune Afrique, 1977.

authority rests not only on his seniority, but as Van Wing says in speaking of the clan chiefs, "His sacred character comes from his being the representative of the clan and like an incarnation of the ancestors."[1] Even recent accounts describe village affairs as being controlled by the head of the dominant lineage and the lineage elders. This control of the old over the young (up to about 30 years of age) expresses itself not only in terms of groups, but in individual relations. Everyone is said to be under the authority of his or her maternal uncle in all matters. This is particularly important with respect to free access to lineage-owned land and in case of marriage. The control of marriage is especially important as a means of maintaining or consolidating lineage property (bilateral cross-cousin marriage reportedly is favored) and a few men apparently dare to marry without their uncle's blessing.

Traditionally, marriage was conceived to be more an alliance between two matrilineages than one between two individuals. It was the lineage heads who made the arrangements and agreed upon the goods to be exchanged, in principle of equal value. Nowadays the spouses themselves are directly involved and the future husband is supposed to take the initiative in proposing marriage. Still, however, the matrilineages of both spouses and those of their fathers must agree and provide the money and goods to be exchanged. One cannot easily marry, therefore, without one's family's approval and support, and the fear of retribution by one's maternal uncle in the form of sorcery in case one goes against his wishes is apparently very strong. A desire to escape the domination of uncles and elders in general has also been cited as a reason for the exodus of youth to the cities, but even there the fear persists. It was said that a common reaction to illness in the city, for example, was to visit and take presents to one's uncle in the village to induce him to withdraw the spell causing it.

Actually important changes seem to have taken place in recent times in the picture just presented. Given the long process of urbanization that has taken place since the thirties an the disruption of life in the rural areas that it has caused, this is not surprising. How widespread the changes are (especially in rural areas) could not be determined. The principal change would seem to be that nowadays it tends to be the father who has control over and

---

1. S.J. Van Wing, <u>Etudes Bakongo</u> (Leopoldville: 1959), p. 125.

responsibility for his children. In cases of divorce, children up to school age would stay with the mother, but older ones would go with the father. The extent to which matrilineal ties dominate and the matrilineage remains a corporate body would seem to depend on circumstances. Some such families remain close and maintain a fund administered by a senior elder for the benefit of its members, but this would no longer seem to be the rule. One informant, an urbanite, who said he had been approached about succeeding to such a position, could not face the prospect of taking responsibility for such a large group. It would mean the end of the kind of life he had grown accustomed to in France and Brazzaville.

The sexual division of labor is strong and is characterized by the dominance of men. The primary agriculturalists are women. Men clear new land, but except for certain cash crops as maize or tobacco, tend to leave all the agricultural labor, including the transportation of the crops from the fields (which might be as much as 5-10 km away from the village) to the women. Indeed, it was reported that one attempt to introduce mechanization on a small scale failed because the men refused to use the "motorculteurs" for plowing. Traditionally, a husband clears one field for each of his wives plus one for himself. His wives all work with him on his own field and plant, harvest and exploit it for his entire benefit. The other fields serve primarily to support the respective households of the wives. Any surplus is sold by the wives and the proceeds kept by them until the fields are finished. The money is then supposed to be divided equally between each wife and the husband, except that each wife is supposed to pay a small amount for the hoe she has received from him. It is said, however, that wives frequently cheat their husbands by withholding part of the money to be divided. In case of a good crop the husband should present each wife with a piece of cloth. The economic advantages to a man of having several wives is obvious, and polygamy is still quite common in rural areas.

Wives also plant their own fields of peanuts, gourds, and maize, both to feed their households and for sale for their own benefit. They may also earn money by making and selling small baskets, raising chickens and goats, and by fishing. Some of this money a wife gives to her own family and some to her married children, while the rest is devoted to the accumulation of clothes to be used for her burial. Although the general rule is that there is a strict separation between the property of husband and wife, there is variation from region to region.

In Bouenza, for example, it seems that the husband's control over his wife's property is much greater than in the Pool, where a much stricter separation is the rule. There it is reportedly common that in case of divorce (which is also more common than in the Bouenza region) husband and wife will have minute records of all gifts and expenses that could be charged to the other during the course of the marriage.

An important factor affecting the relations between spouses is the fact that marital residence is normally virilocal. This means that the wife goes to live with her husband. She will, therefore, presumably have free access only to her husband's land (or rather that of his lineage), though she may be able to use other land on payment of rent. He, on the other hand, will normally have moved from his father's village to his maternal uncle's, where he will have access to the land of his own lineage.

Traditionally there has been no private property in land. It is owned by the lineage or clan and is inalienable. Actually it is the ancestors who are thought to own it. As a member of a lineage one has the right to use that land, so no one is in effect landless. However, the land is not equally divided between all lineages and is not of equal kind or quality. In a single village more than one lineage will usually be represented, one of which will be dominant over the others. The land held by these lineages, however, will not constitute so many integral blocks, but will tend to be scattered, not only around the village, but elsewhere as well. This situation may be the result of different historical processes: lineage segmentation resulting either from a search for new land or because of quarrels, or from the forced relocation of villages by the colonial government in the 1930's. As has also been noted above, the general trend toward larger rural communities is continuing.

The control of access to and the administration of these lands rests with the lineage chiefs. Because of the dispersed nature of the holdings, however, a chief may delegate some of this control to a nephew, younger brother, or younger natural cousin, who collects rents for him. As might be expected, this delegation also leads to conflicts which tend to provoke the use of sorcery. Access to land is further controlled (at least in part) among the Bakongo by a system of rotation (<u>kitemo</u>), according to which one chief opens his land one year to the members of other lineages against payment of rent and the following year another does the same. The process repeats itself yearly within a region which corresponds in part to the area within which matrimonial exchanges take place (it seems that 50% of the women marry within a radius of 8-10 km. An indication that the control of access to land by the matrilineages is no longer absolute, however, is given by a pre-cooperative in the region of Kinkala, the land for which was inherited by one of the men from his father.

The term *kitemo* used above for the rotation of access to land would also seem to refer to a variety of systems of organizing labor. *Ntsala sani* is an association of producers on the basis of affinity, sex, filiation, or marital alliance. The group works on the fields of each member in turn. The *luyalu* is a village association which functions every 8 or 15 days on the day set aside for labor for the state. It can be used either for communal works or for work on individual fields. The village chief regulates the work of this group whose efforts every one has the right to enjoy every one or two years against a small payment which goes into the village treasury.

The *dibundu* or *zola* is also a village group which works for the church. One member is responsible for distributing its labors among the members of the village at a small cost which goes to the church or cult treasury and to pay for food for the participants.

It also happens that young men will hire themselves out, either individually or as a group for specific tasks. It should be noted that none of the above forms of cooperative labor involves joint production on common land. The government's early experience in cooperative programs which stress joint production did not, therefore, rest on any traditional practices. Recent government emphasis on cooperatives as an instrument of marketing and distribution of agricultural inputs seems to be closer to the traditional line.

The Bateke

Among the people of Enkou in the Plateaux region just west of Djambala, lineage structure is also matrilineal. Here, too, it is the maternal uncle and the elders in general who are in charge, and here, too, there is sharp conflict between the old and the young, leading both to the splitting up of villages and an exodus of the youth to the city. "This splitting of settlements is the mark of the new tensions born partly from the realization by the young of the inferiority of their situation, and

partly from a consequent rigidification by their
elders of the customary practices which permitted
them till now to base their authority. The existence
of a very high matrimonial compensation (bride price)
and a high incidence of polygamy are allowed by the
fear of the fetish which can cause disease or kill,
which paralysis the young and strongly impregnates
the social atmosphere."[2]

On the other hand, in contrast to the
traditional situation among the Bakongo, and parallel
perhaps to modern trends among them, considerable
weight is accorded to the authority of fathers as
Banou put it: "...Koukouya society accords a large
place to the patriarchal family home of which the
husband and father is the chief. The family home is
no longer entirely the simple association of clan
families that it is in Ladi (Lari) law. The father
exercises considerable authority over his children,
which is translated by the fact that in the country
the sons live in the village of their father, in
principle, whatever their age and even after the
death of their father, and especially by the
quasi-exclusive right of the father to give his
daughter in marriage."[3] Another difference with
Bakongo custom is that material exchanges at marriage
are not conceived to be equal, but almost all gifts
are expected to come from the side of the groom. As
among the Bakongo, however, the sexual division of
labor is quite marked. In the traditional system,
men planted rafia palms, fruit trees, and harvested
and cured tobacco, but they never used hoes. Now
they are getting involved in new crops -- imported
varieties of beans and tobacco (Maryland or Java),
potatoes, and coffee -- which they cultivate
essentially on forest soils. All of the produce is
sold. Very few men are willing to risk the gives of
friends and women if they are seen using hoes, so
their work is mostly limited to forest clearing,
planting, and harvesting. These are seasonal
activities only the first of which requires much
effort. There is little organization involved,
father and son usually working together. On the
fourth day of each week a wife is supposed to work on
her husband's field.

Whereas men have their fields in the forests,
women's fields are typically in the savanna. They

---

2. Bernard, Guillot, <u>La Terre Enkou (Congo)</u>, Atlas
des Structures Agraires au Sud du Sahara, #8, (Paris
and the Hague: Monton, 1973), p. 48.

3. Alexis Gabou, <u>Le Marriage Congolais</u>, (Brazzaville:
Lad et Koukouya, 1979), p. 27.

are responsible for the staple food (manioc), peanuts, gourds, and some others. An investigation of the work weeks of men and women in this region clearly shows the preponderant role of women in agriculture. The women work 38 hours in the fields, 8 in such tasks as soaking manioc, making palm oil, collecting firewood, and shelling peanuts and gourd seeds. Fourteen hours are devoted to household tasks, making a total of 60 hours. The men, on the other hand, typically work a total of 39 hours.

In Enkou, although descent is reckoned matrilinearily, marital residence as we have seen above, is patrilocal, so that the wife comes to live with her husband in his father's village. Lineage land rights are here particularly associated with forests, which beat the names of the lineages, and which are grouped around the villages owned by noble lineages. Several of these villages would be grouped together under an appropriate chief. Forests were transmitted only in the <u>uterine</u> line, but each man had rights to use not only lands belonging to his mother's lineage, but also to those of his father's matrilineage as well. This inevitably gave rise to disputes which might make it necessary for men to move to the village of their matrilineage. For one group of lineages descended from the noble lineage of Mubie, however, descent and the inheritance of land rights is patrilineal.

The general rule for all land is that it belongs to the person who brought it under cultivation and his descendants. In the case of savanna lands, it is the women who do it, and the land belongs to them and should in theory be inherited by their daughters. However, with patrilineal residence daughters are not apt to be around to work it and it goes to those who are at hand. Because women are seldom living near land to which they have rights, there is much swapping back and forth without any obligatory compensation.

Farmers' Income and Welfare

Income

In general, the farmers grow food crops, especially manioc, bananas, ground nuts and yams, mainly for self-consumption and selling some surplus to the urban dwellers for extra income. In addition to food crops their monetary income derives mainly from the production of cash crops. Cocoa is the main cash crop for the farmers in the Sangha and Likouala regions. Coffee is a source of monetary income for the farmers in the Cuvette, the Plateau and the Lekoumou regions, while tobacco is the main source of income for the Plateaux and the Pool regions (Map 7.2). In recent years rice has become an increasingly important source of income for the farmers in the Plateaux, Pool, Bouenza, Lekoumou and Niari regions.

As shown in Table 7.3, agricultural income is very low compared to national per capital income. In 1982, an average farmer earned an estimated to CFAF 95,000 ($290) a year, which amounted to only 22% of the national average. Though in absolute terms farmers' per capital income more than doubled during 1979-82, due partly to the sharp decline in rural population, the 1982 ratio of rural to national income was 4% less than the 1979 level due to the expansion of oil in the modernized sector of the economy. As such, farmers' income continued to decline in comparison to that of the rest of the country. In producing cash crops for monetary income, small farmers have been heavily taxed in the sense that they were being paid for their products prices which are far below what government agencies received from exporting agricultural products. For example, during the seventies cocoa farmers were paid a producer price averaged at only 30% of the cocoa export price (see Table 6.2 in Chapter 6) An important portion of the difference went into the profits of the marketing boards. To the coffee growers, the treatment was even worse; coffee producer prices averaged at only 21% during the same period. Farmers' income derived from the sale of food crops has also declined partly because of the reduction in the surplus of the crops, partly because of the difficult marketing conditions, unattractive producer prices, interruption in agricultural research and partly because of the declining fertility of soil.

Education

The educational level of the Congolese population is unusually high for Africa. In general, school education has been obligatory from the ages of 6-16 since 1965.[4] In 1968, 68% of the children were

---

4. Law No. 32/65 of August 1965 stipulated free and compulsory schooling.

Map 7.2

Small Farmer Cash Crop Producing Areas

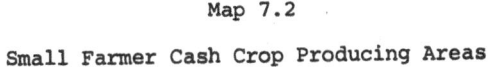

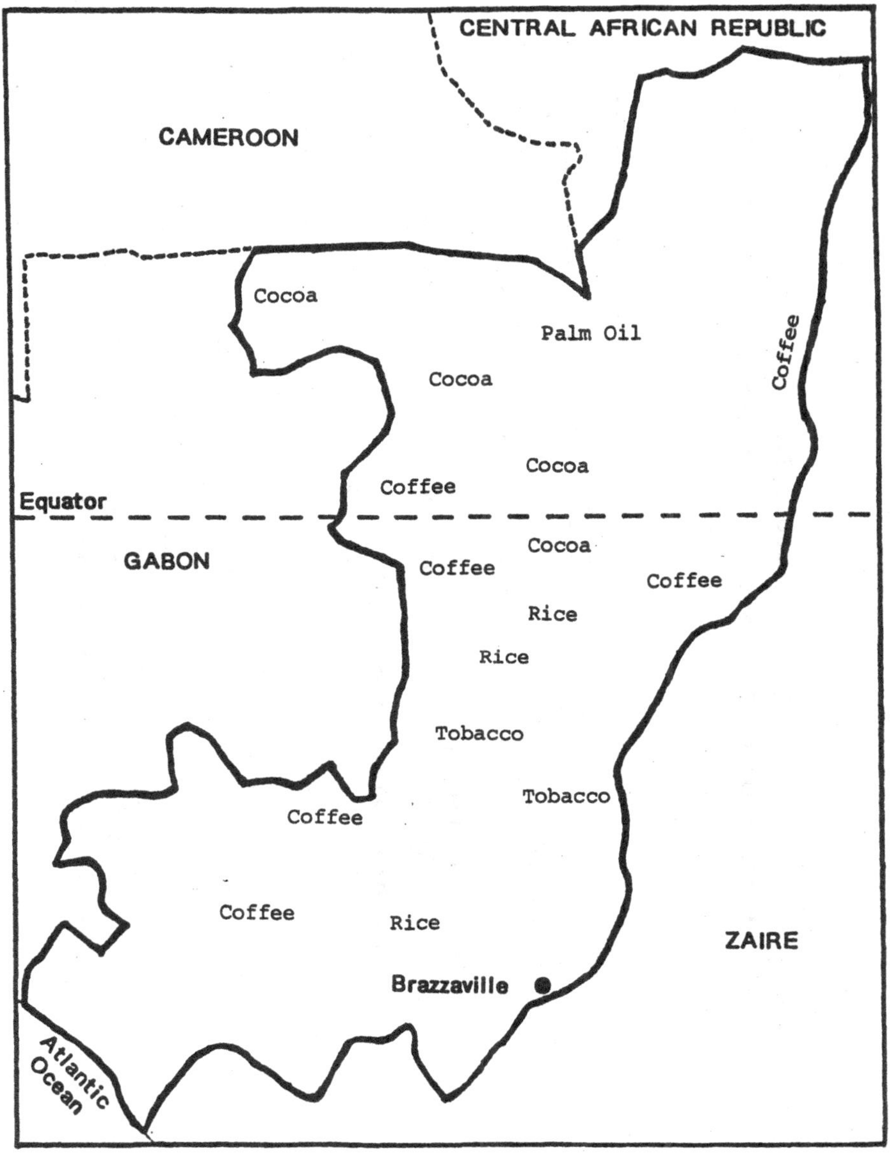

Source: Jeune Afrique, 1977.

Table 7.3

Estimation of Per Capita Agricultural Income 1970-1982

(in CFAF)

	1970	1974	1976	1977	1978	1979	1980	1982
Agricultural Production (millions)[1]	12.1	15.0	19.4	22.9	25.6	29.0	34.4	52.7
Agricultural rural Population (thousand persons)[2]	797	756	737	719	698	674	565	555
Per Capita Agricultural Income (thousands)	15	20	26	32	37	43	61	95
Per Capita GNP (thousands)	61	101	120	123	129	165	232	435
Per Capita Agricultural Income as Percent of Per Capita GNP	25	20	22	26	29	26	26	22

1. Including forestry.
2. Including only population engaged in agriculture.
3. Sources: Tables 1.1 and 2.3.

Table 7.4
Number of Students at Different Levels of Education

Type d'enseignement	1979	1980	1981	1982
BASIC EDUCATION	**482,973**	**517,403**	**544,848**	**571,712**
• Primary, General	358,761	383,018	390,676	406,835
of which, girls	171,601	183,646	188,431	196,690
• Secondary, General	118,958	129,636	145,638	155,789
of which girls	48,209	53,313	62,503	67,338
• Secondary, Technical	5,254	4,749	8,534	9,088
of which, girls	3,421	2,647	5,454	6,368
HIGH SCHOOL	**25,272**	**25,018**	**27,443**	**37,910**
• High School, General	19,567	19,221	20,308	29,766
of which girls	4,360	4,012	5,080	6,915
• High School, Technical	4,065	4,180	4,083	4,185
of which girls	1,468	1,660	1,612	1,676
• High School, Prof.	1,640	1,617	3,052	3,959
of which girls	255	298	996	1,171
COLLEGE	**5,461**	**6,848**	**6,838**	**8,288**
Total	513,706	549,269	579,129	617,910

Source: Ministere de l'Education Nationale.

in school but by 1972 it was 100%. Inevitably this was achieved to a certain extent at the expense of quality and the problems of school support, particularly in rural areas are serious. In 1982, the number of students in school reached 618,000 or 38% of the population; of these, 407,000 were in primary schools, 38,000 in secondary schools, and 8,000 in colleges (Table 7.4). In comparison to 1979, the student population increased by 20% or nearly 7% per annum. There is an agricultural lycee which is located in Brazzaville, nine normal or specialized schools offering training in teaching, paramedical, and public health work, laboratory techniques, administration and sports (all at Brazzaville) as well as two normal schools at Loubomo and Mouyondzi, a forestry center at Mossendjo and a paramedical school at Pointe Noire.

There is only one university, the Marien Ngouabi University in Brazzaville, which in 1982 received about 7,000 students in the three faculties of law, literature and sciences.

The educational and literacy levels are considerably higher in and near the major cities than in the countryside. This is not only because of staffing and supply problems in the village school, but also because all educational facilities above the primary level are available only in the cities, almost exclusively in Brazzaville and Pointe Noire.

Health

It is not possible to give an accurate or complete picture of the health of the Congolese farmer. Certainly, by western standards, the number of physicians and medical facilities is inadequate and of very unequal distribution. Respiratory diseases, malaria, tuberculosis, and afflictions due to intestinal parasites have been the primary causes of death. Trypanosomiasis, yellow fever, small pox, leprosy, and yaws have also been, at least until recent years, prevalent as well. It is estimated that only 27% of total population and 6% of rural population have access to safe water.[1] Undoubtedly, the unsanitary conditions and polluted water supplies that are particularly common in rural areas are factors in the incidence of disease. In addition, there is the problem of malnutrition. According to the World Health Organization's 1976 study in the

---

5. World Bank Country Social Indicators Data Sheet/Congo/1983.

Congo, 17% of the children between 0 and 4 years of age were admitted to a hospital in that year for malnutrition (associated in 70% of the cases with diarrhea, respiratory complaints or measles); and that malnutrition was present in all cases of death by diarrhea and measles (63% of deaths from 0-4 years). It noted that an earlier study (1965) showed that average growth in weight and stature were well below that of well nourished Congolese children and international norms. The decline appeared around four months. Current studies showed normal growth till six months. Low birth weights (2/55 kg.) in rural zones and primipares in Brazzaville were also an indication of nutritional deficiencies in pregnant women. The principal diseases associated with malnutrition were malaria, measles, diarrhea and sickle cell anemia. The normal Congolese diet varies from region to region, but tends to emphasize starchy foods (manioc in particular) and to be somewhat short on animal protein (Table 7.5). Game used to be an important source of the latter, but it has now largely vanished in the more heavily settled regions.

Behind the Rural Exodus

As was discussed elsewhere (Chapters 1 and 3), a major aspect of the rural scene is the relative absence of youth, particularly young men.

The rural exodus, is a historical phenomenon, but it has nevertheless proceeded at a more rapid pace since independence and has created a major social and economic problem for the cities, which has had to absorb the influx; it also caused problems for the villages which were deprived of essential manpower needed for increasing agricultural production.

The reasons for this exodus would appear to be many and difficult to rank in the order of their importance. In addition to the economic reasons discussed earlier there is also a host of social factors. Certainly the domination of youth by the elders in the traditional lineage system is an important factor and are universally cited. The youth seem to resent the lack of opportunity to earn directly for themselves and the lack of freedom to live their own life. What they also try to escape, however, is the manifold ties and responsibilities associated with the lineage system in general, which they perceive primarily as an impediment to their welfare.

The traditional sexual division of labor may also be seen as a factor facilitating a male exodus.

Table 7.5

The Congolese Diet[1]

Foods	Calories	Proteins (GR.)	Lipids (GR.)
Cereals	219	6.1	0.9
Starches	1,450	9.4	5.6
Sugar	43	0.1	-
Legumes	140	6.5	10.8
Vegetables	18	1.2	0.2
Fruits	39	0.5	0.3
Various vegetal sources	3	-	0.3
Meat	46	3.9	3.4
Eggs	12	0.2	0.2
Milk	14	0.6	0.5
Fish	69	11.3	2.1
Oils and fats	117	-	13.2
Total	2,160	39.8	37.5
Of animal origin	134	16.0	6.6
Beverages	61	0.4	-

1. Data from 1964-66.
Source: The World Health Organization (WHO), 1976.

Since women have been the primary agriculturalists responsible for the staple foods, men have not been so necessary as food producers and are, therefore, more easily expendable as labor. What the lineage elders counted on when the exodus first started in the 1920's, of course, was that the youth would contribute to the wealth of the lineages through their salaries. After almost 60 years of urbanization, however, the two spheres have become radically different and it is no longer possible for the elders to control the resources of the young in the cities. Since women have been the primary agriculturalists responsible for the staple foods, men have not been so necessary as food producers and are, therefore, more easily expendable as labor. What the lineage elders counted on when the exodus first started in the 1920's, of course, was that the youth would contribute to the wealth of the lineages through their salaries. After almost 60 years of urbanization, however, the two spheres have become radically different and it is no longer possible for the elders to control the resources of the young in the cities. For example, an urban youth would not try to marry on his own even if he could afford it, because this would be an indication of how much money he actually had which would leave him open to demands to share with his father and relatives.

The extension of compulsory education to all children between the ages of 6 and 16 has certainly had the effect not only of providing information about the outside world and creating new desires, but it has also given the children the schooling to make them employable in the city.

Finally, another factor is the lasting effects of colonization which have also been accelerated since independence. The population, especially in the densely populated south, has been grouped into larger rural settlements leaving an effect on reducing the traditional fallow periods and hence fertility of the soil in the process; the grouping also draws off the younger, primarily male, population to the towns and cities, reducing the rural labor supply and eventually disrupting the traditional patterns of social control.

At the same time, little has been done to make it possible for the rural sector to keep pace with or adapt to the modernization of the urban sector. For example, techniques for the permanent maintenance of soil fertility under tropical conditions, which is a necessary condition for increased production, have not been developed. The rural road network and transportation facilities necessary to enable the farmers to participate in the marketing process remains a serious problem (see Chapter 4).

8

The Farming Systems

Traditional agriculture in the Congo takes place in both forested and savanna areas. Table 8.1 shows the distribution of farms by regions and according to crops. Fields surrounded by forests are held by the local population to be superior to fields cleared from the savanna. Farmers believe this to be especially true for manioc, the center of traditional agriculture. Fields may be either rightly grouped or widely scattered in isolated locations depending on numerous factors, including topography, water, soil fertility, fallow cycle, and land tenure. Farm size is estimated to be averaged at 1.37 hectare per economically active family (Table 8.2)

Within a farm family, each active member cultivated, on the average, 0.53 hectare of land. Farm size did not vary proportionally with the increase in the number of family members. Families with five members farming were found to work 2.5 hectares while those with seven worked only .044 hectares more. By breaking the figures down by region, it was shown that in the three principal agricultural areas farm size is about the same.

In the forest area farmers often clear steep slopes, adding considerably to erosion problems. In the savanna only relatively flat areas are cultivated. During the dry season peasants take advantage of the cooler temperatures and dryness to complete the difficult task of clearing land. Trees and bushes are cut down with machetes. The underbrush is then burned off. Slash and burn techniques are used in both the savanna and forest regions.

At the end of the rainy season agriculture shifts to low areas near streams. These areas are usually flooded during the rainy season and are only usable in dry months.

Table 8.1

Distribution of Farms by Regions and According to Crops

(in thousand units)

Regions	Number of Farms	Manioc	Yam	Taro	Plaintain	Banana	Maize	Peanuts	Palm	Cocoa	Coffee	Tobacco
Kouilou	13,001	12.7	5.6	4.6	5.5	4.3	10.2	7.1	0.4	0.2	0.2	0.1
Niari	23,256	22.9	16.4	8.3	12.2	5.0	20.3	21.8	2.9	0.3	1.7	3.5
Lekoumou	10,452	10.0	8.4	2.6	6.3	1.6	8.7	8.3	0.6	0.1	4.5	2.1
Bouenza	18,012	17.4	11.0	0.4	8.6	3.5	15.7	17.5	1.6	n	2.3	0.8
Pool	34,698	34.5	16.1	2.4	7.6	8.5	28.8	28.1	2.0	-	n	5.4
Plateaux	15,088	14.9	5.7	0.2	7.1	4.3	10.8	8.6	1.1	-	6.4	9.0
Cuvette	16,726	16.1	8.5	3.0	8.6	3.9	10.1	6.1	2.0	1.1	4.9	5.6
Sangha	7,230	6.8	2.9	1.5	6.7	1.9	5.4	2.4	0.3	5.0	-	1.3
Likouala	5,022	4.8	0.7	1.6	4.3	1.2	2.6	0.2	1.2	1.4	0.6	0.1
Congo	143,485	140.1	75.3	24.6	66.9	34.2	112.6	100.0	12.1	8.1	20.6	27.9

Source: Service Statistique Agricole (Recensement agricole, 1972-1973).

Table 8.2

Land Cultivated According to Number of Family Members and by Regions

(in hectares)

No. of active family members	Niari Area/family	Niari Area/person	Lekoumou Area/family	Lekoumou Area/person	Pool Area/family	Pool Area/person	Congo Area/family	Congo Area/person
One	0.78	0.78	0.71	0.71	0.80	0.80	0.68	0.68
Two	1.20	0.60	0.94	0.47	1.09	0.55	1.09	0.54
Three	1.74	0.58	1.50	0.50	1.54	0.51	1.60	0.53
Four	2.01	0.50	1.90	0.48	2.07	0.52	2.03	0.51
Five	2.50	0.50	2.22	0.44	2.46	0.49	2.55	0.51
Six	2.49	0.41	3.07	0.51	3.27	0.55	2.88	0.48
Seven	3.33	0.47	2.85	0.41	2.33	0.33	2.99	0.43
Eight	–	–	–	–	–	–	3.93	0.49
Nine	–	–	2.29	0.25	–	–	3.75	0.42
Ten and more	–	–	2.29	0.25	–	–	3.75	0.42
Average	1.43	0.57	1.32	–	1.28	0.53	1.37	0.53

Source: Recensement Agricole, 1972-73; FAO, Centre d'Investinement, Rapport 47/49, PRC-4.

Food Crops System

Manioc

Typically, manioc is grown in a multiple cropping system. Interplanted with the manioc are a number of different types of plants, such as several different types of gourds, calabashes, yams, maize, peanuts and other legumes such as sweet potatoes. In the southern part of the country a type of eggplant with edible leaves is popular, as is a relative of the buckwheat called <u>nsosso</u>. A local type of sorrel is also widely grown (<u>mbadi</u>). Fields devoted exclusively to manioc are not uncommon. The reason for this seemingly unproductive practice is not known. We observed manioc fields in monoculture that could have easily been used for multiple cropping (convenient water supply relatively good soil. etc.).

Planting takes place from September to November depending upon the start of the rainy season. The Plateaux areas would be started earlier, the Niari valley, later.

A survey of manioc types in the Congo by the French ORSTOM organization found that 10% to 15% of the manioc in traditional fields was of the sweet type that can be eaten without further processing. Among the better types, considerable genetic variation was found, both from one area to another and within the same field. The survey included only bitter types in the classification program. Looking at three main agricultural areas in the country it found that three genetically distinct types were grown in traditional farms in the Plateaux area (<u>nganfouo</u>, <u>odzion</u>, <u>mumdele mpakou</u>), two predominated in the Pool area (<u>m'pemba</u>, <u>maloeda</u>) and two in the Niari valley (<u>mouyoundzi</u>, <u>invoutoulou</u>). The unimproved land varieties also differ morphologically from improved types developed by the major international agricultural centers in Nigeria and South America. Although there is considerable variation, Congolese land races of manioc are generally tall and spindly in appearance. There is little branching of the plants. The canopy is less dense even though the leaf lobes are wider than those of improved types. The tubers are generally small.

Manioc is planted in mounds. Very often these mound plantings are begun with a crop of peanuts. After harvesting this first crop the mounds are enlarged and then planted with manioc cuttings. These larger mounds tend to be uniform in shape. Peanuts and some of the other plants mentioned previously are then planted about the base of the manioc.

Two or three weedings are done before a ground cover has been formed by the secondary crops. There is little other weeding activity until the dry season. The manioc plants take anywhere from eight to eighteen months to mature, after which the tubers are harvested individually. Since the plants may be left in the ground for up to three years no storage is necessary. As is well known, tubers can be stored in this manner for long periods. After the three-year period fields are usually abandoned.

Maize

Maize is planted between the manioc mounds. One or two crops are usually obtained, depending on the availability of water. A first crop is planted in November and harvested in January or February; a second crop is planted in March for harvesting in June. Improved varieties of maize are not used by the traditional farmers, presumably because there are none available for distribution. Land races are notably tall (almost two meters) with very small ears. Traditionally, maize is eaten fresh. Maize does not compete well for either light or nitrogen when interplanted with manioc. During the dry season maize is often included in market gardens that are grown in low lying areas near streams.

Groundnuts

Groundnuts (or peanuts) are the most important oil seed crop grown in the country. As in the case with maize, most of the groundnuts grown in the Congo are land varieties. An incomplete collection by the research station in Loudima has identified 30 different genetic types being grown. In the sixties an improved type, originally developed in the Congo during the colonial period, known as Rouge du Congo, was reintroduced. The extent of its use by the small farmer is not known.

Groundnuts account for about 7% of the cultivated area. At first glance they would seem to be an ideal cash crop for the Congo. As mentioned in the section on manioc cultivation they already play an important role in the small farm cropping system. They seem especially suited to the growing conditions of the Congo. They appreciate light sandy soils, fix most of their own nitrogen, and complete growth within the limits of the rainy season. They store well, especially if left in the shell. From an agricultural point of view increasing their production would not be particularly difficult. Nevertheless, they are not a high value crop. A considerable amount of their value is in processed oil, with little of the money going to the primary producer. As it appears to be the case with other crops, current OCV strategy is aimed at increasing groundnut oil production by centralized collection and marketing, but little attention seems to be paid to production inputs that would help the small farmer. There is also little information as to how much of the edible oil produced from the peanut crops gets back to the rural areas. The government's program to develop this crop includes a plan to increase the number of oil extraction facilities in the country. These facilities would be small scale operations that would assure local farmers a portion of cooking oil in return for their product. The advantage of producing groundnut oil is that it is a relatively stable product and can be stored easily. Closer processing facilities would help to reduce post harvest losses which is high in the case of the Congo. When small scale extraction was set up with American assistance in Rwanda, production was found to increase sharply.

Bananas

Although both plantains and sweet bananas are commonly grown in the Congo there are wide differences in their importance from one area to another. About 43% of the small farms in the Congo grow plantains, 89% of the farms in the Sangha province and 76% of the farms in Likouala grow plantains. According to the "Recensement Agricole" (1972-73) plantains are more important than manioc in the tropical rainforest areas of the north, although manioc is still an important food.

Not much information is available about banana cultivation in the Congo other than production figures and the number of farms that grow them. Fragmentary data suggest that most of the sweet bananas cultivated are of the Gros Michel variety, perhaps <u>Musa Sapientum</u>. The types of ordinary plantains grown are not known and no collections of types exist. The Congo's only agricultural research station in Loudima does not study bananas. Given the state of transportation in the country, commercial banana production with its requirement for refrigeration and rapid shipment is neither feasible nor profitable.

Other Tuber Crops

Yams, sweet potatoes, and white potatoes are widely grown in the Congo. Little study has been done on what types are grown, however. As mentioned in the discussion of manioc, sweet potatoes are used as a rapid ground cover. In areas fairly close to the urban regions such as Pool and Plateaux, white potatoes are grown as a cash crop. In most regions tubers, other than manioc, play a minor role in the peasant farming system. Lack of storage facilities in the Congo's hot, humid climate has been a major constraint in the development of these crops.

Rice

Although rice is not part of the traditional diet of the Congolese, there are indications that it is becoming increasingly popular. Up until the mid-sixties, rice was considered a commercial crop that had potential for export, but was not eaten by the local population and locally produced rice was hard to sell. The situation changed considerably thereafter until about 1974-75. In 1972 the "Recensement Agricole" done by the Congolese government estimated that rice production covered about 1% of the cultivated land (2.000 hectares) and production was assumed to be about 3,000-4,000 tons. Using 1978 figures, the FAO estimated acreage to represent 1.1% of the land area cultivated. More important than this slight increase in area cultivated, has been the government's effort to make rice a cash crop produced at the village level through the use of OCV.

The OCV distributed rice seed grain in the five principal agricultural regions in the country (Table 10.4 in Chapter 10). Often the demand for OCV's rice seed was greater than the amount distributed; during the 1978-79 season, 188 tons were distributed to the Pool region alone. This would indicate an increase in hectarage since the normal seeding rate is 80 kilos per hectare using small farmer techniques. It must be noted also that OCV distribution of seed grain effects only a small portion of the crop that is grown. In the late seventies and early eighties, rice production declined sharply. From 1,621 tons in 1974-75, production decreased to 1,030 tons in 1980-81, or by 37% (Appendix 8.1). The decrease was certainly due to the government's policy of subsidizing imported rice through OFNACOM, a state enterprise. Direct impact of such a policy was to make domestic rice unable to compete with imported rice.

There is little information to indicate the types of inputs available to the rice farmer other than seeds.

Although no study exists outlining in detail the methods that small farmers use in rice production, certain general aspects of the operation are known. Rice in the Congo is not transplanted. Although there is an effort to plant it close to streams and in fairly marshy areas, the classical rice paddy cultivations which are found in Southeast Asia do not exist here. Small farmers plant rice in December and January when there is a slack period from the traditional manioc culture. Rices of medium time are favored by small farmers because they can be planted during this period. Varieties suitable for the major rice producing areas in the south of the country are Moroberek, which requires 140 days to mature, and Ignape Catato, which needs 125 days under local conditions. Rice is harvested in March and April during a relatively slack period in the traditional culture.

In addition to valley cultivated rice, there is also rice that is grown in forested areas. Forest rice cultivation differs from the valley cultivations in that longer maturing types are used and planting of the crop must be done at the onset of the rainy season. Maturity of these land varieties takes almost 200 days.

Citrus Fruits

Citrus production has never been important in the Congo. As in other tropical countries, citrus fruits produced in areas that are completely lacking cold weather are blotchy in color and thus difficult to market without color enhancement treatments such as dyes, now prohibited in many countries. Currently oranges, limes and grapefruits are produced, mostly in the Niari, Pool and Bouenza areas. Fruits are usually produced on trees scattered in and around the villages; there are few organized groves.

Citrus production was introduced into the Pool region by the French colonial administration in the early thirties. Almost immediately trees started to show signs of the viral disease called quick decline (tristeza in French). The disease was not widespread until the introduction of a number of different citrus plants into the Brazzaville Botanical Garden in 1938. This collection from Algeria, South Africa, and the Belgian Congo is credited with the swift introduction of strong races of the pathogen that made the disease common. Its viral origins were not known until 1952, but a recent study (Gaetari, 1979) shows that the disease was responsible for the failure of grafting programs in the forties and generally mediocre yields of even improved types that were introduced. The disease, which discolors the mid vein of the leaves, weakens fruit bearing stems and interferes with flower set, is now found throughout the country. Preliminary indications are that the virus is vectored by insect **Toxoptera auranti** or **Toxoptera citricidu** kril.

Vegetables

Small vegetable gardens grown near streams in the dry season are a common feature of small farm activity. In areas near the city these are grown for market. Such common vegetables as cabbage, lettuce, tomatoes, etc., are found. Even in the agriculturally rich areas such as Loubomo, vegetable seed for leaf crops such as lettuce was difficult to obtain, and at times was purchased from black market sources from Zaire. In the same area, American-produced seed obtained in this manner was being used in some of the plots.

Soil Fertility Maintenance

Fertility maintenance in the traditional system in the Congo is generally dependent on fallowing. Commercial fertilizer is generally not available and the lack of a tradition of animal husbandry makes manure scarce.

It might be added that manioc does not respond well to nitrogen fertilization. As with many tuberous crops, excessive nitrogen fertilization can stimulate excess vegetative growth and discourage carbohydrate storage in the tuber. An unpublished study by the Loudima station has confirmed that this is the case on Congolese soils with local types, but considerably more testing is necessary on this question before any conclusions can be drawn.

While fallowing is not a very effective means of maintaining fertility, the fertility problems have been made worse by a general shortening of the fallow periods. Again this is attributed to the relocation of peasants into larger villages during and since the colonial period. Fallow periods have decreased from six to ten years to only three to five years. There has also been a decline in the fallowing period since the mid-sixties.[1] In the traditional system forest fields were left fallow for longer periods, while savanna fields were put back into production sooner. The results of this shortened fallow period have generally thought to be a decrease in yield. This fertility loss is attributable to a decline in surface organic matter and a deterioration of structure in these highly friable soils. Poor structure also reduces water permeability and retention.

In the traditional farming system, seed storage does not seem to be given much attention. Manioc can be simply left in the ground the year round, as mentioned earlier. Cuttings are prepared from the living plants for the next season. Corn is stored in the husk, a practice that would protect it from insect damage to a certain extent. There is no indication that Congolese farmers follow an "eat the worst, save the best" system. Groundnuts are stored unshelled, again as protection against insects. In general, seed storage of these and other crops is haphazard, with no special containers or practices designed to maintain viability.

---

1. For details, see Sautter, Giles, <u>De l'Atlantique Au Fleuve Congo, une Geographie du Souspeuplement</u>, Ecole Pratique des Hautes Etudes (Paris: Mouton, Co., 1967).

9

Farmers' Organizations: The Cooperatives

Over the last decade, the government has launched a determined effort to induce the farmers into joining cooperatives for the purpose of supplying inputs, marketing and production. Though the program has not been very successful because of the farmers' lack of enthusiasm in joining the cooperatives, especially the production ones, it seems clear that the government, in pursuing its socialist option, will continue to accord priority to the grouping of farmers as an instrument of rural development in the years ahead. This chapter describes in some detail the existing structure of cooperatives as well as their strengths and weaknesses.

Types of Cooperatives

Three types of cooperatives (and pre-cooperatives) now exist in the Congo.

The first of these is the <u>marketing cooperatives</u>. The marketing cooperatives appear to be well established. Some of them have been in operation for many years and appear to have the necessary experience in running their business. A typical, well-managed marketing cooperative, has an office, a storage space, some facility to store and sell products deposited by its members.

The second type of cooperative is the <u>production cooperative</u> directly organized by the Ministry of Rural Economy. Currently, the production cooperatives are being organized around agricultural operations; at some of these cooperatives, such as at Loubomo and Kirkala, managers are often on the payroll of the Ministry of Rural Economy. Members of the Young Men's Vegetable Production Cooperative in

Kirkala district also received government salaries. These directly organized production groups do not fit the cooperative model. By definition, a cooperative is an endeavor voluntarily organized by members who share risks and benefits proportional to their participation.

The third group of cooperatives in the Congo is the pre-cooperative. The pre-cooperatives are essentially farmer groups whose members have applied to become cooperative members; in 1981, the number of pre-cooperatives reached 1,003 as compared to only 362 in 1975, representing nearly a threefold increase (Table 9.1).

At present, the government appears to be cautious in transforming the pre-cooperatives into the production cooperatives because of resistance on the part of the farmers to such a grouping.

Membership of the Cooperatives

According to data from the Ministry of Rural Economy, the total membership of cooperatives stood at 14,000 in mid-1980. There were some 600 cooperative groups of all three types described earlier. Figures were not available separately for the marketing and production cooperatives.

The participation of women seems to be dominant. Their dominance reflects the current composition of the rural population and the traditional sexual division of labor. For example, membership of women in the cooperatives of the Pool and Plateaux regions, which started from a modest beginning in 1971 is now dominant (Table 9.2).

A progressive aspect of the cooperative movement in the Congo is the equal right for men and women to participate in the movement. Like men, women can join a cooperative in their own right with or without their spouses.

Organization and Level of Development

The cooperatives are directly under the Cooperatives Services Department, which operates under the Agriculture and Livestock Division of the Ministry of Rural Economy (Appendix 9.1). The cooperatives are organized into five zones with varying numbers of groups under each zone. Zone I has 13 groups, Zone II has 6, Zone III has 4, Zone IV has 5 and Zone V has 12 groups. The groups can be equated with

Table 9.1

The Pre-Cooperatives

1. **Number**

	1975	362
	1976	409
	1977	448
	1978	483
	1979	416
	1980	856
	1981	1,003

2. **Activities** (1981)

	Agriculture	855
	Elevage	16
	Peche	4
	Artisanat	32
	Consommation	20
	Mixtes	76
	Total	1,003

3. **Capital** (millions of CFAF)

	1979	44.6
	1980	55.2
	1981	60.9

Source: 1982 Report, Direction de l'animation rurale et de l'action cooperative.

Table 9.2

Participation of Women in the Cooperatives
of Pool and Plateaux Regions (1971-1980)

Year	Number of co-ops	Membership	Men	Women	Percent of women
1971	9	211	130	81	38.4
1972	40	1,233	938	294	23.8
1973	49	1,442	1,058	381	26.4
1976	72	2,054	1,370	681	33.2
1977	110	2,699	1,710	989	36.3
1978	137	2,922	1,747	1,175	40.2
1979	151	3,260	1,797	1,463	44.9
1980	159	3,514	1,633	1,981	56.4

Source: FAO/UNDP/Congo.

districts in traditional cooperative organizations. Individual cooperatives then come under the groups. The number of individual cooperatives differs widely under each group as the groups themselves differ under the Zones (Appendix 9.1). As it is organized, the arrangement, though permitting a good degree of administrative control at the Ministry level, lacks a framework of operation and a unity of purpose in dealing with the production and marketing problems of specific agricultural produce such as maize, rice, vegetables, cocoa, coffee, and tobacco.

As regards the level of development, the marketing cooperatives seem to do fairly well on their own. Most cooperatives look to the government for technical and material assistance. The production cooperatives, on the other hand, depend entirely on the government to operate. For example, members of an aquaculture cooperative would wait for the government to provide technical assistance to design its fish ponds so they could be effectively operated. After designing, they would want the government to provide fish species, feeds, and money to carry out their operation. The government, however, does not have the human and material resources to provide assistance to the farmers. It seems clear that the production cooperative movement has not been a successful experiment in the Congo as in the rest of the developing countries. Following the socialist approach to development, the government's interest in cooperatives is high. The official objective in pushing cooperative development is to increase food production and eventually, rural prosperity. As rural life becomes more attractive, it is expected that the young generation of Congolese would choose to remain on the farms instead of moving into the cities in search of wage-earning employment. Nevertheless, the government's ability to shoulder the burden of supporting the cooperatives remains in doubt. On the other hand, by limiting the scope of the current program and channeling its limited resources into development of the marketing cooperatives, the government can provide the farmers with incentives to market their products and to improve their welfare.

Potential Roles for Marketing Cooperatives

A very helpful partnership can be foreseen between the government and the cooperative movement short of production cooperative, in enhancing the national efforts to improve agriculture, and to develop the rural environment. In this regard, it seems appropriate to consider here the potential roles which the cooperatives could play in the Congolese economy.

As Institutional Intermediaries

The cooperatives could serve as a useful institutional intermediary between the government and the farmers. This role will be particularly important in the Congo where the rural population is scattered in small villages. The types of cooperatives suitable would be relatively larger than the existing cooperatives, organized around a crop, (for example, the Cocoa Producers' Marketing Cooperative of Sangha) or around a group of crops (the Fruit and Vegetable Growers' Marketing Cooperative of Kouilou). The national union for cocoa producers will comprise the cooperatives from Sangha, Likoula, Cuvette, and Kouilou.

The government, through the Coffee and Cocoa Office (OCC), could consult with representatives of the national cooperative unions to discuss output goals, quality standards and production problems. For effective government producer pricing, OCC would could also consult with the cooperatives during the price-setting process, and before final recommendations are made to the government in fixing the seasonal prices for farm produce. The government and OCC will find the arrangement mutually satisfying: the farmers will more readily accept the prices, and the government will induce increased farm production through a realistic pricing mechanism. The establishment of lines of communication and consultation between the Ministry of Rural Economy and the cooperatives, as farmers' representatives, will lead to a greater farmer confidence in the central authority.

As Channels of Agricultural Extension Service

One need which is glaringly apparent is agricultural extension service. In the Congo, where farmers are widely scattered in very small villages the logistic problems that extension services would entail are serious. Potentially, the cooperatives would serve as viable institutions through which extension services could reach farmers at reasonable costs. Instead of a direct government effort in organizing farmers to avail themselves of new and improved techniques at agricultural demonstration stations, the cooperatives could easily organize themselves for that purpose. Currently, the Ministry of Rural Economy imports improved coffee seeds from the Ivory Coast, germinates the seeds at a nursery near Loubomo, and gives the seedlings to coffee growers to raise. In this instance, the presence of a well-organized coffee growers' cooperative could facilitate the Ministry's task of distributing the seedlings to farmers who could raise them. Distribution of the seedlings through the cooperatives might also be more fair than dealing with large numbers of individual farmers over a wide area. As it is now, only the farmers living near Loubomo are likely to get the available supply. Farmers near Nyanga and Divenie, where more coffee is grown than near Loubomo, might not have free supplies of the improved coffee seedlings for some time.

As Intermediaries for Handling Individual Members' Credit Needs

Because of the small size of the average farm in the Congo, coupled with the joint clan ownership of land, and the fact that the cooperatives do not own the land on which they work, land as collateral for loans would be very difficult to establish. Moreover, the peasants' credit needs are for hand tools, improved seeds, sacks to bag their produce, and transportation costs to move their produce to collection centers. These goods and services are not available in the villages; cash loans would, therefore, be of no help to the peasants in acquiring them. However, the cooperatives, as larger entities, representing the peasants, could raise the necessary funds to acquire the required farm inputs and services, and pass them on to the individual members. The peasants would discharge their indebtedness when they delivered their produce for sale through the cooperatives. The cooperatives would, in turn, repay the creditor(s).

The enhanced repayment capacity of the cooperatives would make them better credit risks than the individual farmers with very limited cash loan repayment capacity. The arrangement would ensure the repayment of the loan taken in behalf of the farmers by the cooperatives. It would also obviate the high cost of administering small loans as would be the case when dealing with individual small farmers.

Again, the arrangement would prevent misapplication of loan funds, since the farmers' credit needs would be given to them in kind and in light of their needs. Furthermore, because the transactions would be in the form of goods and services, the opportunity for the misappropriation of cooperative funds would be limited.

As Intermediaries for Marketing Assistance to Farmers

The cooperatives can serve as intermediaries through which marketing services may be channeled to farmers. Lack of suitable storage facilities constitutes one of the serious constraints on the marketing of agricultural produce in the Congo. The need is greatest at the village level, where much of the food loss occurs. However, it would be impractical to construct storage facilities in every village. It would be easier to provide the needed storage for a cluster of villages through a marketing cooperative for the area. The actual construction could be undertaken by members of the cooperatives with technical assistance and materials provided by the government.

For those farmers who grow cash crops, the cooperatives could also serve as their source of sacks to bag their produce. There is a general indication that farmers do not always get good weight for their produce. Selling through their cooperatives should obviate this problem. It is unlikely that the cooperatives would cheat their members when weighing in their produce.

The cooperatives, if organized along these lines, would be large enough to acquire a vehicle or vehicles for collecting the members' farm produce from the villages. This would remove one of the difficulties in marketing farm produce. Currently, cash crops have to move from villages to collection centers carried on the head or in baskets which are hung on the backs of women with head straps. Once the products reach the market, uncertainly arises as to when OCV would come to collect them. Whenever OCV was late in arriving, products had perished.

The Non-Viability of Production Cooperatives

While a useful role may be foreseen for the cooperative in the marketing of agricultural produce, it seems unlikely that they will succeed as production units. The farmers' cooperatives, as now planned and being implemented in a limited way, expect their members to work for a certain number of days in a week on the communal farm and the rest of the working days of the week on the members' private plot; a Congolese farmer is also required to provide one day a week of his time for the state and also one day's work to the church. This leaves a cooperative member one to two days a week for work on his private plot. The production cooperative will further fragment the peasants' time, and divide their attention to more than one plot producing the same crop or crops. The arrangement does not seem conducive to increased farmer productivity.

Ownership feeling is strong among small farmers everywhere in the world, and Congolese small farmers cannot be expected to have less ownership feeling for their individual farms, no matter how small their fields may be. Lack of ownership feeling does not elicit from small farmers their best effort. Should the lack of ownership feeling pervade the cooperative movement, the result is likely to be lower farmer productivity than the existing levels. The productivity of the state farms, which have the benefit of modern technology and a bundle of services that are not available to the small farmers is not any higher than that of small farmers producing the same crops. One of the factors said to have been responsible for the less than satisfactory performance of the state farm system in the Congo is this lack of ownership feeling. A prudent course to increasing farmer productivity will be to spare the small farmers some of the problems of the state farm system.

It is true that the Congolese small farmers have a tradition for joint clan or extended family farm work; nevertheless, the joint effort is provided to each member only on the basis of reciprocity when extended family members work on each other's farms. The harvests from each farm belong to the individual owner, and not shared equally among members of the clan. Even when the clan jointly operates a farm, the output is put into a joint clan account for the discharge of joint clan obligations. The traditional cooperative experience of Congolese peasants is not parallel to the type of cooperatives envisaged for them by the government. It is possible that the small farmers could count on the help of their extended family members during the critical farm work periods of planting and harvesting; however, it is not likely that farmers would be willing to work together to produce and to equally share the fruits of their work under the production cooperative arrangement.

Organizing small farmers into workable productive cooperatives will require the allocation of human and material resources in the form of a sizable staff of agriculturists and technicians, vehicles, tools, and seed, which the government does not possess. The same amount of resources and level of effort would be far better used in providing the peasants with extension services, which they seem to need most.

It seems clear that Congolese peasants are capable of organizing their crop production activities by themselves without production cooperatives and can achieve increased output at the existing level of their farming methods, if they are provided with extension services in the form of improved seeds, better hand tools, good improved techniques of growing existing and new crops. They are also capable of producing a modest surplus beyond their subsistence needs for sale, if they are provided with rural access roads and marketing services, so that their farm produce are not left to rot in the villages; moreover, significant improvements in the productivity of Congolese peasants could be obtained if the existing monoculture could be changed to a suitable form of mixed farming.

However, such a move should be followed by a careful study and successful pilot projects that can be replicated elsewhere in the country. Organizing peasants into collective production units, and requesting the state farms to provide them with agricultural extension services does not seem to be a viable solution. Experience in cooperative movements elsewhere in the world does not offer a successful production cooperative model which the Congo could adopt.

Constraints on the Cooperatives Movement

Because of the important role attached to cooperatives by the government in the current strategy of agricultural development, both constraints and prospects for their development needed to be analyzed.

Too Small for Viability

The farmers' cooperatives, as they are now organized in the Congo, are too small as viable marketing units. Nationally, the average ownership per cooperative is 23 members. The figure for Pool and Plateaux regions is 22 members, which is close to the national average. The two regions have seen the most rapid cooperative development as a result of a FAO/UNDP program. Judging from the size of the average Congolese farm, the total acreage that a typical cooperative can effectively cultivate will be less than 100 acres.

The output of such a relatively small farm cannot sustain a large volume of business which is essential to cooperative development. One of the concepts underlying the development of cooperatives is that the farmers, pooling their output together, can sell in volume at lower marketing costs and, at the same time, obtain their farm inputs in volume at lower unit prices than the individual farmers acting alone. Unless relatively large resources are pooled together under the umbrella of a cooperative, the advantages to be derived by individual members will be only marginal.[1] Until members perceive the advantages they derive from their cooperative membership to be better than marginal, they are not going to give it much support for very long. The Ministry of Rural Economy has tried to create some visible advantage for cooperative membership through a pricing system which offers a 15% premium for cooperatively produced agricultural commodities. But the system is being foiled at the village level, where non-cooperatively produced commodities are being passed off as cooperative produce by members for

---

1. Example: A well established vegetable growers' marketing cooperative observed near Pointe Noire had a total business volume of $59,131 in 1979. The total expenses for the year amount of $59,187. The account for the year was positively balanced by retained earnings in the sum of $4,815. This cooperative appears to be well administered. The description of the volume of its operations is mentioned here to show the smallness in the size of a rather large Congolese cooperative with as many as 530 members. From the year's account, the net return to an average member was $8.99. The return did not appear large enough to hold the members' interest completely to the cooperative. The director admitted that some members had been selling portions of their produce through private channels.

their relatives. The two classes of producers thereby get the premium prices. Because of the closely knit Congolese extended family system and traditional obligations one owes family members, it will be very difficult for the Ministry to police this differential pricing system to achieve the advantage it is intended to confer on cooperative members.

Advancing Age of Members

According to the Ministry of Rural Economy, the national average age of cooperative members now stands at 40 years. It will probably be increasing at a rapid rate hereafter as the migration of young men from the rural areas continues. Furthermore, the majority of members are often women. For example, in a vegetable cooperative in the Loubomo area, one could observe that of a membership of 50 farmers, as much as 40 (80%) were women. The mitigating factors for the Congolese cooperatives are women traditionally doing much of the farm work -- planting, weeding and harvesting. Women can also join the cooperatives in their own right with or without their spouses.

Aware of the advancing age of the cooperative membership, planners in the Congo have instituted a program of informal education to point out the advantages of the cooperatives to potential young members; they have pointed out to the differential pricing systems as an anchor to the selling of the cooperatives to potential young members. But, as mentioned earlier, the differential pricing system to create an advantage for cooperative membership is counterproductive.

Relatively High Membership Fees

The government's efforts to encourage young men to join the cooperatives is not being helped by the relatively high application and entrance fees (CFAF 2,110 or $9.3 in 1980). Only a limited number of young men and women in rural Congo can afford this level of fees to enter a cooperative.

Lack of Inputs

The cooperatives' problem of lacking government support and of access to inputs such as credit, hand tools, fertilizer, and seeds is similar to problems faced by the small farmers as a whole. These problems are analyzed later in the subsequent Chapter.

Policy Implications for Cooperatives Program

The potential roles which the marketing cooperatives can play could be realized by removing the constraints discussed above. However, in dealing with some of these constraints, the Congo can also benefit from external technical and material assistance. The level of assistance which foreign aid donors would consider may very well depend upon the lines along which the cooperative movement in the Congo develops. If priority is given to strengthen the marketing cooperatives rather than the production cooperatives, the farmers can expect to reap benefits internally from their own economies of scale, and externally, from outside aid.

Strengthening the Organizational Structure

Measures to strengthen the organizational structure of the cooperatives in order to render them efficient seemed to be necessary. The current organizational structure of the cooperatives lacks the framework within which to deal with individual crop, or groups of crops and with the marketing problems. The cooperative units are also too small to stand on their own after an initial assistance. Maintaining the cooperatives in their existing small units means continuation of government support which could not be provided indefinitely.

The organization of the cooperatives may follow the existing political administrative regions, where the Ministry of Rural Economy now has effective administrative machinery. For instance, the Ministry's regional office located at Loubomo in the Niari region is the case in point. The office is capable of handling the affairs of several cooperatives in the surrounding area. A technical assistance project for reorganizing the cooperatives could have its field office staff also stationed at the regional offices of the Ministry and work through the existing Cooperative Services Units there. Because of the smallness of the average Congolese peasant's farm output, the administrative activities of the cooperatives could be stationed at the regional centers and preferably housed initially in the same premises as the Ministry of Rural Economy. Collection centers could be located at the district level. Each local cooperative would have its own village level storage facility to which individuals will deliver their farm produce to be graded and weighed for storage. The district level will pick up the produce from the storage facilities of each village, or cluster of villages. The OCV, or OCC would pick up the produce at the collection centers, which could be the existing centers from which they now operate.

Some reorganization of cooperatives around groups of agricultural produce would be desirable. For example, all cocoa and coffee growers could have one marketing cooperative. The membership will be organized at the local levels, with each locality electing a district representative, and each district committee will in turn nominate an agreed number of representatives to the regional committee, which will exercise policy control over the activities of the officials at the regional administrative office. Since cocoa and coffee are produced in the six regions of Sangha, Cuvette, Likouala, Kouilou, Bouenza, and Lekoumou, only six operating units would be adequate for the two agricultural products. OCC could work closely with the six groups in handling the output of the cooperatives. The regional office of the Cooperative Services Department of the Ministry of Rural Economy could assist the administrative functions of the cooperatives, which may share the same premises with the regional staff of the Ministry. For logistic and administrative reasons, one grain producer's marketing cooperative could be created to handle the marketing of maize, groundnuts, rice, and beans. Because these agricultural products are grown in all the nine regions, the grain farmers cooperative will have offices in all regions.

In reference to the organizational framework, three to five national cooperative unions would be sufficient to cover the whole country. For compatibility with the existing organization of the Ministry of Rural Economy, cooperative marketing unions could be created for:

- Cocoa and Coffee Producers
- Grain Producers
- Food Crop, Fruit and Vegetable Growers
- Palm Fruit and Kernel Producers
- Tobacco Growers

Providing the Material Support
For Effective Operation

The paucity of material resources with which the cooperative members have to work with is discussed elsewhere (see Chapter 10). The need of the farmers is for the simple hand tools, including cutlasses (machetes), hoes, axes, pickaxes, and spades. A supply of these basic farming tools to Congolese peasants would have an appreciable effect on their performance in a very short time, probably within one crop season.

Possibly, international aid donors may consider making a supply of these tools available to farmers in pilot project areas. For an accurate assessment of the effect of each project, a quick farm production survey is required to establish a baseline data against which to measure performance of the peasants in the project area after an initial period. The arrangement will also permit the assessment of the project's cost effectiveness.

Another class of resources urgently needed by the farmers, especially the grain producers, are village level storage facilities. Much of the post-harvest food losses in the Congo are said to occur in the villages where a few cob-borers (<u>leptidoptera larvae</u>) could devastate a basket for corn kept in the "kitchen storage" in a matter of a few weeks. As a component of their marketing services to members, the cooperatives could be aided by materials and technical assistance to construct simple storage facilities in the villages. For example, a simple grain silo, popularly referred to as Ghana No. 6, which was developed in Ghana during the 1960's with West German development assistance funding, could be adapted to the Congo. Essentially, it made termite-proof the traditional earthen silo for storing grains -- corn, peanuts, beans, sorghum, millet, and rice -- by mixing the clay for building it with cement. When completed, it is usually covered with a specially designed aluminum roofing which was also produced locally. A similar program for storage silos may be designed for use in the Congo. The results and experiences from such a program may be used in similar situations in other parts of the developing world.

Credit Facilities for
the Cooperatives

The cooperative program in the Congo has no credit component. Credit is a common problem for farmers' organizations in other developing countries. However, in most of these cases, the causes for failure could be traced to the government's reluctance to allow the farmers' groups to operate on their own and accept responsibilities for their own commitments. The government of the Congo, on the contrary, has shown interest and necessary support for any workable credit program that could be developed for the cooperatives. The type of credit program which could be implemented in the Congo would have certain basic characteristics. The credit system will be a low budget, short-term program, unburdened by top-heavy administrative personnel and will require no new organization for its operation. All the institutional framework is now in existence in the country.

As an example, the model of credit and assistance to the cocoa and coffee cooperatives at Cuvette is of interest and could be followed by other cooperatives. The Cuvette regional cooperative consults with its districts and local members to assess their needs for tools, pesticides, sacks and transportation. The regional office then collates the requests into both a list of materials and a financial account of their costs. The final account, in the form of a loan request, is to be backed by a proforma invoice from the suppliers of the materials and services. The loan application is then sent to the regional branch of the Commercial Bank of the Congo (BCC), with copies to the regional and national offices of the Ministry of Rural Economy and OCC; OCC advises the Ministry and BCC on the crop and price outlook for the coming year and ability of the particular cooperative to repay the amount requested. On the advice of OCC, the Ministry guarantees the loan at the going interest rate. On approval of the loan, the Bank pays the appropriate amount directly to the suppliers of the goods and services when they are delivered to the cooperative for onward transmission down to the individual local cooperatives and their members. The cooperative members are jointly responsible for the total amount charged to its members, while each member is personally responsible for the amount of goods and services it requested and received. The repayment is then made when the members sell their produce through the cooperative. Along the lines of the Cuvette arrangement, a credit system could be established to provide short-term (one year to 18 months) credit to cooperatives. When cooperatives become strengthened, medium-term credit commitments could then be considered. For example, a successful cooperative may decide to get its own vehicle(s) for collecting its members' produce, instead of contracting for the transport service. In such a case, medium-term credit could be provided to finance the vehicles. If the banking system can supply the necessary capital, there will be no need for the government to do so beyond its loan guarantee. However, external assistance, if available, could be turned over to the BCC as a special revolving loan fund to support the cooperatives. Some technical assistance may be required to make a detail project design, install the system, and train the farmers to run it by themselves.

Using BCC as the operating organization for the credit program will facilitate putting the system into operation as quickly as possible., BCC has the necessary technical expertise and logistic facilities in all the regions to run a loan program. Employing an already established financial institution like BCC to run the program will obviate the cost of creating a new institution with the necessary complement of staff positions at the top. If BCC were to run the project, only a special unit could be created to deal with the program. This may not even be necessary at first, due to the limited number of applications expected to reach BCC during the initial period to be processed. A schedule office at each of the regional branches of the bank may be all the staff the program will need to begin operation.

The participation of the government's National Development Bank (BNDC) is not a viable option. First, development banks are more attuned to handle long-term loans; the initial credit needs of the cooperatives will constitute only short-term loans. Perhaps, when they become well-established, the strong ones among them may consider medium-term to long-term loans which they could repay over a period of years.

Elimination of the Differential Pricing System

The differential pricing, which was instituted to create a monetary advantage for cooperative membership, can only result in complications for management and to a large extent, is impossible to function. There is no way the market can effectively handle, nor can the government control, two or three prices for the same product and at a given point of time.

10

Small Farmers' Participation in the Economy

The scope of farmers' participation in the economy is rather limited. Up until now, the small farmers have been neglected and have received few benefits from economic development and little access to government support.

Domestic Resources

Access to Investment and Credit

Table 10.1 shows estimates of the financial flow into agriculture. In terms of public investment, agriculture accounted for only 7% of the total investment in 1970; it was increased to 11% in 1974, then declined again to 7% in 1976 and to 2% in 1977. During 1978-79, it rose dramatically to 14% but was then sliced to a half (7%) as planned average for the 1982-86 Plan. Of these meager resources, very little was devoted to food crops and cash crop development; the bulk of public investment (between 70% and 90%) were allocated for the state farms and other agricultural parastatals.

In terms of banking credit, agriculture has received only a negligible amount, accounting for between 2% to 6% of total medium and long-term credit during 1960-86. Moreover, most of this credit was allocated for forestry as well as to state farms and cooperatives. The small farmers have been kept outside bank loans.

The credit problems which the farmers face as individuals is similar to problems which the farmer cooperatives encounter as already discussed.

Table 10.1

Financial Inflow to Agriculture (1960-1986)

	1960	1970	1974	1976	1977	1978	1979	1980	1982-86[1]
Government Investment in Agriculture (in million CFAF)	--	667	781	595	142	9,000	9,000	9,000	14,600
As Percent of Public Investment Budget	--	7	11	7	2	14	14	13	7
Agricultural Banking Credit (medium- and long-term)	--	188	498	942	692	787	1,293	--	2,545[2]
As Percent of Total Development Credit	--	2	3	5	3	4	6	--	6[2]

1. Planned.
2. 1983 figure.
Source: Table 2.2; for simplicity, footnotes on "Financial Inflow to Agriculture" in Table 2.2 are eliminated in this table; five-year plan, 1982-86; Centrales des Risques; BEAC.

Access to Other Inputs

There is little agricultural inputs provided to the small farmer on a regular basis, or in a significant amount. Government inputs have been uneven in their distribution and directed more towards the creation of administrative structures in the rural sector. A basic, in-field, hands-on approach to agricultural problems seems lacking. In all the four components of production -- tools, fertilizer, seed and extension services -- there is little evidence of the government's support to the farmers.

Hand Tools

Small hand tools are notably lacking in the Congolese countryside. As shown in Table 10.2, the distribution of hand tools is inadequate. Peasants labor with rakes and hoes in varying states of disrepair. There is no nationwide program to provide tools to the small farmer. In the Pool and Koukouya Plateau, a very limited program that allows agricultural credit to cooperative groups to purchase hand tools and seed, is run with UNDP assistance, Although tools are sold through the regional cooperatives union, they are distributed to individual farmers. Table 10.3 shows loans to cooperatives for the purchases of tools and seeds during 1974-78. Though these figures do not show the actual number of farmers that are reached by this program, they appear to be small in number.

Table 10.2

Average Number of Small Tools Per Farm Family in Niari and Pool Regions[1]

Item	Niari	Pool	Congo
Cutlass (Machete)	1.7	2.2	2.9
Hoe	3.0	3.4	2.4
Axe	1.6	1.2	1.5
Shovel and Spade	0.6	0.6	0.6
Pickaxe	0.3	0.1	0.2

1. As surveyed in 1972 and 1973.
Source: Recencement Agricole, 1972-73.

Table 10.3

Loans for Tool and Seed Purchases in the Pool Area

(in CFAF)

Union of Cooperatives Region	1974	1975	1976	1977	1978
Lekana	223,240	593,460	47,100	53,885	0
Moandza-Ndounga	0	15,415	0	197,235	426,319
Madzia	108,705	22,165	0	0	0
Kindamba	0	279,510	95,785	405,725	683,092
Kinkala	259,190	403,835	24,505	302,105	0
Mindouli	0	204,6555	177,595	676,685	0
Kibuende	255,105	103,450	85,710	0	0
Louingui	56,065	735,960	2,245	60,315	244,231
Kissenguele	75,840	185,385	0	67,580	0

Source: Institute for Rural Development, Mairie N'Gouabi University, 1976.

Fertilizer

Most fertilizer is purchased from private sources. Because of scarcity and of transportation problems, fertilizer is not always available to the farmers. The market garden cooperative in Pointe Noire provides an example: it had no nitrogen fertilizer, although potassium and phosphorous were stocked in the common warehouse. Eventually the OCV plans to begin distribution of fertilizers for the crops that it oversees, but this has yet to come. Moreover, fertilizer which OCV plans to deliver to the local farmer would be a package of 150 kg/ha of urea, 250 kg/ha of 15-15-15 and two tons/ha of lime. The cost of this package would be too high to be profitable (CFAF 30,000 per hectare in 1980). This is especially true in face of the absence of soil conservation in the Congo; fertilizer applied to soils in their present condition would be quickly leached out with few residual benefits from one year to the next.

Currently the most readily available soil amendment for the small farmer is lime from a factory built with Chinese assistance in Mandingou, in the Niari Valley, a major agricultural center of the country. The factory went into operation in 1977; originally its 10,000 ton production was to be distributed by the OCV, with some portion earmarked for the Champs du Parti program. Due to transportation problems and a lack of vehicles, neither OCV nor the Party organization were able to take delivery of the lime. Since production began, lime has been sold to individual farmers at a price of CFAF 16 a kilo, or CFAF 16,000 per ton. Lime ($CaCO_3$) should be of use to most farmers where soil pH is low and calcium deficient a common condition in the Congo. Some types of manioc will respond to calcium treatments. Liming trials in neighboring Zaire, on what appears to be a similar soil type, were not effective with maize production, however. An annual production of of 10,000 tons is modest indeed. An average of two to four tons per hectare would not be unusual on these types of soils. The state farm at Mantsoumba found three tons-hectare best for manioc production.

Seeds

The principal government input into the small farm system is seed. Distribution of seed for rice, maize, and peanuts is done by the OCV. As shown in Table 10.4, OCV distribution of and for these three crops is uneven and deficient in most areas.

Table 10.4
OCV Seed Distribution[1]
(tons)

Region	Estimations			Quantities furnished				Deficits or surpluses			
	P	M	R	P	M	R		P	M	R	
Kouliou	–	7.5	–	–	9	–		–	1.5	–	
Niari	–	9.5	31	–	9.5	30		–	-1.5	-11	
Lekoumou	–	4	28	–	4.5	27		–	0.5	-1	
Bouenza	700	19	22	6.822	4.5	30		693.172	15.2	6.100	
Pool	–	25	19	5.178	23.243	188.222		–	1.757	-0.773	
Plateaux	–	62	–	–	41.080	–		–	-20.720	–	
Cuvette	–	38	56	–	34.334	56.068		–	-3.666	–	
Total	–	164	156	12.000	126.257	161.295		–	–	–	

1. 1978-79 season.
P = Peanuts
M = Maize
R = Rice
Source: OCV

Table 10.5

Administrative Employees Funded By the Government in the Pool and Plateau Rural Development Program

Support personnel	Number	Total		Total 1970-1973		1974		1975		1976		1977		1978	
		M/H	CFAF	M/H	CFAF	M/H	CFAF	M/H	CFAF	M/H	CFAF	M/H	CFAF	M/H	CFAF
National Director	1	108	10,350	48	4,600	12	1,150	12	1,150	12	1,150	12	1,150	12	1,150
Assistant Director	1	108	10,350	48	4,600	12	1,150	12	1,150	12	1,150	12	1,150	12	1,150
Extension Field Agents	1	108	10,350	48	4,600	12	1,150	12	1,150	12	1,150	12	1,150	12	1,150
Extention Training Agents	1	108	10,350	48	4,600	12	1,150	12	1,150	12	1,150	12	1,150	12	1,150
Shop Foreman	3	324	31,050	144	13,800	36	3,450	36	3,450	36	3,450	36	3,450	36	3,450
Women's Welfare	3	323	31,050	144	13,800	36	3,450	36	3,450	36	3,450	36	3,450	36	3,450
Rural Community Development	2	216	20,700	96	9,200	24	2,300	24	2,300	24	2,300	24	2,300	24	2,300
Assistants to Rural Groups	2	216	20,700	96	9,200	24	2,300	24	2,300	24	2,300	24	2,300	24	2,300
Fish Culture Agents	2	216	10,700	96	9,200	24	2,300	24	2,300	24	2,300	24	2,300	24	2,300
Livestock Agents	2	216	10,700	96	9,200	24	2,300	24	2,300	24	2,300	24	2,300	24	2,300

Key: M/H = Manhours; CFAF = CFA Francs
Source: Institute for Rural Development, 1979.

(See last column on "Deficits or surpluses). Although no figures are available, it was apparent that OCV seed distribution does not reach a large number of farmers and that on farm seed production and storage remain important for the three OCV crops. A seed producing farm near the agronomic research station at Loudima has embarked on a program to increase its production. Other seed is simply saved from the previous year's crop which is purchased by OCV. Since there is no testing done for adaptability and performance, so this seed would have to be considered land variety, and not improved stock.

Transportation remains an obstacle to efficient seed distribution. This is confounded by the fact that many roads are not passable during the rainy season when the seed is needed. Storage problems also persist. Where a storage facility was available, seeds were stored in tin roofed buildings where the temperature was very high during the warm seasons, contributing to a decline in seed viability. Sacks were placed directly on the floor with no protection from insects or moisture.

Extension Services

Because of various constraints (discussed in the subsequent chapter), there has been little extension service available to the small farmers. The only effective service which reaches the rural area is the "Radio Rurale" project, directed by the Ministry of Rural Economy.

The project is an integrated media, extension, and publication on rural development scheme. The station has weekly broadcasts to two key areas of the country, La Cuvette and Lekoumou. In these pilot areas radio clubs have been organized with an "animateur" who is in charge of keeping the government-issued radio working. The "animateur" also writes a monthly report which comments on the quality of the reception and suggestions and questions that come from the group discussions that follow the broadcasts. Broadcasts cover a wide range of subjects that might be of interest to the rural population such as agriculture, animal husbandry, hunting, fish culture, fishing, marketing, etc. The material is presented in a lively manner mixed in with local music and folk tales. Backing up the information on the radio programs are extension agents who answer directly to the Radio Rurale administration. There are 12 of these agents in the Lekoumou area and 15 in La Cuvette. They service 78 and 105 radio clubs

Table 10.6

Support Personnel for the Pool and Koukouya Plateau
Rural Development Program

(amount in CFAF)

Support personnel	Number	Total M/H	Total Amt.	Total 1970-1973 M/H	Total 1970-1973 Amt.	1974 M/H	1974 Amt.	1975 M/H	1975 Amt.	1976 M/H	1976 Amt.	1977 M/H	1977 Amt.	1978 M/H	1978 Amt.
Assistant extension agents	20	2,160	86,400	960	38,400	240	9,600	240	9,600	240	9,600	240	9,600	240	9,600
Ag. production agents	6	640	25,920	288	11,520	72	2,880	72	2,880	72	2,880	72	2,880	72	2,880
Fish culture monitors	10	1,080	43,200	480	19,200	120	4,800	120	4,000	120	4,800	120	4,800	120	4,800
Fruit tree production monitors	3	324	12,960	144	5,760	36	1,440	36	1,440	36	1,440	36	1,440	36	1,440
Assistant monitors	3	324	12,960	144	5,760	36	1,440	36	1,440	36	1,440	36	1,440	36	1,440
Animal husbandry assistants	6	648	25,920	288	11,520	72	2,880	72	2,880	72	2,880	72	2,880	72	2,880
Veterinary Nurses	6	648	25,920	288	11,520	72	2,800	72	2,880	72	2,880	72	2,880	72	2,880
Assistant Ag. Education monitor	6	648	25,920	288	11,520	72	2,800	72	2,880	72	2,880	72	2,880	72	2,880

Key: M/H = Manhours
Source: Institute for Rural Development, 1979.

respectively. The average membership is 25 per club. The activities of the extension agents are summarized and commented on in the monthly report by the villagers themselves. Such items as the frequency of agents' visits and the coverage of the radio program itself were included in the villagers' comments.

Radio Rurale publications serve two purposes. First, they serve as a backup to technical information given in the broadcasts, and secondly, they are used to train extension agents. As an example, of the first case, Appendix 10.1 shows an illustration of a simplified accounting system that helps illiterate farmers relate weights and measures of certain products with the amount of currency that they should receive. The objective of the system was to encourage marketing of agricultural products by the small farmers. Appendix 10.2 shows an example of Radio Rurale as a manual demonstrating the types of food that can be used for the growing of the fish tilapia in local ponds.

In spite of its small size, Radio Rurale's extension service program seems to be effective. At the present time the program is limited in the amount of information that it can spread by a lack of locally done research that might be used for individual crops. Given the Congo's low population density, the program seems to be an excellent approach to extension services and could be economically sound.

In addition to the Radio Rurale project there are limited extension services available to the farmers in the Pool and Plateaux areas. They come under a special rural development program that the Congolese government sponsors in cooperation with the U.N.D.P. Table 10.5 shows the administrative employees funded by the government in the two regions. It is evident that both the number of people involved and the actual number of hours spent on the project are low. Table 10.6 shows support personnel who work in the field. In practice, these agents rarely visit the field and spend most of their time doing administrative duties at the head office.

External Assistance

For years, most of the external assistance to agriculture has been directed toward the state sector including state ranches and state farms as well as state agro-industries. Very little, if any, has been channeled to assisting small farmers' production and marketing. However, since the government adopted a new policy orientation toward agriculture in 1977, international financial assistance has begun to reach the farmers and more attention has been given to increasing food crops and cash crops production.

Increasing Food Crops Production

A major part of the international assistance in this area has been focused on three main issues (1) to reinforce the OCV's administrative and institutional development; (2) to support major OCV's rural development programs; and (3) to improve the rural road conditions. To reinforce the OCV which was created officially in 1979 to undertake the responsibility of rural development, several international institutions are now interested in helping OCV to operate efficiently. A project was proposed to the World Bank for assistance to the OCV in the following areas:

(a) <u>Institutional Development</u>: to improve the administrative and accounting system of OCV. The project includes the establishment of six centers in the Niari, Pool, and Lekoumou areas as extensions of the Loudima Research Station;
(b) <u>Agricultural census</u>: to be conducted in the Niari, Pool and Lekoumou regions;
(c) <u>Marketing and price research</u>: to determine the channel of food crops, marketing, and price-cost structures;
(d) <u>Project preparation</u>: for food crop development in the Niari, Lekoumou, and Pool regions;
(e) <u>Technical assistance</u>.

To support the OCV rural development programs, the African Development Bank (BAD) has assisted the OCV to develop the Bouenza region. The project covered 18,000 small holdings and affecting 28,000 hectares of agricultural land producing three food crops: rice, corn and groundnuts. There were three components of this project: extension services, increased distribution of seeds, and facility to decrease post-harvest loss. The objective of the project was to help the small farmers in this region to increase the production by 300 tons of rice, 2,700 tons of corn, and 800 tons of groundnuts.

To improve the rural road condition, the government launched in 1978 a "Pistes Agricoles" program aimed at rehabilitating 2,400 kilometers of rural roads, comprising a portion of roads which provide a link between remote villages and the points of marketing near the rivers, the railroads, and roads. The program was integrated into the 1982-86 Development Plan.

Expansion of Cash Crops Cultivation

Development of Coffee and Cacao

The African Development Bank has provided a total of CFAF 1.4 billion foreign exchange costs to finance a CFAF 4.7 billion five-year coffee and cacao development project. The project was designed to have impact on a population of 33,000 small farmers, calling for the improvement of 7,000 hectares of cacao and 3,750 hectares of coffee in the northern regions. Areas under cultivation of these crops would be increased to 5,000 hectares (cacao) and 3,000 hectares (coffee). By 1984, the project had already been half completed.

Oil Palm Development

In 1978-79, a French company, the CECI, prepared an agricultural project calling for CFAF 3 billion for an 11 year development program to increase palm oil plantation in the Cuvette and Sangha regions; it also included a program to develop new plantations at Ouesso, Etoumbi and Kaunda. Responding to the project, OCC approached the European Development Fund as well as the African Development Bank for financing. The African Development Bank also commissioned a FAO study for oil palm development in the Ouesso and Sangha regions; the plan called for rehabilitation of 1,500 hectares of palms, planting another 1,650 hectares, and the modernization of the existing oil palm processing factory.

In 1979, a Belgian company, the SOCFINCO, undertook a study on the Sangha Oil Palm Development Project. The program proposed a plantation of 10,000 hectares of oil palm and a processing plant costing about CFAF 13 billion, to last over a period of 11 years. The end output would be 30,000 tons of palm oil. This project required the transfer of manpower since the Sangha region has a population of only 40,000 persons.

Animal Husbandry Development

Eggs Production

Cuba has assisted the Congo in developing egg production. A development program at the cost of CFAF 350 million was implemented in 1980 to increase egg production on the five existing state poultry farms and to establish a new one at Ouesso. The annual output planned was 10 million eggs per year. A French company also proposed establishment of a complex of poultry development at Pointe Noire, the plan costed CFAF 3.9 billion of which 80% was financed by French supplier credit and 20% by the government. The complex also included a chicken farm to produce 1.7 million chickens per year, a feed factory and a chicken processing plant. Egg production increased dramatically in recent years, reaching 10 million in 1983, as compared to only half a million in 1980.

Hogs Development

Bulgaria participated in financing two integrated complexes for the Louboumo and Owando regions for raising 3,800 and 2,300 pigs a year respectively, and producing 350 tons and 240 tons of pork. The complex also includes a chicken component producing 300,000 eggs per year.

Other Assistance

Agricultural Credit

A FAO team studied briefly the question of agricultural credit in rural development in August 1979. There was some interest from West Germany in providing agricultural credit to the small farmers.

Fishing and Aquaculture

FAO completed a number of studies in fishing activities in the Congo as well as in the coast of Equatorial Africa in 1980; as a result of these preliminary studies, UNDP approached bilateral assistance from Hungary, Yugoslavia, and Canada to provide financing for selected fishing projects. In 1978, FAO also studied the traditional fishing activities at Pointe Noire and the European Development Fund supported a deep sea fishing project at Pointe Noire. During 1980, the International Fund for Agricultural Development undertook the assessment of prospects for fishing projects in the Cuvette region.

Sugar Processing

A number of studies on the sugar sector were undertaken by the African Development Bank, the French Aid and Cooperation Fund (FAC), the European Development Fund (FED), and by the Common Market in 1980, but only a Canadian company, REDPATH, proposed a concrete plan to resume the operation of a one thriving sugar mill, the SIACONGO. The 1982-86 Plan included programs to increase sugar output by the state factory, the Sucrerie du Congo (SUCO).

Rural Electrification

By 1980, a Swiss firm completed a study on rural electrification and irrigation for the plateau region. The total cost was estimated to reach $35 million. China provided a $95 million credit (a ten-year loan) for dam construction and rural electrification. In a July 1980 state visit by the Congolese President to Peking, an agreement was made between the two governments for China to extend the main North-South route through the plateau region, that is the Itsoula-Djambala-Lekana portion.

PART III
PROBLEMS AND PROSPECTS

11

Constraints to Agriculture and Rural Development

The development of agriculture in the Congo, especially of the small farmer sector, is severely hampered by a host of constraints which are evident throughout this book. This chapter only focuses on the main constraints with emphasis on those which are susceptible to intervention (marketing, government policies) and merely touches on those over which there is little prospect for change (ecological factors, size of population, resource endowment).

At the Farms

Environment and Cultural Conditions

The Land. The primary constraint to increased agricultural development is the soil itself. Soils in the Congo are inherently fragile and infertile, as such unimproved soil would not support permanent intensive agriculture. In addition, there is another factor which has impact on limiting production to a single crop: the absence of irrigation. In the face of a long dry season each year in the southwestern part of the country, the fact that the dry season is characterized by low insolation would also make irrigation of dubious value. A third factor is the problem of serious post-harvest loss because of pests and diseases. According to FAO, climatic conditions in the Congo are very conducive to the spreading of a large number of pests and diseases which constitute a major constraint to intensification of farming:

Eight to 12 months of warm weather, high rainfall and high relative humidity provide an excellent environment for proliferation of a large number of pests, weeds and diseases. As the season advances the rising incidence of insect pests and diseases is considered as important a constraint to second season crop production or adoption of continuous agriculture, as any other factor. The build up of weeds is the other main reason for abandonment of cleared land.

The mission inspected a standing second season maize crop on a state farm and found that practically every stand of maize had been attacked by either a stem or cob-borer. An apparently healthy cob selected from a recently harvested pile of cobs was selected and kept for observation by the mission. After two weeks 3.8% of the grains on the cob were already damaged by four young Lepidopterous Larvae. Inspection of a "kitchen" type storage in a village also showed a relative high degree of damage compared to damage observed under similar conditions in other parts of West Africa.[1]

The Tiller. The Congolese peasants had long ago adapted their subsistence patterns and social organization to their environmental conditions. They practiced shifting cultivation with a low population density and impermanent settlements. This adaption has been profoundly modified, however, during the French colonial period and since, partially by the regrouping and consolidation of the peasants into fewer and larger permanent settlements.

The lineage structure, which was left essentially intact, at least among the Bakongo, developed rotational schemes to regulate access to a now fixed and increasingly inadequate amount of land requiring shorter periods of fallow, while assuring itself of new monetary sources of income derived from the wages of its youth, and reinforcing the traditional domination of elders over the young. This has, however, only accelerated the departure of the young wishing to escape as far as possible from this control. The

---

1. FAO, Republique Populaire du Congo, Mission d'Identification Agricole Generale, Rapport D'Identification, Programme de Cooperation FAO/Banque Mondiale, Rapport No. 47/49 PRC-4, Octobre, 1979.

traditional sexual division of labor was developed in a forest environment, with men clearing the forest, hunting, and fighting, while women were responsible for food crops and the household. With permanent settlements, the forest largely gone in the more heavily populated regions, and game hunted out, there is relatively little left for the men to do.

Marketing constraints

<u>Lack of Storage Facilities</u>. A lack of storage facilities of all types places a severe constraint on the marketing of agricultural produce in the Congo. The results have been heavy food losses, high food prices, and discouragement of farmers to increase their food production. It is estimated that the post-harvest food losses might be as high as 60% of the total food crop.

In some cases such as maize, the loss may even be higher. No detailed research has been done on the subject of post-harvest loss in the Congo. An exhaustive study on post-harvest food losses in the developing countries, sponsored by the U.S. National Academy of Sciences did not cover the Congo.[1] The educated guess of the situation is that about half the food produced is lost through poor storage practices and lack of transportation to move food from the villages to points of sale. The storage problem becomes paramount for producers of such perishable commodities as meat and seafoods. For example, it was observed at Pointe Noire that the fishermen had to work all night so that they could land their catch very early in the morning, when buyers could obtain their supply early enough to take it to destinations inland before the fish deteriorated. Some crates of fish were seen left on the beach waiting for a vehicle to move them inland for sale. However, the crates of fish which had been left unrefrigerated since dawn would have perished by late afternoon when the vehicles arrived for pickup. Such a loss could have been prevented by the construction of a small coldstore near the beach, where the fishermen could hold their catch for a fee until the vehicles could come for them. While there are coldstores in Pointe Noire to serve the needs of commercial fishermen, there is none to serve traditional Congolese fishermen (the fish drying station at Mossaka in the Cuvette region had been closed down for some time).

Lack of Access to Credit. The farmers have almost no access to credit. The credit problem is also the missing link in the current effort to develop a cooperative movement in the Congo, a movement which the government viewed as a determining factor in the success or failure of its agricultural policy. One of the potent factors that gave birth to farmers' cooperatives in Europe was the search for a way to meet farmers' credit needs with a view to freeing them from the financial clutches of merchants who were also the moneylenders in the rural area. For example, in France the farmers' marketing cooperatives were placed on their current firm footing with the establishment of the National Agricultural Credit Bank (Caise National de Credit Agricole-CNCA). The activities of the CNCA are similar to programs administered by the USDA Farmers Home Administration, and include credit for rural housing, modernization in agriculture, consolidation of holdings and natural disaster relief programs for farmers. In the Congo, where institutional source of credit is not available, a rural credit institution could be expected to partially fill the gap of farmers' needs for credit to finance their production.

Other Inputs. As discussed in Chapter 10, the Congolese farmers are short of agricultural tools to work in the fields. Furthermore, the limited number of hand tools available were badly worn down with use, and were in need of replacements. In a typical government agricultural station in the agriculturally rich Niari region, for example, one may find only one shovel among an assortment of worn-out cutlasses (machetes), hoes, axes, and pickaxes available. Apparently the depletion of the number of hand tools as a stock of capital per farm family had been going on for some time. The nearly nonavailability of seeds and fertilizers as already discussed, is also a serious constraint on production. Lack of basic technical information on appropriate means to restore and maintain soil fertility as well as limited extension service poses another set of constraints on the Congolese agricultural prospect.

Beyond the Farms

Poor Trunk and Rural Roads

The Congo has only a very limited rural infrastructure in the form of trunk roads and rural access roads. Lack of access roads places constraints, not only on the marketing of agricultural produce, but also on the incentive to produce more. Peasants suffer heavy losses when vehicles fail to reach them in the villages and collect their farm produce. The loss discourages peasants from producing more food than what they need for their own subsistence. The solution to the problem lies in the improvement of existing trunk roads and the construction of rural access roads. But the construction of roads can be very costly and time consuming.

In the current Five Year Plan (1982-86), transport equipment and the extension of road systems are given high priority. The RNTP is to spend CFAF 16.8 billion to purchase modern equipment and CFAF 107.3 billion to pave existing primary roads (Appendix 11). The Plan also calls for an increase in rural access roads to open up some of the hinterlands near urban markets. At present, the lack of transport vehicles and decent all-weather roads greatly inhibits, along with the lack of storage facilities, the ability of the farmers to sell their excess produce. Harvests from frequently remote fields have to be transported to the villages on the heads or backs of women, and once there, they have to wait sometimes for weeks for the irregular visits of government trucks to pick up the produce.

The country also lacks the right types of vehicles to transport high value items. For instance, the price of saltwater fish is high enough in Brazzaville to make fish a high value item to be carried in refrigerated vehicles and railway cars from Pointe Noire to Brazzaville. None of these now exists in the Congo. Furthermore, the number of trucks available for transporting agricultural produce from the rural to urban areas, and to the port for export are not enough to handle the present level of farm production. This is reflected in the significant difference in the rural and city prices of the same food item only 50 kilometers apart.

A long-term solution for the road problem will include the establishment of repair facilities in the primary and secondary urban centers for maintenance. An aspect of the approach will include the training of technicians and mechanics, who will carry out the repair function. The approach may also involve formal and informal technical education for vehicular care and regular maintenance.

Absence of Marketing Research

There is limited information on the Congolese market for agricultural produce, and there is little marketing research in process. In 1980, FAO undertook a survey project to establish a baseline data on agricultural production in the three regions of Pool, Lekoumou, and Niari. The outcome of the effort, which is yet to be published, should shed some light on basic indicators of agricultural production in the three regions. Marketing is essential to any agricultural development program, and effective marketing requires up-to-date information on the supply and demand situation in the market for the various farm produce, as well as some indication with regard to demand-price relationships in the market. In the Congo, whose government-administered prices avail at all levels, the state marketing organizations should have reliable and up-to-date information on the activities of the participants at each level of the marketing chain -- from producer to transporter to wholesaler to processor/convertor to retailer and finally to consumer.

Information on the specific problems at each stage along the marketing system would also be useful to the state's marketing organization, so that these problems could be tackled with. It will be very helpful, for example, to know which of the post-harvest food losses are attributable to attacks by pests and fungi, which are due to poor storage practices and which are due to lack of transport means and to the road conditions. Marketing research to provide both quantitative and qualitative information is therefore prerequisite to any program designed to improve marketing conditions in the Congo. The research process which focuses more on the gathering of market intelligence than on the collection of statistical data, would be more useful. For example, technicals to develop output projections of crops prior to their harvest would be crucial to permit planning of the logistic needs to market the output effectively.

Support to the farmers in this area would involve a combination of technical assistance, institutional building and training of technicians to run the marketing research project thereafter. Detailed research design and project preparations would have to be carried out to pin point the areas of research needs, how to go about initiating the project, in which institution or ministry to locate it, and which organizations are to receive its findings.

Policy Constraints

There is a number of constraints on rural development which are policy related and administrative in nature. First, there is an inadequate planning and programming capacity at both the Ministry of Rural Economy and at the Ministry of Planning. For example, no long-term or medium-term rural development strategy or projection has been formulated; no coherent study of linkages between different projects has been undertaken. In principle, projects, programs, and strategies are developed in the Ministry of Planning in a planning body composed of one representative of all Ministries. These plans and their related budgets, once developed, are presented to the Executive Council where, if they are approved, they become policy. Thus, policies as they are contained in plans for projects and programs can and usually are formulated by working level technicians who develop programs and projects for approval at higher levels.

Examples of poor policies currently affecting the agricultural sector in the Congo are low prices fixed for agricultural products, government support of inefficient state marketing institutions and inefficient state farms and ranches.

Administrative problems have also posed serious obstacles to rural development. For example, at this time there is only a few extension agents who actually work in the field. Part of the problem stems from the disagreement within the government as to who is actually to perform the basic extension work. OCV felt that training local farmers as an extension agent would be the most effective means of spreading information, therefore, OCV would supervise the training and activities of these farmer/agents. On the other hand, the Ministry of rural Economy felt that graduates from the various agricultural schools would be the most suitable agents, and logically would be under the direction of the Ministry. Outside the government, there is also the Party which maintains that all basic contact with the villages should be a role reserved for itself, and, therefore, the Party's cadres could act as extension agents.

This disagreement seems to be just part of the inherent conflict between OCV and other agencies within the Ministry of Rural Economy assigned similar, if not identical responsibilities. At the moment, extension agents are being included in the government's funding of the general rural development program at least in the Pool, Plateaux and Koukouya areas; however, these persons are currently engaged mainly in administrative duties, and their visits to the villages are for inspection and control. For example, in Loubomo one could find announcements posted in public buildings informing local farmers that the government's field agents would be visiting them to offer assistance and to inspect farm animals, assuring that they were properly licensed and that taxes on them had been paid. Nevertheless, the Institute for Rural Development of the Mairen N'gouabi University found in a study of the government rural development project in the Pool and Plateaux areas that these agents had failed to make sufficient contact on the village level. The report cited a lack of extension services as a primary reason why the small farmers were not being reached.

The lack of field agents might be a reflection of the low numbers of students in the Congo who are choosing agriculturally related fields of study. This includes not only the Institute for Rural Development at the Marien N'gouabi University in Brazzaville, but mid-level and elementary type education in that field. It is these mid-level students that would seem to be the most likely persons to do field work. Appendix 11 shows the various mid-level agricultural institutions in the country and the low enrollment in these institutions. The Institute for Rural Development, which trains agronomists, agricultural economists, agricultural engineers, has an enrollment of only 70 for the whole country.

Natural Constraints

Among the natural constraints are a scattered rural population of low density, small land holdings, a poor transportation system and soil and climate differences within the country. Low population density is a natural barrier to providing extension services. In certain areas such as Likouala, with a population density of only 0.43 persons per km^2 and large areas not accessible by road, extension services would have to take forms other than the traditional visiting agent. Even in relatively more populated areas such as Bouenza (9.43 persons/km^2) or Niari (3.71 persons/km^2) villages are also scattered.

According to the regional director of the Ministry of Rural Economy for Niari, unless peasants could be grouped in some way, extension visits would not be practical. He also noted that because of the distances involved, it was not unusual for only one member of a cooperative or a village to attend agricultural demonstrations or Ministry meetings. As noted elsewhere in this book, the area cultivated by a household or individual farmer tends to be small, making extension visits even less rewarding in remote areas. Under these circumstances, radio can play an important part in the extension service; the Ministry of rural Economy is currently producing agriculturally oriented radio programs, the "Radio Rurale," to propagate agricultural technology.

Finally, differences in climate and soil can be viewed as a constraint to extension services in that field testing of improved varieties would have to be done over a wide number of locations before planting decisions for different crops could be made with confidence. With most of the population and agricultural activity in the southern part of the country, this factor becomes especially important. As noted in Chapter 4, rainfall in this area can vary considerably in amount and distribution, creating a total different soil/water environment from one location to the next or from one year to another.

12

Supporting Agriculture and Rural Development

In the long run, agriculture, not oil, remains the foundation of the Congolese economy. For when the known oil reserves are depleted or when the world market for oil is soft it would be agricultural production which provides the main source of employment and income for the majority of the population. Given the structural problems of the Congolese economy and the current state of the depressed agriculture, what can international assistance do to support the Congolese in restoring the viability of the small farmer sector? The problems are multitudinal and the constraints are numerous. Nevertheless, given the fact that agriculture has been abandoned for nearly two decades and its revitalization must now start anew, adequate inflow of outside assistance at the initial state of reconstruction could bring about significant and visible impact on long-term development prospects.

In focusing on the small farmer subsector, external assistance can help to remedy a bias against the farmers, for up until now most of the international aid has been directed toward the modern sector. Within agriculture, aid has been channeled to state farms and to other government agricultural enterprises; nearly all of them have failed to employ the assistance efficiently and their performance has been rather disappointing.

In the past, the government has attempted to solve the agricultural problem by taking over agriculture itself and pushing it along the socialist path. This attempt has failed and the government, during the 1982-86 Plan, has declared its readiness to circumvent ideological strictures, and calling for the "liberalization" of agriculture. As the end of the current Plan approaches, the basic shift in economic orientation is clearly underway, a shift which is expected to bring about increasing international aid to develop the neglected agricultural sector.

Given the constraints on agriculture, however, it seems imperative that some criteria be established in order to determine priority and to maximize the impact of support.

Feasibility

Ideally, external aid could be tailored to reach all the farmers, especially those in the northern part of the country (in the Sangha and Likouala regions) who have been completely ignored by the central government in the past. However, aid intervention could not reach the northernmost farmers without basic infrastructure to even permit contact with them such as access roads and government outlets to cooperate in implementing the aid. What seems feasible is to allocate the aid according to population distribution. Roughly speaking, two-thirds of the population lives in the southern part of the country (the Kouilou, Niari, Lekoumou, Bouenza and Pool regions) and one-third, in the central and northern regions (the Plateaux, Cuvette, Sangha, and Likouala regions). On this basis, two-thirds of aid could be allocated to the southern part (say to support the Sibiti cooperative development and other marketing projects in the Lekoumou and Niari regions) and one-third for improving economic conditions in the north (say to improve marketing outlets in the Sangha region and develop fish pond activities in the Cuvette area).

Cost-Benefit

Another criteria for international assistance strategy would be the cost-benefit test. Because of the lack of basic facilities in the country and the dispersion of population, infrastructure projects to aid production such as irrigation and rural roads are very costly. Furthermore, building and upgrading rural roads, though this appears desirable and even prerequisite for rural development, may not bring real and lasting benefits to the farmers at this stage because the roads, once repaired, will be quickly used by log transport trucks, the owners of which (mainly foreigners) do not contribute to the maintenance of roads while using them. The cost-benefit test, therefore, points to the direction of improving marketing as a more efficient way to assist agriculture at least for the time being.

Speed of Implementation

Given the urgency to restore agriculture in order to slow down the rural exodus, projects which can be quickly implemented would bring more benefits to the country. Furthermore, there is a timing factor: for the rest of the eighties, the government plans to progress in liberalizing agricultural policies; international assistance could certainly support this effort in order to bring about an alternative to increase agricultural production other than through state farms and ranches. In this context, a list of projects which may be considered for financing as presented in Appendix 12.

Past Experiences

Finally, past experience of aid supporting projects in the Congo is also of value to future effort. The European Development Fund (F.E.D.), for example, has not been very successful with its "motoculteur" (mechanization) projects to aid the Congolese farmers. On the other hand, a French pilot project in the late 1960's to stimulate agricultural production through price incentive and improved input delivery and marketing systems was a success. Some of the projects which may be considered by the international aid community is listed in Appendix 12.

The long-term goals of an agricultural development program should include not only increased production to feed an every growing urban population, but also the creation of conditions that will make rural life attractive enough to bring about a slowing of the rural exodus movement and to make rural environment a productive and healthy alternative to urban living. The agricultural sector is in need of assistance in all areas. It is important, however, that assistance be provided in the proper sequence with sound planning lest it be ineffective or even counterproductive. For example, money spent in organizing the farmers for increased production without providing them access to viable markets would not increase farmers' income. Providing chemical inputs without prior research on soil and plants and without extension services would not assure increase in production. Urging the farmers to plant crops in a manner appropriate to mechanized cultivation (as is now being done) when mechanized agriculture is a remote prospect if ever a realistic one, can only have an adverse effect on present farming patterns.

It is crucial, therefore, that a major effort be directed from the start toward careful selection of projects to be implemented. In the short run, projects to improve the marketing conditions at the farm and beyond the farm seem to be the most appropriate. In addition, it is reasonable to consider expanding production through a variety of means; increase in land cultivated through light mechanization, application of lime, fertilizers, and other inputs. At the same time, research could be undertaken to develop the best possible utilization of the differing rural environments in the Congo, involving a wide variety of food crops, fruits, fish, poultry, animals, and trees in an integrated approach. This would not only enrich and diversify the resources of the small farmers, but offer ways out of the bonds of the traditional sexual division of labor. Such efforts can be accompanied by measures to improve the general quality of life in the rural area, such as improved water supplies, health care, housing, rural electrification, improved communications and roads.

The Congolese government is preparing a second Five-Year Plan (1987-92); undoubtedly, the Plan provides a logical framework for international effort to help revitalize the agricultural sector. Within this framework, appropriate and timely external assistance could contribute greatly to the Congolese economy in general and could improve the living conditions of the rural poorin particular. At the same time, no amount of assistance could alter the existing depressed condition in the rural environment unless the government's "liberalization of agriculture" policy could be translated into practical measures in terms of market oriented incentives and of shifting the critical role of the government from that of an owner-manager of farms and ranches to that of a supporter of agriculture and of farmers working on their own plots.

Appendixes

Appendix 1.1
Administrative Division in the Congo

REGIONS	CHEFS-LIEUX	DISTRICTS	P.C.A.
KOUILOU	Pointe-Noire	Loandjili M'Vouti Madingou-Kayes	. Kakamoeka . Nzambi
NIARI	Loubomo	Louvakou Kimonko Kibangou Mossendjo Divenié Mayoko	Makabana Londéla Kayes Banda Mougoundou Nyanga Mbinda
LEKOUMOU	Sibiti	Sibiti Komono Bambama Zananga	
BOUENZA	Madingou	Madingou Boko-Songo Nkayi MFouati Loudima Mouyondzi	. Mabombo . Tsiaki . Kingoué
POOL	Kinkala	Kinkala Boko Mindouli Kindamba NGamaba NGabé Mayama	. MBandza- Ndounga . Loumo . Louingui Vindza
PLATEAUX	Djambala	Djambala Lékana Gamboma Abala	. NGo . MPouya . MBon . Makotipoko Ollombo
CUVETTE	Owando	Owando Makoua Kelle Ewo Boundji Okoyo Mossaka Loukolela Mtumu Oyo	NTokou Etoumbi MBama NGoko Tchikapika
SANGHA	Ouesso	Ouesso Sembé Souanké	Pikounda NGbala
LIKOUALA	Impfondo	Impfondo Epéna Dongou	Liranga . Enyellé . Bétou

Source: CNSEE, *Annaire Statistique*, 1982, p. 52.

Appendix 1.2
Population Pyramid

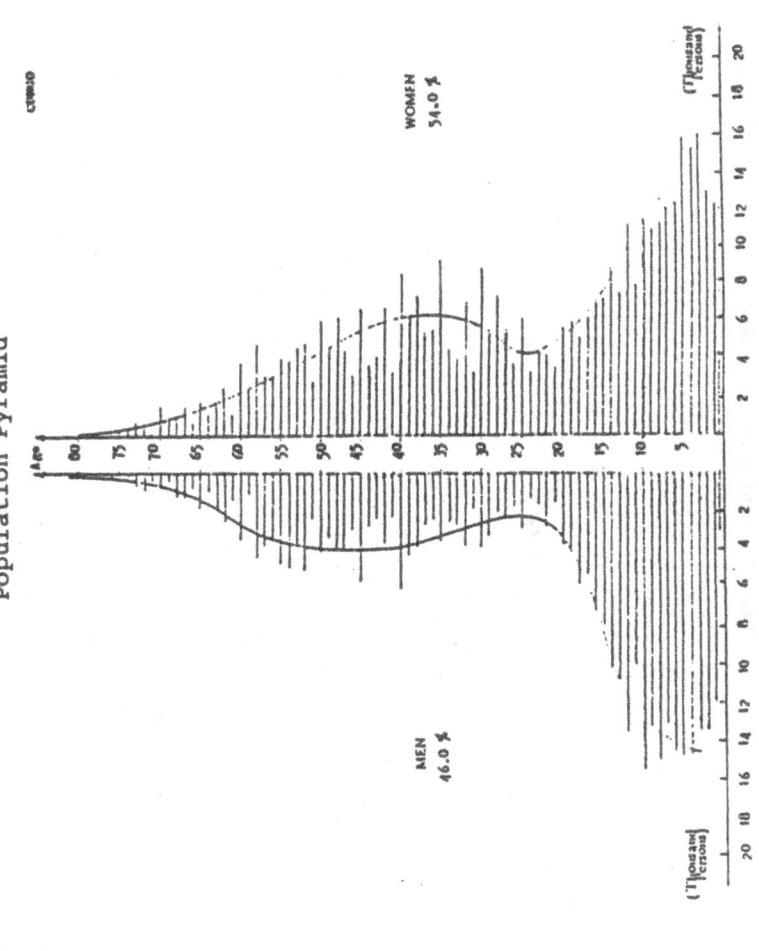

Source: FAO, Recencement Mondial de L'Agriculture (Congo), 1977.

Appendix 1.3

Ratio of Men Per 100 Women

Source: FAO, Recencement Agricole de L'Agriculture (Congo), 1977

Appendix 2.1

SUMMARY OF TWO MAJOR DEVELOPMENT PLANS
(Billions of CFAF and percentages)[1]

	First-Five Year Plan 1964-1968			Three-Year Plan 1975-1977		
	Planned Outlays	Percentage Allocation		Planned Outlays	Percentage Allocations	
		Planned	Actuals		Planned	Actuals
Agriculture forestry fishing	4.9	9	5	11.6	15	3
Industry mining	25.1	46	51	12.6	17	28
Economic infrastructure	8.5	16	18	19.9	26	24
Social infrastructure	10.3	19	13			
Services	5.5	10	13	31.9	42	43
Other	-	-	-			
Total	54.3	100	100	76.0	100	100
Financing						
Domestic	-	-	18	-	-	31
Foreign	-	-	82	-	-	69

[1] The Three-Year Plan was postponed at the end of the second year.

Source: Surveys of African Economies, Vol. 1 (IMF, 1968); IBRD; and Ministry of Planning.

APPENDIX 3.1
FINANCIAL OPERATIONS OF STATE ENTERPRISE IN AGRICULTURE*
(in thousands of CFAF)

	Total Receipts	Total Expenses	Total Expenses Total Receipts (Percentage)	Net Margin Before Taxes
I. AGRICULTURE AND LIVESTOCK				
UAIC	86,519	104,576	120.8	- 18,057
Ferme Gamaba	25,122	41,582	165.5	- 16,460
Ferme Kombe	50,961	151,265	296.8	- 100,304
Ferme avicole Mafouta	12,839	26,954	209.9	- 14,115
Ferme Manioc Mie	None	42,372	-	- 42,732
Ferme avicole Louboomo	27,336	33,191	121.4	- 5,055
Ferme parcine Louboomo	10,055	23,000	229.6	- 13,033
OC Tabacs avicole	203,000	205,707	100.7	- 1,907
Ferme avicole Loandjili	3,005	16,676	430.3	- 12,071
Ferme Manioc Mafouta	13,945	108,094	775.1	- 94,149
SOCOTOM	369,027	365,987	99.0	+ 3,040
St. Fruitiere Loudima	10,433	47,163	452.1	- 36,370
Ferme manioc Makoua	29,390	35,700	121.5	- 6,310
SUNIL	42,406	76,325	179.6	- 33,839
St. de M Passa	600	34,350	5,725.0	- 33,750
RNCP	173,998	616,234	354.2	- 442,236
Ferme d'Odziba	469	43,479	924.9	- 42,910
Ranch Dikesse	3,112	267,699	8,602.1	- 264,587
Societe Champs du Parti	7,566	-	-	-
TOTAL	1,152,263	2,320,342	201.4	-1,168,079
II. FORESTRY				
SNEB	258,640	474,872	103.6	- 216,232
UEB Betou	89,200	199,261	223.4	- 110,061
SONATRAB	236,883	292,666	123.5	- 55,783
SOCOME	35,416	58,178	164.9	- 22,762
OCB	2,050,554	2,610,213	91.8	+ 232,341
OCF	-	205,300	-	-
TOTAL	3,470,693	3,840,490	110.9	- 172,497

Source: UNDP

*1979 situation

Appendix 3.2

ORGANIZATION OF MINISTRY OF AGRICULTURE AND HUSBANDRY

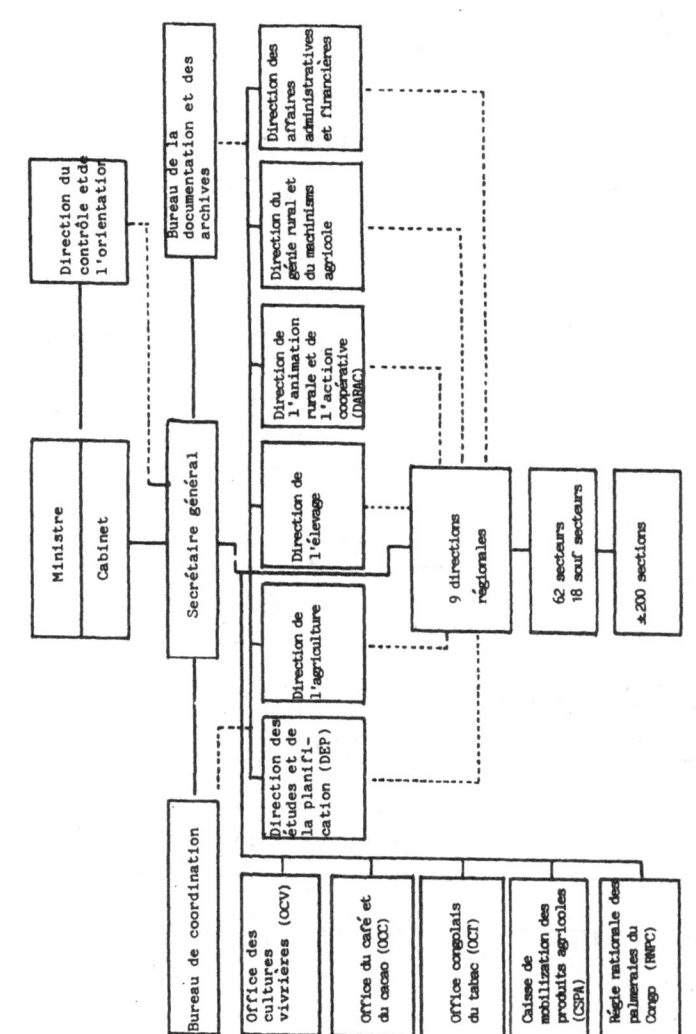

Source: Ministry of Agriculture and Husbandry.

Appendix 3.3

Organizational Chart of OCC

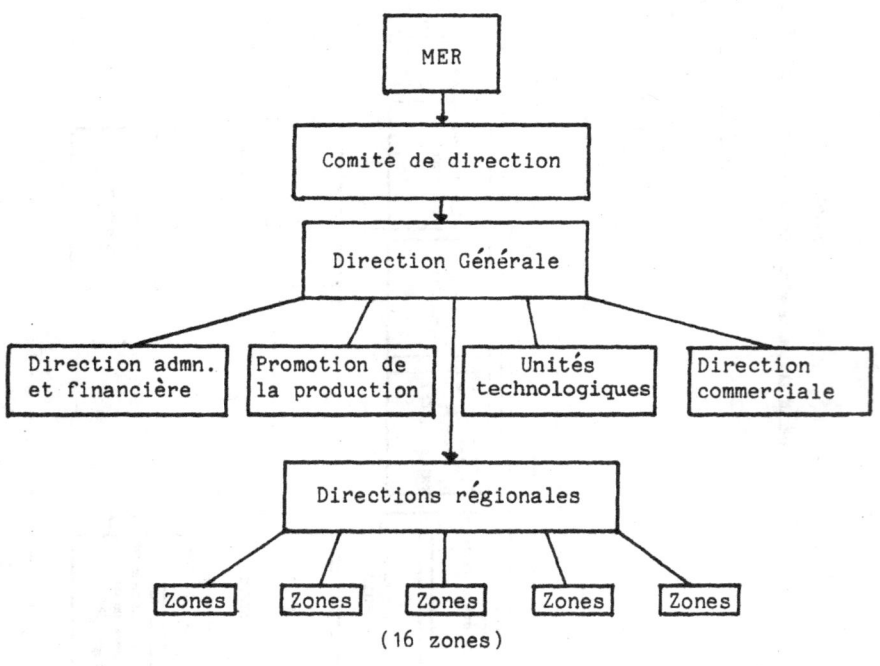

Source: OCC

Appendix 4.1
Evolution of Rainfall, 1979-1983

Stations	Average		1979		1980		1981		1982		1983	
	Number of days	Accumulation in millimeters	Number of days	Accumulation in millimeters	Number of days	Accumulation in millimeters	Number of days	Accumulation in millimeters	Number of days	Accumulation in millimeters	Number of days	Accumulation in millimeters
Souanke	143.0	1,647.2	142	1,685	139	1,719	139	1,663	151	1,550	144	1,619
Impfondo	140.2	1,922.6	152	2,156	151	2,285	137	1,879	138	1,868	123	1,425
Ouesso	122.0	1,549.6	121	1,626	116	1,638	124	1,656	126	1,639	123	1,184
Makoua	131.5	1,591.75 [1]	126	1,224	151	1,871	99*	1,601**	133	1,920	116	1,352
Gamboma	122.8	1,656.2	122	1,800	123	1,259	120	1,663	143	1,996	106	1,552
Djambala	146.4	2,123.4	139	2,385	158	2,178	141	2,005	151	2,262	143	1,787
Makabana	104.75 [1]	1,334.0 [1]	113	1,153	107	1,496	103	1,548	96	1,139	---	---
Mpouya	126.8	1,499.6	131	1,509	120	1,783	130	1,468	137	1,631	116	1,057
Sibiti	123.2	1,336.2	128	1,411	129	1,235	111	1,568	115	1,245	133	1,222
Mouyoundzi	103.0	1,253.8	103	1,291	109	1,655	112	1,412	91	1,169	100	792
Brazzaville	112.25 [1]	1,460.75 [1]	105	1,391	112	1,512	80**	1,141**	115	1,515	117	1,425
Loubomo	102.4	1,110.6	104	1,131	97	1,012	122	1,510	85	717	104	1,183
Pointe-Noire	109.6	1,076.0	108	897	109	1,242	115	1,314	105	917	106	1,010

* 10 months
** 11 months
(1) Average for 4 years.
Source: Direction nationale de la meteorologie.

Appendix 4.2
SOIL CLASSIFICATION

A great deal of data on soils have been collected from different sources during recent years resulting in the development of a variety of classification systems. All of the material found in the Congo is based on the French Classification.

Approximate Correlation of the Food and Agriculture Organization of the United Nations, New Soil Taxonomy of the United States, and French Soil Classification Systems

FAO[a]	New U.S. Soil Taxonomy	French Classification
FLUVISOLS	Fluvents	Sols minéraux bruts et sols peu évolués d'apport alluvial et colluvial
REGOSOLS	Psamments Orthents	Sols minéraux bruts et sols peu évolués d'apport éolien
ARENOSOLS		
Ferralic A.	Oxic Quartzi-psamments	Sols ferrallitiques moyennement ou fortement désaturés (à texture sableuse)
GLEYSOLS		
Eutric G.	Tropaquepts	Sols hydromorphes peu humifères à gley
Dystric G.		
Humic G.	Humaquepts	Sols humiques à gley
Plinthic G.	Plinthaquepts	Sols hydromorphes à accumulation de fer en carapace ou cuirasse
ANDOSOLS	Andepts	Andosols
PLANOSOLS		
Eutric P.	Paleudalfs	Sols ferrugineux tropicaux lessivés (pro parte)
Dystric P.	Paleustalfs	
CAMBISOLS		
Dystric C.	Dystropepts	Sols ferrallitiques fortement et moyennement désaturés, rajeunis (pro parte)
Eutric C.	Eutropepts	Sols ferrugineux tropicaux (non lessivés); Sols ferrallitiques faiblement désaturés, rajeunis
Humic C.	Humitropepts	Sols ferrallitiques fortement et moyennement désaturés, humifères, rajeunis
LUVISOLS	Tropudalfs Paleudalfs Paleustalfs	Sols Ferrugineux tropicaux lessivés
ACRISOLS		Sols ferrallitiques fortement désaturés
Rhodic A.	Rhodudults	Sols ferrallitiques désaturés lessivés
FERRALSOLS	Oxisols	Sols ferrallitiques
LITHOSOLS	Lithic subgroups	Lithosols et Sols intitués

Source: National Academy of Sciences.

APPENDIX 4.3
THE RNTP ORGANIZATION CHART

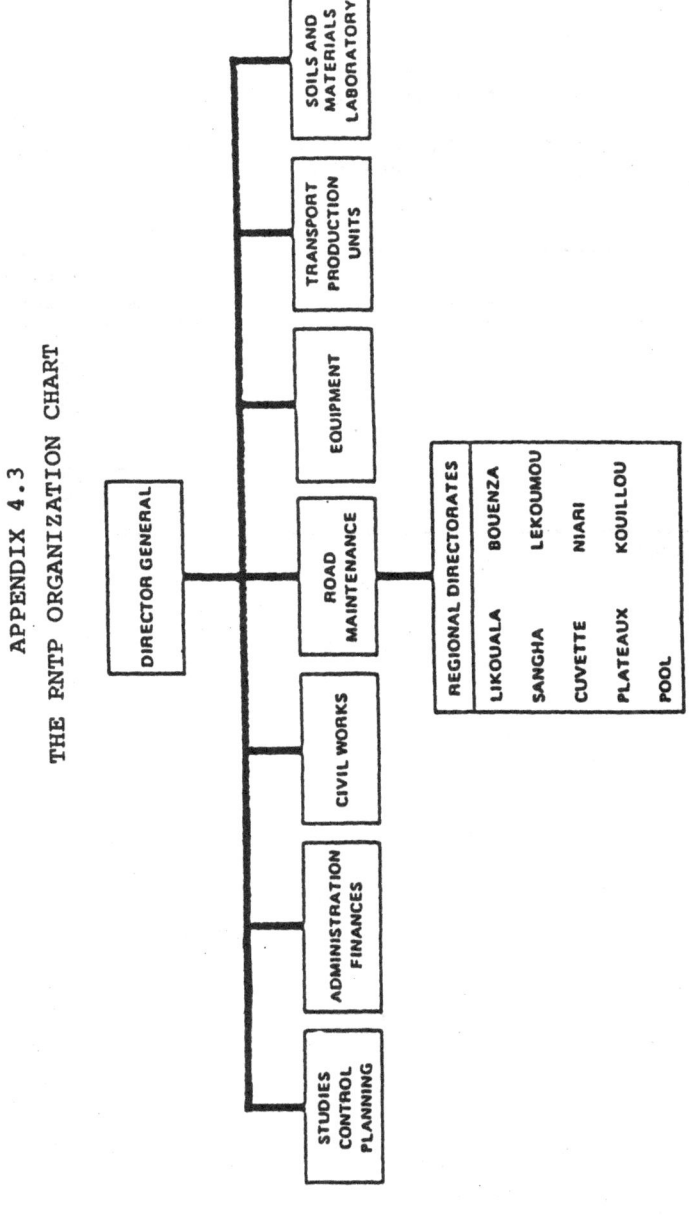

Source: RNTP

Appendix 4.4

Equipment Needed for the Road Work
in the Plateaux Region

Equipment Type	Number needed	Unit cost in U.S. dollars
Dumptruck	7	57,900
Land Plane	2	85,500
Pickup Truck	2	23,500
Bull-dozer	1	175,000
Water Tank	1	70,000
Roller	1	77,000
Flat Truck	1	118,750

Source: RNTP

Appendix 4.5

Necessary Equipment and Deficit for the Road Work in the Plateaux Region

Equipment type	Need	Equipment available	Deficit
EMBANKMENT WORK			
Land Plane	3	2	1
Pickup Truck	1	0	1
BED CONSTRUCTION			
Dumptruck	6	0	6
Wheel Loader2	2	0	1
Bull-dozer	1	0	1
Water Truck	1	0	1
Tractor & Roller	1	1	0
Roller	1	0	1
Land Plane	1	0	1
Flat Bed Truck	1	0	1
Pick-up	1	0	1
BRIDGE CONSTRUCTION			
Dump Truck	1	0	1

Appendix 5.1

VALUE OF AGRO-INDUSTRIAL PRODUCTS
(In Million CFAF)

Item	1973	1974	1975	1976	1977	1978*	1979
Refined sugar	35,507	28,067	19,610	23,008	9,925	13,500	
Palm Oil	2,681	2,700	2,200	2,200	2,565	2,600	1,700
Peanut Oil	1,249	617	600	660	365	400	
Soap	4,475	4,108	4,462	5,051	5,568	4,800	
Cigarettes	676	516	504	636	641	800	
Fish Products	33,800	37,700	15,500	12,600	10,296	12,600	

*Estimates

Sources: Ministerie de L'Agricole, Service des Statistique Agricoles

Appendix 6.1
Consumer Price Index For Brazzaville, 1973-1982
January 1964 = 100

Consumer Prices		Annual Averages								
Item	Weight	1973	1974	1975	1976	1977	1980	1981	1982
Foodstuffs	0.51	148.0	157.0	183.9	199.0	238.0	289.0	359.0	398.0
Clothing	0.06	155.0	150.0	172.6	189.0	203.0	268.0	310.0	382.0
Electricity, fuel and water	0.06	110.0	110.0	110.0	110.0	151.0	180.0	200.0	200.0
Household Services	0.07	132.0	132.0	196.4	196.5	197.0	172.0	182.0	182.0
Other	0.30	147.0	148.0	183.5	225.1	252.9	336.0	360.0	381.0
General Index		144.6	149.3	179.5	201.0	223.0	281.0	328.0	367.0

Source: Centre National de la Statistisque et des Etudes Economiques.

Appendix 7.1

Distribution of Rural Population, Number of Holdings and Areas Under Cultivation

(1973 Census)

ITEM	NIARI	LEKOUMOU	POOL	CONGO
No. of holdings (households)	23,256	10,452	34,690	143,485
Population engaged in agriculture (persons)	129,966	58,045	183,502	798,032
Persons per household	5.6	5.6	5.2	5.6
No. active in farming per household	2.50	2.76	2.36	2.58
Area cultivated (ha)	33,299	13,819	44,254	196,910
Area cultivated per household (ha)	1.43	1.32	1.27	1.37
Area cultivated per active person (ha)	0.57	0.48	0.54	0.53

Source: FAO, Centre d'Investissement, Rapport 47/49, PRC-4.

Appendix 8.1
Rice Production by Regions
(tons)

Area	1974-75	1977-78	1978-79	1979-80	1980-81
Kindamba	212.0	119.8	370.6	186.1	281.1
Mayama	286.5	--	--	19.3	1.0
Mossendjo	363.8	106.4	296.0	144.7	137.6
Zanaga	274.5	204.6	214.6	163.2	45.1
Bambama	33.4	--	24.8	10.8	9.5
Komono	45.1	--	30.3	9.6	28.8
Sibiti	7.8	--	5.5	0.2	6.7
Boko-Songho	87.7	9.8	51.9	67.2	213.7
Mouyondzi	--	30.5	20.7	41.7	62.6
Ewo	304.5	176.3	229.5	143.5	176.7
Boundji	--	--	44.3	18.0	39.1
Autres zones	5.3	33.0	65.4	98.6	27.7
Total	1,620.6	680.4	1,353.6	902.9	1,019.6

Source: OCV; Annuaire Statistique, 1982.

Appendix 9.1
Organizational Structure of the Co-operatives

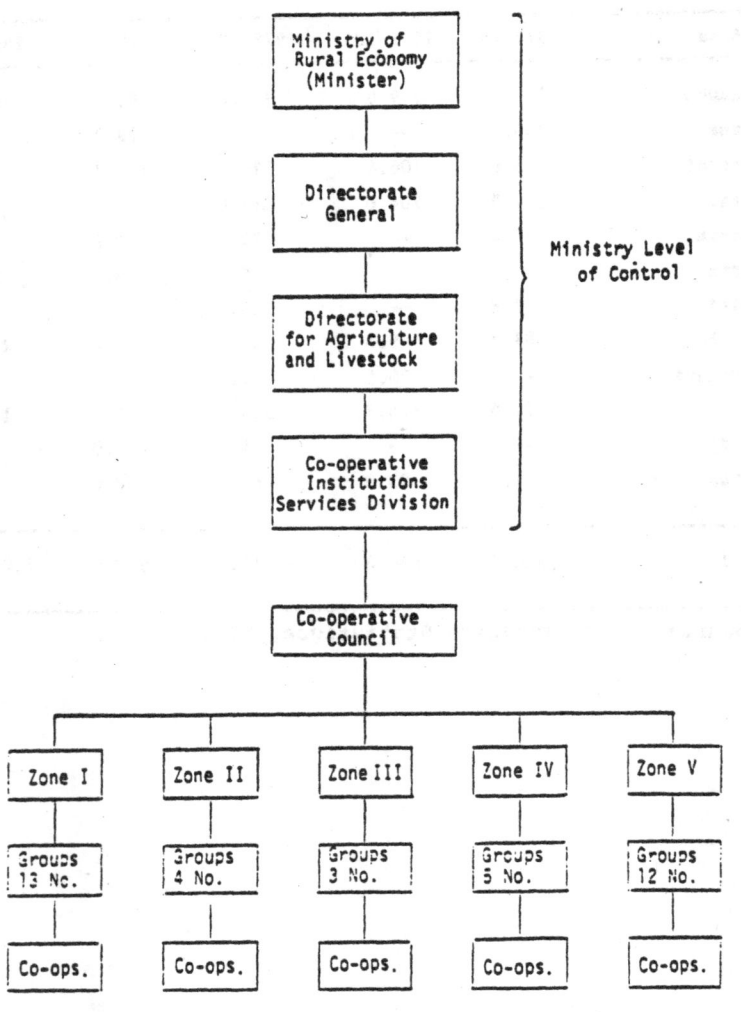

Source: From discussions with Ministery of Rural Economy and Co-operative officials.

Appendix 10.1

ILLUSTRATION OF EXTENSION SERVICES: FARMERS' ACCOUNTING

Example of a simplified counting system used in the Radio Rurale pre-literacy agricultural marketing program. The numerals on the left are about the same as Roman numerals with "0" equal to five. In the upper left hand corner is the unit of measure, in this case a kilo. A mark is made under each unit of currency shown across the top that the farmer is supposed to receive for his product.

MINISTÈRE DE L'ECONOMIE RURALE
Projet Radio - Rurale   FONDATION FRIEDRICH NAUMANN

[kilo]	M'BOUTOU / M'BOUMA		100	5
I				
II				
III				
IIII				
0				
0I				
0II				
0III				
0IIII				

Source: Ministry of Rural Economy.

Appendix 11
Public Investment in Transportation
1982-1986 Plan

	Cost (CFAF million)
Public works	
Equipment for RNTP	20,000
Paving of existing primary roads	107,300
Road maintenance	10,000
Feeder roads rehabilitation and maintenance	8,140
New roads	5,000
Bridges and other structures	13,100
Training and studies	1,400
RNTP buildings	3,330
Administrative buildings	9,100
Equipment and Housing	16,800
Sub-total	194,170
Transport and civil aviation	
Financing of Lina-Congo	1,090
CFCO-Comilog Railways	41,430
Sea ports	16,550
Commercial navy	725
River transport and ports	29,221
Air transport and airports	38,125
Road transport	1,100
Studies and services	1,410
Administration building and equipment	3,524
Training	5,600
Sub-total	138,775
Total	332,945

Source: Five Year Development Plan.

Appendix 12

AGRICULTURE AND RURAL DEVELOPMENT: SELECTED PROJECTS

Given the current state of the Congolese agriculture and rural development analyzed in this book, there are some projects which could be considered for financing by the international donor dommunity. Following is a list of some of these projects.

1. **Medium Term (One to Three Years)**

    Project 1: **Strengthening the Organizational Structure of the Cooperatives**

    Purpose: A pilot project, say at Sibiti in the Lekoumou region to revamp the cooperative movement into viable organizations which will act as intermediary institutions in channeling agricultural extension, marketing, and credit services to their members (see Chapter 9).

    Activities: Providing financial and technical assistance in reorganizing the cooperatives and training of Congolese to administer the movement.

    Project 2: **Supply of Simple Agricultural Implements to Farmers**

    Purpose: To replenish the dwindling supply of simple farm implements used by Congolese peasants (for details, see Chapter 10).

    Activities: Acquiring a number of cutlasses (machetes), hoes, spades, axes, and pickaxes to distribute to farmers in a pilot project area. Selection of the approximate project area should be made in consultation with the government of the Congo. There has been a continuing depletion of the number of farm implements as a stock of capital with which peasants have to work their fields. The reversal of this decline will provide a needed assistance to farmer productivity at the current level of farming expertise by Congolese peasants.

Project 3: <u>Creation of a Revolving Account to Meet the Short-Term Credit Needs of the Farmers</u>

<u>Purpose</u>: Provide the initial funding of a revolving account to cater to the credit needs of peasants through the cooperatives (see Chapters 10 and 11).

<u>Activities</u>: Providing a modest initial fund of about $500,000 to $1,000,000 for the establishment of a revolving account which will cater to the credit needs of the farmers. The fund can be administered either by the Ministry of Rural Economy, the Congolese Development Bank, or preferably by commercial banks to meet the short-term credit needs of the farmers through the cooperatives.

Project 4: <u>Adaptive Research and Extension Services</u>

<u>Purpose</u>: To provide farmers with access to extension services and with diversifying the sources of income of the peasants and ensuring their permanent availability through improvement and protection of the soil. The diversification of activities and resources could also provide an opportunity for rewarding agricultural work for males outside of the traditional sexual division of labor, thus redressing the present imbalance and possibly reducing, it not stemming, the exodus of youth to the cities. An important component of the project would be an extension service package to farmers. Under the criteria established above, this project is considered by the team as one of the best projects for the Congolese farmers.

<u>Activities</u>: The project should be set up to last for a number of years in a relatively densely settled region having reasonable means of communication with the outside world (say at Sibiti in the Lekoumou region). The project should collaborate with the national research station in Loudima and as experience is gained it should be shared not only locally, but through Radio Rurale and other extension

services with other rural populations in similar areas. At a later stage satellite projects should be set up in different regions of the country having different ecological conditions.

The operations of the project should be highly visible and involve direct collaboration with the surrounding population. Research should be directed not just to specific crops, pest control, or other techniques, but toward developing an integrated approach to land management involving soil improvement and fertility maintenance, food crops, the planting of trees of appropriate types to improve soil, prevent erosion, and to provide fire and construction wood and wind protection. Fish ponds should be dug and animals raised to provide food for the fish as well as manure for the fields and meat for human consumption and sale.

Project 5: **Improvement in the Collection of Food and Cash Crops**

Purpose: To strengthen the ability of the government's marketing institutions (the OCV and OCC) to effectively collect farm produce from small farmers in the villages.

Activities: Providing a limited number of trucks to OCV and OCC to augment their existing fleet of vehicles used for collecting farm produce of small farmers. The assistance can be in the form of a long-term development loan.

Project 6: **Establishment of Freshwater Fisheries Research Unit**

Purpose: To conduct applied research and communicate the result to traditional fishermen with a view to helping them increase their fish harvesting.

Activities: Providing an initial grant to create the Freshwater Fisheries Research Unit at the Marient N'gouabi University, recruit an educator with the necessary expertise to help set up the unit within an academic year, and provide any material assistance necessary to set up the unit.

Project 7: **Assistance for Fish Storage and Preservation**

Purpose: To help preserve fish harvested by

traditional fishermen and to increase the availability of fresh fish in rural areas away from the sea and rivers.

Activities: Providing material and technical assistance for the construction of cold storage and fish drying and smoking facilities at Mossaka, Pointe Noire, and other key centers for the use of traditional fishermen and fishmongers.

Project 8: Training in Marketing Research

Purpose: To strengthen the mechanism for price setting by the Ministry of Rural Economy based on reliable market information gathered through market research.

Activities: Providing technical assistance and training for Congolese to run a market research unit to be located in the Ministry of Rural Economy.

Project 9: Development of Village Level Storage Facilities

Purpose: To provide technical assistance to villagers to build their own storage facilities.

Activities: Providing material and technical assistance through the peace Corps to help villagers build their own sample storage facilities.

Project 10: Expanding the Service Production Project and Extending it to Cover Poultry, Sheep and Goats

Purpose: To improve the production of market hogs, poultry, sheep and goats by peasants.

Activities: The government of the Congo is likely to expand the current swine production project and extend it to cover poultry, sheep and goats. Aid donors may introduce a credit component into the project and introduce a national rabbit project as an extension of the effort to help peasants raise small livestock.

Project 11: Upgrading the Existing Fish Ponds and Building New Ones

Purpose: To help reactivate a long-time thriving peasant enterprise.

Activities: Providing technical assistance through the Peace Corps to help the peasants rehabilitate their existing fish ponds and to develop new ones (possibly at the Pool region).

2. Medium Term (Three to Five Years)

Crop Diversification with Emphasis on New Cash Crops

Project 1: Introduction of New Cash Crops

Purpose: (1) Provide new income generating activity for peasants; and (2) compensate for the nearly half-year of their idleness due to the long dry season.

Activities: The newly activated agricultural research stations can select varieties of tree crops that do well during the dry season and on relatively poor soils. Conduct laboratory and field tests to select the most promising varieties, carry out seed multiplication, propagation and distribution of the seedlings to peasants to grow. Provide extension series during the growing period and marketing services after the harvest. Two tree crops, castor seed and cashew nut, can form the first group of long-term crop diversification program. Another valuable crop worth exploring is the Macadamia nut (Macadamia integrifolia). Originally, an Australian evergreen tree, which grows well in the Central African countries of Malawi and Zambia; these two countries have climates similar to those of southern Congo. Kernel is also a very valuable confectionary nut with its largest market in Europe and the United States. The only world commercial producers of this valuable cash crop are Australia, Hawaii, and Malawi.

Project 2: Introduce Sorghum and Millet

Purpose: Diversify the raw material base for the country's nascent animal feed industry.

Activities: Obtain sorghum and millet varieties for trial and selection of varieties most suitable for the Congo. The seeds of the appropriate varieties should be multiplied for distribution to farmers. An extension service package should accompany the introduction of the two cash crops.

Improvement in Varieties of Existing Cash Crops

Project 3: **Improvements in the Varieties of Cocoa and Coffee Trees**

Purpose: Improve farmer productivity of cocoa and coffee production by introducing high yield varieties which are also disease resistant.

Activities: Import improved cocoa seeds of varieties which are tolerant to capsid attack from Ghana for field trials and subsequent distribution of seedlings to farmers to grow. (Varieties of cocoa trees now grown in the Congo are types known to be susceptible to capsid attack. Some trees are now under attack, although the situation is somewhat under control). Expand the current coffee program by importing coffee seeds from the Ivory Coast. The imported varieties should, however, be subjected to rigorous field tests before the seedlings are released to farmers. Extension services should accompany the new seedlings to demonstrate to farmers how to grow and care for the new seedlings.

Rural Infrastructure

Project 4: **Drawing Up a National Rural Infrastructure Program**

Purpose: To determine the magnitude, cost, and time it should take to develop a rural infrastructure program and the ways and means to finance the program.

Activities: The government of the Congo may consider setting up a planning commission of technical personnel to draw up a comprehensive program on how to go about developing the rural infrastructure of the country. Aid donor countries may consider providing technical advisers to help draw up the plan. Once completed, the plan could be circulated to multilateral and bilateral economic assistance agencies for help in carrying out the program in stages. (The development of rural infrastructure is a very costly, and time consuming affair. It requires careful planning to establish the right priorities of which project comes first and which second, and so on. Unplanned approaches could easily result in serious financial problems).

Testing Program

Project 5: **Liming Test**

Purpose: To determine if lime applications represent a useful and profitable input at this stage of development of the Congolese small farms.

Activities: Lime is one of the few soil amendments that is available to the small farmer, since it is produced by a factory in Mandingou and sold locally. Trials at the state farm at Mantsoumba shows that manioc yields could be significantly increased with application of three tons per hectare. A pilot project would be selected to find out whether smaller amounts applied by hand at the time of planting could improve productivity for the small farmer.

Project 6: **Improved Rotations**

Purpose: To determine whether the current multiple cropping system, although seemingly an efficient use of the growing season, could stand considerable improvement, especially in the area of fertility maintenance which is given little attention in the traditional cropping system.

Activities: This inexpensive and often successful method of fertility maintenance might work well in the Congolese environment. Again, this would have to be done on the basis of on-farm testing with farmer acceptability as a major input.

Special attention could be paid to levels of potassium, the major mineral requirement for manioc. In addition, attention will also be given to crops which suffer from juxtaposition with other more aggressive plants. Maize would seem to be a good case in point.

With the OCV attempting to get farmers to grow maize as a commercial grain, its current place in the multiple cropping system must be reconsidered. In the traditional system, maize is planted in between mounds of manioc. Research done by the excellent maize program in Zaire has shown that maize plants compete poorly with manioc for both light and presumably nitrogen.

Project 7: **Seeds Selection**

Purpose: To provide information on how farmers select seed for the next growing season from the current crop and to make peasants aware of how selection of seed grains is important in preventing the spread of pathogens and genetic drift.

<u>Activities</u>: A study of the selection of rice, maize, and legume seeds and storage from one season to the next at the village level. It seems important to get farmers to maximize the seed stock they currently have and at the same time to prepare the way for the introduction of new types, which in turn need careful selection if seed is to be saved by the farmer himself from one season to the next. The emphasis of any introduction program should be on achieving the highest maintainable yield as opposed to the highest possible yield. In other words, yield stability and predictable performance would seem more suited to the Congolese environment.

Appendix 13

EXCHANGE RATES

Throughout this book, the following rates have been used:

Currency Unit: CFA Franc (CFAF)

1969	US$1 = CFAF 256
1970	US$1 = CFAF 277
1971	US$1 = CFAF 276
1972	US$1 = CFAF 252
1973	US$1 = CFAF 230
1974	US$1 = CFAF 240
1975	US$1 = CFAF 214
1976	US$1 = CFAF 239
1977	US$1 = CFAF 246
1978	US$1 = CFAF 226
1981	US$1 = CFAF 272
1982	US$1 = CFAF 328
1983	US$1 = CFAF 385
1984	US$1 = CFAF 420
1985	US$1 = CFAF 450

Appendix 14

LIST OF ABBREVIATIONS

AGIP	-	Agenzia Generale Italiana di Petrolio
BAD	-	Banque africaine de developpement
BCC	-	Banque Commerciale du Congo
CEGI	-	Compagnie d'etudes economiques et de gestion industrielle
CENAGES	-	Centre national de gestion
CSPAF	-	Caisse de stablisation des prix des produits agricoles et forestiers
DAE	-	Direction de l'agriculture et de l'elevage, Ministere de l'economie rurale
FAC	-	Fonds d'aide et de cooperation (France)
FAO	-	Food and Agriculture Organization
FED	-	Fonds europeen de developpement
FIDA	-	Fonds international pour le developpement agricole
IDR	-	Institut de developpement rural
IRAT	-	Institut de recherches en agronomie tropicale
MER	-	Ministere de l'economie rurale
OCB	-	Office congolais du bois
OCC	-	Office de cacao et du cafe
OCT	-	Office congolais du tabac
OCV	-	Offices des cultures vivrieres
OFNACOM	-	Office national de commercialisation
ONCPA	-	Office national de commercialisation des produits agricoles
ORSTOM	-	Office de la recherche scientifique et technique outre-mer
PCT	-	Parti congolaise du travail
RNPC	-	Regie nationale des palmeraies du Congo
RNTP	-	Regie nationale des travaux publics

APPENDIX 14 (continued)

SIACONGO	-	Societe industrielle et agricole du Congo
SICAPE	-	Societe italienne-congolaise d'armement et de peche
SMAG	-	Salaire minimum agricole garanti
SMIG	-	Salaire minimum interprofessionnel garanti
SNE	-	Societe nationale de'energie
SNEB	-	Societe nationale d'exploitation du bois
SOCOBOIS	-	Societe congolaise du bois
SOCOMAB	-	Societe congolaise de manutention du bois
SOCOTON	-	Societe cotonniere nationale
SONATRAB	-	Societe nationale de transformation du bois
SONEL	-	Societe nationale d'elevage
SOTEXO	-	Societe textile du Congo
SUCO	-	Sucrerie du Congo
SYBETRA	-	Syndicat belge des enterprises de travaux
UCB	-	Union congolaise des banques
UDEAC	-	Union douaniere et economique de l'Afrique centrale
UEB BETOU	-	Unite d'exploitation du bois de Betou
UNDP	-	United Nations Development Program
WHO	-	World Health Organization

Appendix 15

The People's Republic of the Congo: Basic Data

Geography

Area: 132,000 sq. mi. (slightly larger than New Mexico).

Capital: Brazzaville (population 400,000).

People

Population: 1.8 million (1986 estimate).

Annual Growth Rate: 2.7%

Ethnic Groups: 15 groups, 75 tribes; major groups are Bakongo, Bateke, M'Bochi, Sangha.

Religions: 48% Animist, 47% Christian, 5% Moslem.

Languages: French (official), Lingala, Kikongo.

Eduation: 80% of primary school-age children enrolled, one of the highest rates in Africa. Literacy rate 50%. University at Brazzaville.

Labor: About 600,000 economically active, 37% in agriculture. About 17% unemployment.

Government

Type: People's Republic.

Independence: August 15, 1960.

Date of Constitution: January 3, 1970

Political Party: Congolese Labor Party (PCT).

Suffrage: Universal

Political Subdivisions: 9 Regions, divided into districts, and capital district.

Economy

> Officially follows Marxist model. An entrepot for Equatorial Africa.
>
> GDP: $2 billion (estimated) at current prices in 1985.
>
> Agriculture: Accounts for 8% of GDP (1983) and 2% of net exports. Provides livelihood for 54% of population. Only 2% of usable land cultivated. Cash crops comprise rice, maize, coffee, cocoa, oil palm and sugar.
>
> Development Plan: Five-Year Plan (1982-1986) under execution. Forthcoming Five-Year Plan (1987-1991).

Natural Resources

> Land: About half the size of Texas, extending from the west coast of Africa northeast across the Equator. Rugged terrain between the coast and plateaus presents an obstacle to transportation.
>
> Climate: Equatorial climate, hot and humid. Wet (February to May, September to December) and dry seasons. Rainfall decreases away from the coast.
>
> Minerals: Petroleum production 5.9 million metric tons in (1984), Potash production ended in 1977. Limited gold, copper production. Estimated billion ton high grade (60-66%) iron ore reserves in Zanaga.
>
> Forestry: Covers 50% of total area. Log production 180,000 cubic meters, processed wood 130,000 cubic meters in 1978. Veneer and pulp production becoming more important.

Basic Economic Facilities

> Transportation: National transportation agency (RNTP) responsible for rail and water transport and ports. Many navigable waterways, 285 km. of

railroad and 7.600 km. of roads (558 km. surfaced). Pointe-Noire, main seaport; Brazzaville river port. Two international airports and about 40 lesser fields.

Communications: Automatic dial telephone in Point-Noire and Brazzaville. Radio, TV-Congo. International radio and wire communications available. About 75,000 radio receivers.

Power: Nationalized utilities since 1967. Almost unlimited hydro-electric potential. Thermal units serve Pointe-Noire and Loubomo while hydro facilities for Brazzaville constitute 70% of installed capacity. Over 40,000 kW capacity; over 110 million kWh consumed 1972. Sowanda project (230 MW, expandable to 830 MW) under study. Bouenza dam (72 MW) began production during 1978.

SELECTED READINGS

Annuaire Statistique, Repulbique Populaire duCongo: Ministere du Plan, 1982.

Department of Agricultural Research. Agroforestry, Proceedings of the 50th Tropische Landoouwdag 1978. Bulletin 303. Amsterdam: Royal Tropical Institute Amsterdam, 1979.

Amin, Samir, & Catherine Coquery-Vidrovitch, Histoire Economique Du Congo, 1968-1980: Du Congo Francais a l'Union Douaniere et Economique d'Afrique Centrale. Paris: I.F.A.N. (Dakar), 1969.

Apercu Sur l'Alimentation et la Nutrition. Congo: Organization Mondiale de la Sante, 1976.

Bertrand, Hughues, Le Congo, Formation sociale et mode de developpement economique. Paris, 1975

Bilan Techniques de l'Operation Experiementale Motoculteurs, Brazzaville, Republique Populaire du Congo: C.E.E.M.A.T., 1975.

Collinet J., and Forget, A. Notice explicative No. 70. Carte pedologique de N'Dende a 1/200,000. 1977-79, 177, 1 tabl., 1 carte h.t. p. 23/B-5. O.R.S.T.O.M., Paris.

Commission des Communautes Europeenes Projects de Developpement rural integre realises avec l'aide du FED en Afrique noire. Evaluation et perspectives. Serie Developpement, 1979.

Decalo, Samuel. "Ideological Rhetoric and Scientific Socialism in Benin and Congo/Brazzaville." Socialism in Sub-Saharan Africa. A New Assessment, Eds. Carl G. Rosberg & Thomas M. Callaghy Berkeley: Universtiy of California, 1979, pp. 231-264.

Department de l'Agriculture. Republique du Zaire Programme National Mais, Cinquieme Rapport Annuel, 1977.

Department de l'Agriculture, Republique du Zaire
Programme National Mais, <u>Sixieme Rapport Annuel</u>,
1978.

Desjeux, Dominique. "La question fonciere dans le
Pool." <u>Rapport d'evaluation EX POST du P.D.R.</u>,
Fiche I of Tome II, Brazzaville, July, 1979.

Direction General de la Recherche Scientifique.
<u>Rapport d'Activities</u>, 1977-78. Republique
Populaire du Congo: Centre de Recherche Agronomiques de Loudima, 1978.

Direction General de la Recherche Scientifique.
<u>Rapport sur la Soja</u>. Republique Populaire du
Congo: Centre de Recherche Agronomique de
Loudima, 1980.

Direction General de la Recherche Scientifique.
<u>Rapport d'Activities, 1976-77</u>. Republique
Populaire du Congo: Centre de Recherche Scientifique de Loudima, 1977.

Duckham, AN.N. and Masefield, G.B. <u>Farming Systems of the World</u>, London and New York: Praeger, 1969 and 1970.

<u>Etudes et Statistiques</u>. Indicateurs Economiques de
la Rep. Popl. du Congo. BEAC, May 1979.

FAO, Republique Populaire du Congo, Mission
d'Identification, Agricole Generale, <u>Rapport D'Identification, Programme de Cooperation FAO/Banque Mondiale</u>, Rapport No. 47/49 PRC-4 Octobre, 1979.

Gabou, Alexis. <u>Le Marriage Congolais Ladi et Koukouya</u>.
Brazzaville, 1979.

Guillemin, Rene, et G. Bocqrie. <u>Les Facteurs Physiques du Milieu Conditionnant la Production Agricole das la Republique Du Congo</u>. Tome II.
Communaute, Haute Commissariat General a Brazzaville, 1947.

Guillemin, Rene. <u>Les Facteurs Physiques du Milieu Conditionnant la Projection Agricole dans la Republique du Congo</u>. Tome I. Communaute, Haut-commissariat General a Brazzaville, 1947.

Guillot, Bernard. La Terre Enkou (Congo). Atlas des Structures Agraires au Sud du Sahara #8. Mouton, Paris and The Hague, 1973.

Institute de Developpement Rural. Genese et Dynamique du Projet de Developpement Rural (P.D.R.) du Pool et Plateau Oukouya. Brazzaville, Nov. 1979.

Institute de Developpement Rural; Universite Marien Ngouabi. Rapport Preliminaire d'Evaluation du Projet de Developpement Rural (P.D.R. de Kinkala at Plateau Koukouya). Tome I. Brazzaville, March 1979.

Jamet, R. Pedogenese sur roches cristallophylliennes et argileuses en milieu equatorial congolais, $7\underline{e}$ fascicule. Pedogenese sur chloritoschistes, $2\underline{e}$ etude mineralogique et physico-chimique. 107 multigr. 199/COD/C.D. -2; A-14 O.R.S.T.O.M., Bondy, 1978.

Jeune Afrique. Atlas de la Republique Populaire du Congo, Paris: Editions Jeune Afrique, 1977.

Lopes, Henri. Tribaliques, 5th ed. Younde, 1979 (1st ed. 1971).

Marche Tropicaux et Mediterraness No. 1805. 13 June, 1980.

Maumon, Griveau, et Arnaud. Quinze Ans de Travaux et de Recherches dans les pays du Niari, Republic du Congo: Synthese Generale. Ministere de la Cooperation, Paris, 1966.

Quinze ans de Travaux, Esquise....,: de Developpement Et D'Amenagement Des Pays Du Niari, Ministere de la Cooperation. Paris, 1966.

May, J.M. The Ecology of Malnutrition in Middle Africa. London and New York: Hafner Publishing Co., 1965.

McDonald, Gardon C. et al. Area Handbook for People's Republic of the Congo. American University Foreign Area Studies, 1970.

Ministere de l'Agriculture et de l'Elevage, Republique Populaire du Congo. Cellule Technique de l'Unite Experimentale du Manioc industriel de la ferme d'Etat de Mantsoumba. Rapport d'Execution 1972-74.

Ministere de la Cooperation. Republique Populaire du Congo: Dossier d'Information Economique. Paris, June, 1975.

Ministere de l'Economie Rural, Republique Populaire du Congo. Projet d'Amenagement du Service Nationale de Controle du Condionnement, 1980.

Ministere de l'Economie Rurale, Republique Populaire du Congo, Techniques et Developpement. Bulletin trimestriel no. 2/79, Projet Radio Rurale.

Ministere de l'Education Natinoale, Republique Populaire du Congo. Rapport sur L'Enseignement Technique Project EC/PRC/ED/04, Aout 1979.

Mission de Preparation: Projet de Developpement des Cultures Vivrieres Dans la Regions de la Bouenza. Programme de Cooperation FAO/Banque Africains de Developpement, 1980.

Molinier, M. et B. Thebe. Donnees Hydrologiques En Repulbique Du Congo. Office de la Recherche Scientifique et Technique Outre-Mer (ORSTOM), Avril, 1977.

Muller, D. Contribution a l'Etude de la differcia tion des horizons nodulaires des sols ferrallitiques congolais sur granito-geniss. These Doc. 3 cycle, 118 multigr. 209/COB/D-5.

Muller, D. Les sols de MOUGOUNDOU, massif du Chaillu, Description des elements dus a l'accumulation des sesquioxydes. Brazzaville: O.R.S.T.O.M.,1978, 229 multigr. 208/COB /D-5

Office de la Recherche Scientifique et Technique Outre - Mer, Centre be Brazzaville, Annuaire Hydrologique de la Republique Populaire du Congo, Annee 1978, Avril 1978.

Office de la Recherche Scientifique et Technique Outre Mer. 1980 Liste bibliographique des travaux, Centre ORSTOM de Brazzaville, 1947-1978.

ORSTOM. Annuaire Hydrologique de la Republique Populaire du Congo Annee 1978. Centre de Brazzaville. Section Hydrologie. Avril 1978.

ORSTOM. Liste Bibliographique des Travaux 1947-1978, Pedologie, Centre de Brazzaville. Section de Pedologie, Janvier, 1980.

O.R.S.T.OM.M. Quelques examples d'application des mesures de vayonnement a la determination de l'evapotranspiratin au climat tropical, Cahiers Hydrologies. Vol. VII, No. 4. Paris, 1970.

Programme des National Unies pour le Developpement - Project PRC - 68-507 Projet de Developpement Rural de la Region du Pool et du Plateau Koukouya, Republique Populaire du Congo. Rapport D'Avancement No. 12, Ler Aout 1977 - 31 Mars 1979, Brazzaville, Mars, 1979.

Ministere de l'Economie Rurale, Secretariat General a l'Econmie Rurale. Rapport Annuel. 1977.

Direction de l'Agriculture et de l'Elevage, Ministere de l'Economie Rurale. Rapport Annuel. 1979.

Recensement Mondial de l'Agriculture: Cameroon, Congo, Gabon, Empire Centrafricain, Tchad. Rome: FAO 1977.

Representation de la FAO/Brazzaville, Republique Populaire de Congo. Revue de Programme Au 10 Mai, 1979.

Representation du PNUD Brazzaville. RPC Revue du Programme, 1979.

Riou, C. Etude de l'Evaporation en Afrique Centrale, Contribution a la connaissance des climas. These de Docteur es sciences, Paris: O.R.S.T.O.M., 1972.

Sautter, Giles, De l'Atlantique Au Fleuve Congo, Une geography du souspeuplement. Vol. I et II, Ecole Pratique des Hautes Etudes. Paris: Mouton Co., 1967.

Ministere de l'Economie Rurale. Statistiques de Production et de Commercialization des Produits Agricoles et Forestiers, 1975-77.

Ministere de l'Economic Rurale. **Statuts des Groupements** Pre-Cooperatives.

Thompson, Virginia & Richard Adloff. **Historical Dictionary of the People's Republic of the Congo (Congo Brazzaville).** Metuchen, NJ, 1974.

Universite Marien N'Goubabi. **Institute de Developpement Rurale, Genese et Dynamique du Projet de Developpement Rural du Pool et Plateau Koukouya.** Novembre, 1979.

Universite Marien N'Gouabi. Institut de Developpement Rural. **Rapport Preliminaire d'Evaluation du Projet De Developpement Rural de Kinkala et Plateau Koukouya.** Tome I. Mars, 1979.

Van Wing S.J., Jr. **Etudes Bakongo. Sociologie-- Religion et Magie.** 2nd ed. Leopolaville, 1959.